ADAPTER
FRANCE

a traveler's tools for living like a local

Terry Link

AVALON
TRAVEL

Acknowledgments

For Phil, who taught me to live well in any country.

ADAPTER KIT: FRANCE
First edition
Terry Link

Published by Avalon Travel Publishing
5855 Beaudry Street, Emeryville CA 94608, USA

Text © 2001 by Avalon Travel Publishing, Inc.
Cover, illustrations, and maps © 2001 by Avalon Travel Publishing, Inc. All rights reserved. Some photos and illustrations are used by permission and are the property of the original copyright owners.

> Please send all comments, corrections, additions, amendments, and critiques to:
>
> **ADAPTER KIT: France**
> AVALON TRAVEL PUBLISHING
> 5855 BEAUDRY ST.
> EMERYVILLE, CA 94608, USA
> email: info@travelmatters.com
> website: www.travelmatters.com

Printed in the United States of America by R.R. Donnelley

Printing History
1st edition — July 2001
5 4 3 2 1

ISSN 1534-5890
ISBN 1-56691-348-9

Editor: Kate Willis
Series Manager: Kate Willis
Copy Editor: Elizabeth Wolf
Graphics: Melissa Sherowski
Interior Design & Production: Amber Pirker
Map Editor: Mike Balsbaugh
Cartographers: Kat Kalamaras, Mike Morgenfeld
Index: Kate Willis
Cover Design: Melissa Sherowski, Amber Pirker
Front cover photo: John Elk III
Back cover photo: C.D.T. d'Eure-et-Loire; Abercrombie & Kent

Photo on page vii: Terry Link; photo on page 1: Abercrombie & Kent; photo on page 3: D. LeFranc; photo on page 13: John Elk III; photo on page 29: CDT Lot; photo on page 37: CDT Lot; photo on page 39: Archie Satterfield; photo on page 51: V. Coutant; photo on page 63: Abercrombie & Kent; photo on page 79: ADT Vercors; photo on page 81: John Elk III; photo on page 103: E. Bruneau pour Office de Tourisme, Dreux; photo on page 113: Abercrombie & Kent; photo on page 123: John Elk III; photo on page 125: Abercrombie & Kent; photo on page 137: CDT 76; photo on page 153: Linnemann—CDT 76; photo on page 159: John Elk III; photo on page 175: Abercrombie & Kent; photo on page 191: N.&F. Michel; photo on page 205: CDT d'Eure-et-Loire; photo on page 217: Abercrombie & Kent; photo on page 229: Leo de Wys; photo on page 231: Vernon Houghton; photo on page 241: CDT Lot

Distributed in the United States and Canada by Publishers Group West

All rights reserved. No part of this book may be translated or reproduced in any form, except brief extracts by a reviewer for the purpose of a review, without written permission of the copyright owner.

Although every effort was made to ensure that the information was correct at the time of going to press, the author and publisher do not assume and hereby disclaim any liability to any party for any loss or damage caused by errors, omissions, or any potential travel disruption due to labor or financial difficulty, whether such errors or omissions result from negligence, accident, or any other cause.

Contents

INTRODUCTION

1. **Welcome to France** 3
   Vive La Difference 7 • The United States and France: Les Amis 8 •
   France's Future 10 • Where Should You Live? 11

2. **An Overview of France** 13
   The Lay of the Land 13 • How the Country Is Divided 21 •
   Language 22 • Religion 22 • Economy 23 • Standard of Living 24 •
   Getting Around 26

3. **Planning Your Fact-Finding Trip** 29
   Know Yourself 29 • Talk to Folks 31 • Study Maps 31 • Read 31 •
   Study French 32 • Consider Your Family, Relatives, and Friends 32 •
   Visit France 33

FRENCH CULTURE

4. **Parlez-vous Français?** 39
   If You Don't Learn the Language 40 • Learning French 41 • French
   Instruction in the United States 41 • French Instruction in France
   42 • A Word about Accents 46 • Literature 46

5. **French People and Culture** 51
   Class 51 • Solidarity and Education 52 • The Second Sex 52 • The
   Ethnic Mix 54 • Workers United 56 • Cuisine and Culture 57 • A
   Day of Rest 58 • French Attitudes Towards Americans 60

6. **450,000 Years of History** 63
   Roman Rule 64 • Charlemagne and the Church 64 • A Powerful
   Aristocracy 65 • Consolidating Royal Power 66 • Renaissance and
   Reformation 68 • Intellectual Flowering 68 • The Sun King Shines
   70 • "Liberté, Egalité, Fraternité!" 71 • Napoleon's Rise and Fall 71 •
   From Monarchy to Empire to Republic—and Back Again 72 • Diplo-
   matic Defeats 72 • The Third Republic 73 • Cultural Ferment 73 •
   War and Depression 75 • The Vichy Government 75 • Colonial
   Crises and the Cold War 76 • De Gaulle Rewrites the Constitution 76 •
   Mitterand and the European Union 77 • The New Millennium 78

DAILY LIFE

7. Keeping in Touch 81
   Telephone 81 • Computers and the Internet 83 • La Poste (mail) 85 •
   Television 85 • Radio 87 • Newspapers and Magazines 87

8. Money Matters 91
   From Francs to Euros 91 • Cost of Living 94 • Banking 98 • Taxes 99 •
   Social Security 101

9. Staying Healthy 103
   Know Your Health Status 103 • You and the French Health-Care
   System 104 • Providing for Your Own Insurance 105 • Pharmaceuti-
   cals and Remedies 107 • Hospitals 107 • Smoking 108 • The
   Environment 108

10. Getting Around 113
   Trains 113 • Buses 115 • Automobiles 117 • Requirements and Rules
   of the Road 117 • The Highway System 118 • Buying and Maintaining a Car in France 120 • Car Rental 120 • Air Travel 121

MOVING IN

11. Making the Move 125
   The Long-Stay Visa 125 • Student Visas and Special Cases 127 • What
   to Bring, What to Leave Behind 129 • Once You're in France 133

12. A Roof Over Your Head 137
   Housing in France 137 • Renting versus Buying 139 • Renting an
   Apartment 141 • Buying a Home 142 • Building a New Home 146 •
   Renovating an Older Home 148

13. Prime Living Locations 153
   Paris and the Île-de-France 153 • Southern France: The Midi and
   Languedoc 154 • Southeast France: Provence and the Côte d'Azur
   155 • Northwest France: Normandy and Brittany 155 • East-Central
   France: Burgundy and the Rhône Valley 155

14. Paris and the Île-de-France 159
   Housing in Paris 161 • The Right Bank, the Left Bank 163 • Les
   Banlieues: The Suburbs of Paris 167

15. **The Midi and Languedoc** 175
    Bordeaux 177 • Around Bordeaux 179 • Toulouse 182 • Around Toulouse 183 • Languedoc 184

16. **Provence and the Côte d'Azur** 191
    Nice 193 • Cannes-Antibes 195 • Around Cannes 195 • Marseille 197 • Aix-en-Provence 198 • Avignon 200

17. **Normandy and Brittany** 205
    Normandy 205 • Brittany 215

18. **Burgundy and the Rhône Valley** 217
    Burgundy 218 • The Rhône Valley 223

EARNING A LIVING

19. **Working in France** 231
    Owning Your Own Business 231 • Social Security and Business Taxes 235 • Working for Someone Else 235 • Income Tax: No Escape 236 • "Working Black" 237

APPENDIX

20. **Useful Resources** 242
    French Consulates in the United States 242 • U.S. Embassy and Consulates in France 243 • Institutions in France Teaching French as a Foreign Language 244 • Taking the Measure of Metrics 248 • Shoes and Clothing Sizes 249 • Radio Frequencies 250 • Chronology of French Kings, Emperors, and Presidents 253

INDEX 255

Preface

I moved to France a decade ago, having signed the papers to buy a vacant bakery on my 50th birthday. The day of the signing was hot. It was also a holiday, and I had to take the *notaire* away from a family gathering because I was returning to California the next day. I signed with as much trepidation as I had experienced 30 years before in asking my girlfriend to marry me, and just as much certainty that this was what I wanted, no matter what the future held.

Ten years of that future have since unfolded, and my two regrets are that I did not make the move sooner and that I did not study more French before doing so.

The old bakery that my wife and I bought and turned into a *chambres d'hôtes* was neither the culmination of a dream nor the beginning of one. Rather, it was the next logical step in a process that began with my first trip to Europe—an eight-week trip that in the end was little more than a tour of France. I was crazy about the country!

My wife was too. As a partner in a cheese and wine shop, she specialized in French cheeses. Soon she left the cheese shop and opened her own *charcuterie*, making pâtés, sausages, quiches, and salads as well as selling cheese and wine. This endeavor required more trips to France, and when our eldest son decided to attend university in France rather than in the United States, we easily agreed.

Eventually, together with our son and his wife, we bought a small house in a village that served the four of us as a vacation home. Working on remodeling projects in that house with its meter-thick stone walls was a new experience for me, and one I thoroughly enjoyed.

By this time, our other children were grown and my wife and I were ready to move to France permanently if we had some means of support. When the newspaper where I was working offered an "early retirement" buyout to older workers we had the solution: Use the buyout money to start a bed-and-breakfast.

I enrolled in a French class five mornings a week and we began making two-week trips looking for a suitable property. One of these we made in January, to see what the winter weather was like. (My wife already knew, having spent two weeks one February on a farm learning about *foie gras* production.)

The building we eventually bought was sound—it had housed the ovens of the abbey, according to a map of the village from 1668. It had continued as a bakery until the late 1980s, when the owner, who had grown up in the house to become a baker like his father, had retired. But it had minimal electricity and no hot water. (The communal bath house up the street has since been converted to a senior citizens' center.)

Thus began my real education in *bricolage*, the French term for do-it-yourself construction. As a learning process, it was largely enjoyable. Not all the lessons were.

When my mother-in-law had a heart attack while visiting us, we received a close look at French medical care. In the end it turned out well, but we had an anxious few weeks. Meanwhile, my father-in-law and I built a second bathroom so she would not have to climb the stairs and they spent Christmas with us until she was able to travel.

A plan to supplement our income by renting bicycles to the general public ran afoul of French bureaucracy: We were a *chambres d'hôtes*, not a bicycle shop. We could rent rooms, but not bicycles, without establishing a separate business.

When our first car threw a rod and had to be scrapped, we learned just how isolated a small village could be—no used car lots and no easy way to shop for another car—and how dependent we were upon the friends we had made.

There were numerous similar incidents, small enough in themselves, but for an immigrant beginning a new life in another country, they loomed large. After deciding to leave your native land, making the move, and getting settled, there comes a point when you begin to wonder if you have done the right thing.

For my wife and myself it came after a rainy winter day of fruitless shopping for furniture. The dollar had dropped from 6.25 francs (when we came to France) to 4.53 francs, it was raining, and the heater in the car wasn't working, and we were cold, hungry, and tired. We started to voice our fears aloud.

Then, as we came over a rise and saw our village, we also saw a double rainbow that seemed to end there. Looking at each other, we both grinned and said, "There's our home!"

— *Terry Link*

Part I
Introduction

1. Welcome to France
2. An Overview of France
3. Planning Your Fact-Finding Trip

1 Welcome to France

"**H**ow are you gonna keep 'em down on the farm after they've seen Paris?" was the question a popular song asked after World War I. Numerous Americans from Ernest Hemingway to Gertrude Stein answered, "You can't."

France is still a magnet for Americans today. The world's number one travel destination draws hundreds of thousands of American tourists each year, some of whom fall so deeply in love with the country they return to stay. Why?

The attraction, just as it has been for generations past, is the extraordinary quality of life the ordinary person can enjoy. France is both modern and old-fashioned. French science and technology rival any nation's, yet the country appreciates fine food, a slow pace, and the good things in life. Indeed, it is a French phrase that describes it best: *joie de vivre*.

That joy of life can be experienced throughout the entire country. In Paris, you can sit in front of Nôtre Dame cathedral and watch pigeons bob along, as they have for the past 700 years, while talking on your cell phone. Then you can catch a high-speed train to charming Beaune, where farmhands snip clusters of grapes from the vines the way they did in Roman times.

At the local market you can buy cheese from the person who made it, and fruit and vegetables from the farmer who grew them. The *charcutier* (butcher) can tell you where his meat comes from. You can sit along the quai in Honfleur and savor a bowl of *moules* (mussels) while gazing at the boats in the harbor. Here, though the boats may be powered by diesel motors, little else has changed since Samuel Champlain sailed off to the New World. And while the barges that ply the Canal du Midi between Bordeaux and the Mediterranean transport passengers today rather than haul freight, their captains still banter with the lockkeepers, just like in the old days.

You can drive through the south of France on two-lane roads edged with wildflowers and shaded by sycamore trees generations old. In olive groves and orchards, wild thyme, lavender, and rosemary grow in rocky

Governing the Ungovernable

"How can anyone govern a nation that has 246 different kinds of cheese?" asked Charles de Gaulle, who underestimated the number of French cheeses but not the difficulty of running France.

In fact, de Gaulle finally gave up trying, walking away from the presidency to write his memoirs. But de Gaulle's efforts were not in vain. The constitution of the Fifth Republic he helped write in 1958 continues to serve the nation well after more than 40 years, delivering the stability France has historically lacked.

The French constitution establishes a parliamentary form of government with parallels to both the British and the American systems, but different from both. Representatives are elected to the *Assemblée Nationale* (National Assembly) and a prime minister is chosen from among the majority to run the government. But the French system differs from the British in that there is also an elected president. It is the president who names the prime minister. Executive power is wielded by a series of ministries whose heads are appointed by the prime minister. It is at this level that most of the decisions affecting life in France are made: The budget, taxation, health care, and Social Security are all determined by the ministries.

This system has proven to be an effective antidote to the parliamentary jockeying that paralyzed the Fourth Republic. Since election to the presidency requires a majority vote, the president enters office with a true mandate from the electorate. His appointment of a prime minister depends on the legislature's majority vote. When the president's party controls parliament, this appointment is a relatively straightforward matter; the president installs his own person and they work in tandem. When another party controls the parliament, a situation the French call "*cohabitation*," the president bows to the will of the majority party and names its leader prime minister, who then chooses his own ministers to govern.

The president, elected for a seven-year term, is charged with guaranteeing the proper functioning of the public authorities and the continuity of the state—a large task, ill defined. He is head of the armed forces, can dissolve the legislature, and convenes and presides at meetings of the Council of Ministers. He can also call for a national referendum on acts passed by the legislature and require the legislature to reconsider its acts in whole or part.

The prime minister is responsible for running the government. Although the president actually appoints the ministers in the cabinet, he does so following the suggestions of the prime minister. The sort of cooperation that the constitution forces upon these high elected officials can be seen in the area of defense. The president commands the armed forces, but the minister of defense heads the agency that manages them, and he serves at the pleasure of the prime minister because it is the prime minister who is responsible for the nation's defense.

At the risk of oversimplifying, the president is responsible for the overall welfare of the country, but the instrument of

patches of soil. The scent of pine and heather perfumes the air. You can linger over dinner, just like the French do. When you reserve a table at a restaurant in France, it's yours for the night—the waiter won't ask you to wait in the bar for 30 minutes before seating you, or hustle you along so he can seat another party before the night is over.

This is France today, a land that has preserved what is good and beautiful and true from its past and made it work in the present. Other nations have also preserved their historical charm, and other industrialized nations

action is the government, which is headed by the prime minister. It is the prime minister and his cabinet who are responsible for the day-to-day operations of the government while the president serves as head of State and represents France on the international stage. The president is seen as guardian of the proper functioning of the various organs of government and maintains the separation of powers between executive and legislative. Nonetheless, it is the government (of the prime minister) that is responsible for the conduct of national policy. Given the ambiguous nature of this relationship, it is easy to see that much depends on the personalities of the individual president and prime minister and their relative political strength at any given time.

There are two houses of the legislature, the *Assemblée Nationale* and the *Sénat* (Senate). Representation in both houses is by department according to population.

The 577 deputies of the National Assembly are directly elected for five-year terms, unless the president of France dissolves the assembly and calls for new elections. Because of France's multiplicity of political parties, two votes are held a week apart. If a candidate wins an absolute majority in the first vote, he or she wins the seat. If no candidate gains a majority in the first round of voting, as is often the case, the top vote-getters have a runoff and whoever gets the most votes is declared winner.

The assembly, which supervises the government, elects its own president for the life of the assembly's term. No deputy may belong to more than one of the six standing committees: Cultural, Family and Social Affairs; Foreign Affairs; Defense; Finance; Constitution and Administration; and Production and Trade.

The nation's 321 senators serve nine-year terms, one-third of them elected every three years. Unlike the deputies of the assembly, they are not directly elected. Instead, an electoral college made up of all the elected officials, including municipal counselors in each department, chooses the senators. This is further complicated by the fact that, in the departments entitled to five or more senators, election is on a proportional basis, whereas in the smaller departments, it is based on majority rule.

The senate cannot be dissolved, again, unlike the assembly. It is the president of the senate who succeeds to the national presidency if that post is vacated.

There are elections almost every year in France owing to the differing term lengths—nine years for senators; seven for the president, six for mayors and city councilors, five for deputies; plus varying terms for departmental and regional councils. If your favorite sport is politics, you'll enjoy an unending spectator season.

The French themselves enjoy a high degree of representation: one representative in the national legislature for every 67,000 citizens (compared to, in the United States, one for every 510,000 Americans). For this reason, the average French person is far more likely than the average American to be personally familiar with his or her elected representatives.

also boast ultra-modern amenities, but no country combines these two so successfully as France. This is true not only in Paris but also, remarkably, in the smaller towns and villages. The successful blending of past and present permeates the entire society and every region.

One of the secrets of this successful blending lies in the fact that the French have managed to combine an agricultural base with a modern industrial economy. High-tech agricultural methods mingle with the rural charm of hand-hewn stone walls and tile roofs. Farmers—individual, small producers—are still important to the French economy. When French farmers take their complaints to the streets, the government pays attention to them. After all, France is the food basket of Europe thanks not to corporate agribusiness, but to the family farm.

At the same time, France prizes its modernity. The country boasts a surplus of electric power from nuclear plants and builds rockets to launch its own satellites into orbit. It is Europe's largest producer of automobiles and host to its commercial aircraft industry. Exports surpass imports by a wide margin. French medical researchers rival peers anywhere in the world, and the health of French citizens is taken seriously. Employers provide mandatory health care, and the government offers extensive benefits for the needy and unemployed.

> *Throughout most of France, you can find a quality of life that is difficult to match anywhere in the world.*

France also educates its people, providing a university education, at nominal cost, for anyone who graduates from high school and wants to continue in school. An extremely popular annual event is the televised *dictée* in which millions of French people sit before their televisions and try to write a paragraph of dictation correctly, just as they did in school. The correct version is later published, along with the results.

France is a well-educated, well-run nation, internationally famous for its culture, art, and cuisine; Americans living in France enjoy the benefits of all this as much as French citizens do. And the weather's nice, too. The country enjoys a temperate climate, an added boon to Americans from harsher climes. The southern Atlantic and the Mediterranean coasts rarely dip below freezing and enjoy pleasant daytime temperatures of 50 degrees nine months out of the year, from February through November. The country's coldest region, north above the Loire River, does not rest long under a blanket of snow. July and August are the only months with stretches of 95-degree highs.

With such nice weather, it's no surprise France offers abundant recreational opportunities for outdoor enthusiasts. Two massive mountain ranges, the Pyrénées and the Alps, border the country on the south and the east, respectively, providing Olympic-caliber skiing on nearly 80,000 miles of runs, plus hiking, biking, and other activities, all just a few hours from any location in the country. On the two coasts, extensive beaches offer chances to laze away the day, comb for seashells, or go boating—not to mention abundant fresh fish and seafood.

From the rolling plains of Champagne to the forests of the Massif Central, France boasts a tremendously varied geography paralleled only by its cultural variety. A distance of 10 miles can bring noticeable changes in the language, in the crops, in the architecture, and certainly in how the local population defines itself.

Vive La Difference

Cultural differences, that is. Indeed, the lifestyle differences between the two countries comprise the main attraction to France for many Americans. Few French people spend hours commuting to work, for example, like millions of their American counterparts. And lunch "hour"? What's that? The French linger over meals and, as a rule, eat healthier, better food than the average American. They don't sit in front of the TV for hours each day, but rather visit friends and spend time with their families. And the French government debates issues for months, not years, and acts decisively at the end of the process.

There is no better example of the French dedication to quality of life than the country's adoption of a 35-hour work—heresy to the American business mindset, where productivity is king. But the French ask, "Is that our only goal? What about expanding employment opportunities? What about family

The Chateauneuf de Pape vineyard in Southern France

J.L. Seille

Symbols of France

For two centuries, France's most enduring symbol has been Marianne, the personification of Liberty. She is often depicted wearing a Phrygian cap, the cloth headgear worn by freed slaves in Greece and Rome. Mediterranean seamen wore a similar cap, as did revolutionaries in the South of France.

One of the best known depictions is Eugène Delacroix's *Liberté guidant le peuple*, in which a bare-breasted Marianne strides on the battlefield, one hand gripping a musket with fixed bayonet, the other hoisting the French flag.

Marie-Anne was a very common woman's name in late 18th and early 19th centuries, and as the figure came to represent the commoner, counter-revolutionaries poked fun at the name. But during the Third Republic, busts of Marianne began appearing in public places in France. Today, coins and stamps bear the image.

Until 1969, Marianne was merely a symbol—no living woman personified her. That all changed when a sculptor gave his version of Marianne the features of France's most famous movie star. Others followed suit, and now mayors across the country vote for the model they deem most personifies Marianne. The current holder of the title is fashion model Laetitia Casta.

If Marianne is the human symbol of France, "*La Marseillaise*" is the musical equivalent. Like Marianne, the song was born of battle. And like Marianne, it was freely adapted for decades before an official version was produced.

The rousing song dates to 1792, when Capt. Claude-Joseph Rouget de Lisle composed a tune he called "Battle Song of the Army of the Rhine" while stationed in Strasbourg during the war against Austria. Volunteers from Marseille took up the song and the "*Hymne des Marseillais*" spread rapidly.

Rouget's work may have saved his life during the Reign of Terror. Although the composer was merely a political moderate, not a revolutionary, he was well known as the creator of the popular tune. On July 14, 1795, "*La Marseillaise*" was declared a national song.

Napoleon banned it, however, and it did not regain its status until the revolution of

---

life?" To the French, other values are just as important as productivity, an attitude many Americans living in France find balm to their overworked souls.

Anyone who moves to France should do so with the same intention he or she would have in moving from Boston to San Diego—to become a fully functioning member of a new community, despite the distance from friends and family. Travelers should pack an ample supply of patience, curiosity, and desire to participate in their adopted culture. The sort of person who should *not* consider moving to France (or to any other foreign country, for that matter) is one likely to keep sighing, "Back home, we do things *this* way."

The United States and France: Les Amis

Along with welcome differences in lifestyle, Americans living in France enjoy a certain resonance with the French. After all, historical ties have connected the two nations for more than 200 years. We may speak different languages, but Americans and the French share many cultural symbols and philosophical beliefs.

1830, when Hector Berlioz wrote an orchestration dedicated to Rouget.

In 1879 the Third Republic proclaimed "*La Marseillaise*" the French national anthem, but without designating any particular version. It took a commission of professional musicians in 1887 to work out a single rendition. Occasionally some public figure will complain about the bloodthirsty lyrics, but to no avail. "And drench our fields with their tainted blood!/Oh come, come see your foes now die" just has a certain ring to it.

France's flag, the red, blue, and white *tricolore*, also had its conception in the revolution, followed by a long period of gestation. The three colors have three origins: Paris and a militia formed just before the storming of the Bastille contributed red and blue—the French capital's official colors and the hues of the militia's insignia. White, the color of the king, was added by Lafayette, commander of the National Guard, just before Louis XVI arrived to inspect the troops on July 17, 1789.

In 1794 the *tricolore* was officially adopted as the French flag. During the 19th century, revolutionaries and royalists battled over flag color and design, but the Third Republic brought consensus. By World War I, the country was united under the flag, which became enshrined in the constitutions of 1946 and 1958.

Perhaps the most ancient symbol of France, the rooster, has not met with universal approval. The image was printed on ancient coins from Gaul, perhaps as a pun—Latin *gallus* means "rooster." In the 14th century the Germans used it in reference to France, and by the 16th century, it began appearing on French coins. It was used following the revolution, but Napoleon refused to accept it: "The rooster has no strength," the emperor growled. "In no way can it stand as the image of an empire such as France."

Revolutionaries took the opposite tack, however, and the rooster appeared on a gold coin of 1899, as well as in propaganda as an opponent of the German eagle during World War I. These days, however, it is mostly used in foreign countries to symbolize France and, in France, to symbolize sports.

The mutual attraction between the two nations has existed since the beginning of the United States. For starters, the American Revolution provided an impetus for France's own. French Protestants fleeing persecution by an intolerant monarchy sought refuge in America just as, generations later, American free thinkers and artists found welcome refuge from puritanical mores in Paris, long viewed as the cultural center of the Western world. The two nations' concern with the human spirit and intellect—and the freedom to explore ideas—formed the first bonds.

Remember, it was French General Lafayette who offered military aid to George Washington. Founding fathers Benjamin Franklin and Thomas Jefferson so admired the French they visited the country as American ambassadors. French political scientist Alex de Tocqueville returned the praise in his famous study of the young United States.

The ties continued into the 20th century. When World War I began, American sympathies lay with France and Great Britain, finally prompting our intervention on their side. "Lafayette, we are here," General John J. Pershing intoned when he and his troops landed in France in 1917, acknowledging a 150-year-old debt.

It was the political connections during that war that led to more personal ones. At last, ordinary Americans got a vivid glimpse of a world already known to the well-to-do elite. A world in which wine was an everyday beverage and meal preparation approached an art form. A world in which common folks' houses were built to last centuries, not a few years. A world in which writers and artists and intellectuals of every stripe were not only welcomed, but celebrated.

These connections endure today, enhanced by air travel that brings Paris as close to New York as the Big Apple is to San Diego, by telecommunications that bridge the distance between family members and friends, and by a global economy that produces similar products everywhere. A McDonald's hamburger tastes no different in Toulouse than it does in Topeka. Rest assured, you won't give up any modern conveniences by moving to France.

France's Future

But modern conveniences cost, and France pays the price. Just like other industrialized nations, France suffers its share of urban sprawl, congested highways, crime, and poverty. Don't move to France to escape the 21st century or Western civilization. But do admire the nation for its willingness to tackle these problems in a rational way: to study and debate them, then implement positive solutions.

France is poised at the beginning of its third millennium as a nation with great natural and cultural resources, a checkered political history, and

The French Pyrénées

a proven desire to surpass the average. Change is coming here as quickly as anywhere in the world.

With an economy firmly tied to most of the rest of Europe, with trade barriers falling and costing jobs but lowering prices, the French voice in international affairs is sometimes only one hoarse whisper among a rising clamor. And with a 19.6 percent value-added tax weighing heavy on every purchase of goods, labor, and service, the French can see that the future will not resemble the past.

Most French people look forward to the future, knowing that change is inevitable and willing to work to turn it to their advantage. It is an enviable attitude, one that can make your move to France a pleasant and profitable experience.

Where Should You Live?

Paris remains the primary attraction for American visitors, if not all emigrants, as it has for generations past. This is where Gene Kelly was "Singin' in the Rain." African-American musicians like Bud Powell, Charlie Parker, and Ben Webster found the French cared more about their music than the color of their skin. Among those who found postwar Paris a congenial milieu was a young wife who took cooking classes to while away the hours when her businessman husband was at work. Julia Child later collaborated with two of her teachers on the two-volume *Art of French Cooking* that has helped transform American cuisine.

Paris is still a magical city—at least to visit. Living in a major metropolitan area, anywhere in the world, isn't for everyone. Business people may be attracted to those towns and regions offering greater employment opportunities or financial incentives to those who wish to engage in commerce in France. Retirees might find a mountain village, a coastal cottage, or a little farm more appealing. You can live in a small village of 1,000 people and still enjoy good public transportation, find doctors and nurses who actually make house calls, greet merchants who call you by name, and dine on fresh produce and seafood—all without losing access to big-city benefits.

> *This is France today, a land that has preserved what is good and beautiful and true from its past and made it work in the present.*

Thanks to France's rapid rail system, cities large and small are connected, as France is to the rest of Europe, with a speed most Americans find astonishing. What's more, international airports are common, and the country's highway system, Europe's most extensive, makes auto travel easy and fast.

In short, throughout most of France, you can find a quality of life that is difficult to match anywhere in the world.

2 An Overview of France

The French call their country the "Hexagon" for the six rough sides that form its boundaries. The northeastern side borders Belgium, Luxembourg, and Germany. To the east, the Alps and the Rhine separate France from Germany, Switzerland, and Italy. The Mediterranean coast forms the southeastern side; the Pyrénées, the southern; the Atlantic coast, the western; and the coast along the English Channel, the northwestern.

The Lay of the Land

The Hexagon contains 543,965 square kilometers (337,258 square miles) of land inhabited by 60 million people, approximately one percent of the world population. Although France lies between the same latitudes as Newfoundland and Boston, the country's climate is more temperate—the south sees little or no snow each year. Even in the semi-arid Mediterranean basin, annual rainfall averages about 600 millimeters (24 inches). Fruits, vegetables, and grains flourish in the fertile soil. Pastureland and vineyards roll across poorer ground.

A network of great rivers—the Rhône, the Seine, the Loire, and the Garonne—along with their lesser tributaries provide abundant water to almost every region of the country. The basins drained by these rivers yield much of France's famed agricultural production, one of the keys to its prosperity. The well-forested lower mountains ringing the Massif Central, the great uplift of land in the center of the country, historically provided much of the timber fuel the nation needed. Slightly more than a quarter of France is forested, most of this land lying east of a diagonal line drawn between Bordeaux in the southwest and Luxembourg in the northeast. Today, much of this thinly populated region is a favorite recreation area.

Paris

The heart as well as the head of the country is Paris and the Île-de-France region surrounding it. Home to 10 million people, Paris is the seat of government, as it has been for centuries. The city and environs are also the economic and industrial core of the nation, the world's favorite vacation destination, and the center for France's famed universities, museums, and cultural institutions.

> *The heart as well as the head of the country is Paris and the Île-de-France region surrounding it.*

It is difficult to overemphasize the cultural richness of Paris. The smart shops, the food markets, the sidewalk cafés, and the restaurants all serve to showcase the wealth of ingenuity that created it all.

The physical city itself, blending modernity with historical preservation, is breathtaking—old, worn stone façades on the outside, chrome and glass on the inside. What better example of how the French maintain their *patrimoine* (national heritage) than the Musée D'Orsay. They took a grimy old train station and turned it into an aesthetically pleasing 21st-century home for some of the greatest art in the Western world. The Musée D'Orsay is emblematic of the French refusal to bulldoze their past in order to satisfy the present. Instead, they adapt what has been to serve what now must be and in doing so, provide for the future.

Wherever you go, you'll detect this sense of continuity, of history unfolding, of a tapestry still in the making, from broad esplanades like the Champs de Mars, leading to the Eiffel tower, to I. M. Pei's glass pyramid in front of the Louvre, from the narrowest alley of Montmarte to the stones paving the plaza in front of Nôtre Dame. Paris, you could say, is synonymous with civilization—and it ain't bad.

But it was from agrarian roots that the magnificent city grew. Paris is situated in a great plain. It was the rich soil of the Seine river basin that first attracted the grain-growing Celtic tribes from Central Europe a millennia ago. The fertile soil, easily turned with a primitive plow, the mild climate, and ample rainfall produced bountiful harvests.

The Regions of France

Let's take Paris as our reference point to explore the regions of France.

Wooded, rolling plains account for much of the terrain surrounding Paris. To the north lie Picardie and Flanders, where the city of Lille is gaining importance as a crossroads. The high-speed train from London, which zips under the English Channel, arrives in Lille; other trains leave for Brussels, Amsterdam, Paris, Germany, and Geneva.

To the northeast stretch Champagne, Verdun, and the Ardennes uplands. Much of this territory was the setting for the terrible trench warfare of World War I and the blitzkrieg of World War II. The landscape has recovered, but war memorials in every town and village are grim reminders that this area has long been in the path of invaders.

West of Paris lies Normandy, famous for its dairies and cheeses, its apples and cider—and its WWII beaches. Omaha and Utah beaches were put on the map of Western military history June 6, 1944—D-Day to Americans, *Jour-J* to the French. Normandy is also home to Deauville and Trouville beaches and to the little harbor of Honfleur, where Samuel Champlain set sail for the New World. Normandy is a weekend escape for many Parisians, and, in turn, ideally situated for Normandy residents who like to make frequent day trips into Paris. It is well served by both rail and highways.

Further west is Brittany. The region's pink granite coastline, apple orchards, fishing villages, and sometimes wet and stormy weather bespeak a rustic peace at odds with its historically violent movement for independence.

Southwest of Paris lies Chartes, home to the stunning cathedral, and Orléans. Situated at the northernmost curve of the Loire, the longest river in France, Orléans is the gateway to the Loire Valley, dotted with grand châteaux. The Loire Valley and its tributaries cut through the limestone plateau and finally flow into the Atlantic past Nantes, one of France's fastest-growing metropolitan areas. The grapes of the Loire are white ones, chenin blanc and sauvignon blanc, from which the crisp Sancerre wine is produced.

In medieval fashion, the town of Chartres was built with the houses gathered around the church, which rests on the hilltop.

France from Ain (01) to Val d'Oise (95)

France is divided into 100 *départements* (departments). Six of these lie outside the borders of the country. The island of Corsica contains two, and the *Départements outre-mer* (DOM) account for the remaining four.

The departments, grouped by region, are numbered according to alphabetical order, except for those established in the last century. Territoire de Belfort, for instance, given departmental status in 1922, became No. 90. The five regions around Paris, subdivided in 1964, are also out of order. The two departments of Corsica, which were established as a region in 1974, became 2A and 2B.

Visualize the French political structure as a pyramid of parallel structures involving communes, cantons, and departments. Every commune, roughly equivalent to a U.S. town or city, has a mayor and a council. In turn, communes are grouped into cantons, and a representative from each is elected to sit on the council of the department, not unlike a county board of supervisors in the United States.

Each department has a *préfet* (prefect), who represents the national government and commands the national police units stationed in that department. The *préfet*'s headquarters, called the *préfecture*, is located in the department's main city. Branch offices, called *sous préfectures*, are sprinkled throughout the department for convenience. Visas, *cartes de séjour* (residency permits), and auto registrâtion are handled at the *préfecture*.

The departments grouped into a region elect a regional council, comparable to a state government, although with less power. Most taxation is in the hands of the national government, which in turn disburses funds for education, police force, and the like, back to the regions, departments, and communes.

Listed below are the departments and their populations:

REGION	POPULATION	DEPARTMENT	POPULATION
Alsace	1,729,800	Bas-Rhin (67)	1,023,600
		Haut-Rhin (68)	706,200
Aquitaine	2,902,000	Gironde (33)	1,284,800
		Pyrénées-Atlantique (64)	598,000
		Dordogne (24)	387,600
		Landes (40)	327,000
		Lot-et-Garonne (47)	304,900
Auvergne	1,307,206	Puy-de-Dôme (63)	603,000
		Allier (03)	344,619
		Haute-Loire (43)	209,046
		Cantal (15)	150,563
Bourgogne	1,609,500	Saône-et-Loire (71)	544,600
		Côte-d'Or (21)	506,800
		Yonne (89)	333,000
		Nièvre (58)	225,000
Bretagne	2,902,636	Ille-et-Vilaine (35)	866,686
		Finistère (29)	852,143
		Morbihan (56)	642,805
		Côtes d'Armor (22)	541,002

Centre	2,437,500	Loiret (45)	616,900
		Indre-et-Loire (37)	554,100
		Eure-et-Loir (28)	407,200
		Loir-et-Cher (41)	314,600
		Cher (18)	313,600
		Indre (36)	231,000
Champagne-Ardenne	1,341,400	Marne (51)	564,850
		Aube (10)	291,850
		Ardennes (08)	290,000
		Haute-Marne (52)	194,700
Corse	256,000	Haute-Corse (2A)	140,000
		Corse-du-Sud (2B)	116,000
Franche-Comté	1,115,600	Doubs (25)	498,200
		Jura (39)	250,500
		Haut-Saône (70)	229,600
		Territoire de Belfort (90)	137,400
Île-de-France	10,925,600	Paris (75)	2,116,200
		Hauts-de-Seine (92)	1,423,200
		Seine-St-Denis (93)	1,382,100
		Yvelines (78)	1,352,600
		Val-de-Marne (94)	1,222,900
		Seine-et-Maritime (76)	1,192,900
		Essonne (91)	1,132,900
		Val-d'Oise (95)	1,102,800
Languedoc-Roussillon	2,293,400	Hérault (34)	896,000
		Gard (30)	622,300
		Pyrénées-Orientales (66)	392,000
		Aude (11)	309,600
		Lozère (48)	73,500
Limousin	710,000	Haute-Vienne (87)	353,400
		Corrèze (19)	232,100
		Creuse (23)	124,500
Lorraine	2,308,100	Moselle (57)	1,022,800
		Meurthe-et-Moselle (54)	712,800
		Vosges (88)	380,400
		Meuse (55)	192,100
Midi-Pyrénées	2,548,500	Haute-Garonne (31)	1,046,200
		Tarn (81)	342,400

France from Ain (01) to Val d'Oise (95) (continued)

Region	Region Pop.	Department	Pop.
		Aveyron (12)	263,300
		Hautes-Pyrénées (65)	222,000
		Tarn-et-Garonne (82)	205,792
		Gers (32)	171,900
		Lot (46)	159,700
		Ariège (09)	137,200
Nord-Pas-de-Calais	3,990,167	Nord (59)	2,549,785
		Pas-de-Calais (62)	1,440,382
Basse-Normandie	1,420,300	Calvados (14)	647,400
		Manche (50)	481,400
		Orne (61)	291,500
Haute-Normandie	1,777,400	Seine-Maritime (76)	1,237,400
		Eure (27)	540,000
Pays de la Loire	3,218,517	Loire-Atlantique (44)	1,132,024
		Maine-et-Loire (49)	732,455
		Vendée (85)	539,362
		Sarthe (72)	529,366
		Mayenne (53)	285,310
Picardie	1,855,900	Oise (60)	765,000
		Somme (80)	556,200
		Aisne (02)	534,700
Poitou-Charentes	1,637,200	Charente-Maritme (17)	556,400
		Vienne (86)	398,300
		Deux-Sèvres (79)	343,500
		Charente (16)	339,000
Provence-Alpes-Côte-d'Azur	4,494,500	Bouches-du-Rhône (13)	1,832,600
		Alpes-Maritime (06)	1,007,700
		Var (83)	893,800
		Vaucluse (84)	500,700
		Alpes-Hautes-Provence (04)	139,600
		Hautes-Alpes (05)	120,000
Rhône-Alpes	5,634,500	Rhône (69)	1,575,000
		Isère (38)	1,091,000
		Loire (42)	728,000
		Haute-Savoie (74)	631,000 (01)
		Ain (01)	515,000
		Drôme (26)	437,000
		Savoie (73)	372,000
		Ardèche (07)	286,000

East of Paris the land rises gradually until the eastern slope of the Vosges Mountains drops steeply into Alsace and the Rhine River, the border with Germany. Strasbourg, for centuries a beautiful city on the Rhine at the head of the narrow valley that follows the river down from Switzerland, has gained new importance as the home of the European Parliament, the legislative body of the European Union.

Burgundy, southeast of Paris, beckons Parisian weekenders with its storied vineyards and colorful past; through marriage to a Burgundian princess Clovis, king of the Franks, converted to Catholicism. Further to the east rise the Jura Mountains.

Following the Rhône River south you come to Lyon, western gateway to the Alps, Switzerland, and northern Italy. To the southwest lies Grenoble, a high-tech industrial center, and the Savoy, the mountainous region bordering Italy. The Savoy and Nice were first annexed to France following the revolution, but lost with the fall of Napoleon. The region was brought back into France in 1860.

France's favorite retirement locale, the region stretching from Nice west to Montpellier, is prized for the same reason American snowbirds flock to Florida, Southern California, and Arizona—the weather. The Côte d'Azur, Provence, and Languedoc all enjoy mild winters (daytime temperatures of 45 to 55 degrees), hot summers (85 to 100 degrees in July and August), and gorgeous springs and falls. Provence and the Côte d'Azur, especially, have attracted a wealthy, international group of residents that includes many Americans, as Peter Mayle's popular books attest.

This region is also one of France's prime vacation destinations. July and August bring streams of tourists. Inland from the coast, both the

A small country road leading up into the Pyrénées

residents and the tourists thin out. In Aix-en-Provence, a center for foreign universities operating in France, you'll overhear students from all corners of the globe practicing their French, chatting together in English, or in their common language.

East of Lyon lies the Massif Central, the great plateau rising in the center of the country. Thinly populated, its best-known city is Clermont-Ferrand, home of Michelin tires. Due to the region's numerous volcanoes—none of them active—natural hot springs abound in the area. The Massif is off the beaten path; in place of bustling commerce, you'll find tiny villages where locals are still bound by a tremendous communal spirit and extend to each other authentic neighborliness.

Between the Massif Central and the Pyrénées, west of the Mediterranean, lies the Midi, another rich agricultural area—but one with a high-tech heart, Toulouse. Poultry, wine grapes, vegetables, sunflower, canola and other oils, barley, and corn are all produced here. Toulouse, the center of the French aerospace industry, hosts a large university and numerous software developers.

Amid the Pyrénées live the French Basques, a unique people of unknown origin whose language is unrelated to any of the Romance or Germanic tongues of Europe. Basque culture extends across the mountains, where a fierce independence movement continues, and west to Bayonne on the coast.

One of the many beautiful churches in Strasbourg, Alsace-Lorraine province

Abercrombie and Kent

Northwest of Toulouse, between that city and Bordeaux, is the Dordogne, a region that became popular with the British middle class in the 1980s when property values in Normandy climbed dramatically. The Dordogne, named for the river that joins the Garonne at Bordeaux, is dotted with small villages and farms. Much of the land is forested and very green in spring and summer. The region contains archaeological sites such as world-famous Lascaux, with its magnificent prehistoric cave paintings, as well as the Grotte de Font-de-Gaume, the Grotte de Peche Merle, and others.

Bordeaux and the region have historic ties to England dating to the Middle Ages. When Eleanor of Aquitaine divorced Louis VII in 1152 and married the future Henry II, she became queen of England and her possessions, English territory. These ties continue today through the wine trade. The famous Bordeaux châteaux may disappoint the casual tourist, however. Their wine is too valuable to hand out free samples, and few of the famous castles, privately owned by individuals and corporations, encourage uninvited guests. Pine forests and lakes big and small border the southern Atlantic coast, a favorite summer recreation area. North of Bordeaux, vintners grow grapes for still more wine and for cognac as well.

Populating the regions of France are, of course, the French themselves. The majority—more than 75 percent—live in major cities or their neighboring towns, and, according to the 1999 census, this 20-year trend to urbanization continues. People are leaving rural areas to relocate to large metropolitan centers. Paris draws by far the greatest number, but Nantes, Toulouse, Montpellier, Lyon, Lille, Strasbourg, and Rennes are also magnets. Urbanization has left many rural villages with aging, declining populations and vacant houses. Rushing in to fill the void are foreigners, as well as the French themselves, seeking vacation homes.

How the Country Is Divided

French *régions* (regions), roughly equivalent to American states, are divided into departments, cantons, and communes. The country comprises 100 departments (see sidebar on page 16 for a list), which in turn are divided into cantons and communes.

The commune is the basic geopolitical unit in France. Unlike American towns, French communes extend to the border of the adjacent commune, taking in farmland and forest as well as the town that gives the commune its name. The commune is important because it, and the mayor who runs it, handles much of the business of daily life. Need to renew your *carte de séjour* (residency permit)? Go to the *mairie* (mayor's office) to fill out the forms. Want to buy a house? Clear it with the commune first—it has the right of first refusal. Selling a car? Pick up the form you need at the *mairie*.

Communes are grouped into cantons. Each canton elects a representative to the *Conseil General,* the governing body of the department, the rough equivalent of an American county that also performs some of the functions of a state. For example, automobile registration is by department.

Each department has a *préfet* (prefect), who heads the police force. Although there are municipal police in France, the primary law enforcers are the *gendarmes*, a branch of the Ministry of Defense, and a national police force under the Ministry of the Interior. The *préfet*, their local chief appointed by Paris, administers not only the police force itself, but also auxiliary functions such as automobile registration, driver's licenses, and visas for foreigners. As a foreign resident of France, you may never have occasion to visit the offices of the *Conseil General*, but almost certainly you will become familiar with the prefecture.

Language

France is a nation of many historically autonomous regions, such as Languedoc, Burgundy, and Normandy. Nowhere is this fact more evident than in the language. Linguistically, the country is divided between the north and south—*les langues d'oïl* and *les langues d'óc* (*oïl* signifies "yes" in the north; *óc*, the same in the south). Within these two broad categories are numerous separate languages.

Today, many of the northern tongues classified as *les langues d'oïl*, such as Picard and Normand, have all but disappeared. The important thing to note about all of the minority languages is that they are not foreign, but native tongues. Spoken before the nation of France was fully formed, they have remained alive through the centuries. After all, it was not until the mid-16th century that French became the official language; before then, it was Latin. Historically, the language spoken in powerhouse Paris prevailed linguistically in much the same way that English supplanted Spanish as the official language of Texas and the American Southwest.

The country's numerous immigrant groups provide the ingredients for a veritable linguistic stew. Today, 75 different languages are spoken in France. North Africans from Algeria and Morocco, the largest immigrant group, speak various dialects of Arabic and Berber, and Portuguese, Spanish, Italians, Dutch, Central Africans, Vietnamese, Germans, English and Irish, Scandinavians, and Eastern Europeans all add a dash to the soup. Although schools and telecommunications have had a homogenizing effect on France, linguistic and regional differences remain deeply ingrained. At the level of the European Union, there is an effort to preserve linguistic diversity among the 15 member nations, but only time will tell what the result will be.

Religion

France's immigrant groups also account for religious differences among the French, but make no mistake: France is a Catholic country. Nearly 80 percent of the French are at least nominally Catholic. Roman Catholicism became a potent force in France with the conversion of Clovis, king of the Franks, in 493. Charlemagne undertook the protection of the pope in Rome. It was not until 1905 that church and state were definitively separated in France. Even today, some Catholic feast days, such as Ascension Thursday and All Saints Day, are recognized as national holidays. Other religious holidays that always fall on a Sunday, such as Easter and Pentecost, are followed by recognized Monday holidays.

Only about a million Protestants live in France; over the centuries, Catholic authorities succeeded in driving out most Christian dissenters via persecution and wars. Indeed, it is Islam that is the second-largest religion in France, with about two million followers. France is also home to some 750,000 Jews, 400,000 Buddhists, and 200,000 members of the Orthodox Church. However, no matter a couple's religion, the only valid marriage is a civil one, performed by the mayor or his deputy. A church wedding may follow, but a bride and groom are not legally wed until they have a civil ceremony.

Economy

Economically, France is in an enviable position. Though dwarfed by the United States in any statistical showdown, it remains one of the world's largest economies, ranking with Japan, Germany, and Great Britain. The world's fourth-largest exporter overall, France enjoys a trade surplus, a shrinking public deficit, and low inflation. Since the early 1980s, France has used nuclear power to supply 75 percent of its electricity, cutting its use of coal and imported oil and gas. Slower than the United States to recover from the world recession of the 1990s, France's greatest economic problem remains high unemployment, above 11 percent in 2000.

France has other reasons to crow about its economy. It is the world's second-largest exporter of services and agricultural products, and fourth-largest of automobiles, a rank that Renault's recent alliance with Nissan seems sure to enhance. The nation produces 20 percent of Europe's food products and leads the continent in the aerospace industry. Privatization of industry continues, following both international trade rules opening national markets and European Union regulations limiting national subsidies.

At the level of the European Union, France's commitment to join most other member nations in establishing a single currency appears beneficial as globalization continues. The euro, as the new monetary unit is called, welds France and 10 other nations into a single economic unit, comparable to or greater than the United States in population, productivity, and consumption. The franc is not scheduled to vanish until 2002, when the new money makes its appearance, but the value of the euro was fixed at the end of 1998 as equaling 6.55957 francs, and prices throughout the country now appear in both francs and euros. It is now the euro that fluctuates in relation to the dollar and the yen and other world currencies, so the exchange rate continues to be important. After initially being valued at $1.17, the euro fell to about $0.90, making the dollar equal to about 7.25 francs. (In this book,

A United States of Europe?

The European Union is a done deal. Fifty years in the making, the economies of the 15 member nations are already running on parallel tracks, and, slowly but surely, their laws being brought into conformity with one another.

France and Germany are the two great engines driving this unification. The United Kingdom hung back from the EU for years and, although it ultimately joined, it has refused to accept the common currency, the euro.

No one can say whether this unity is forever. The lessons of Yugoslavia and the former Soviet Union teach very well how quickly things can fall apart. Austria's coalition included a neo-fascist element, to the dismay of other nations, and rising oil prices and the falling euro have wreaked some havoc economically.

But at this point, the entwining of the national economies, the free movement of the populations among the nations, and the cooperation among European institutions are gaining enough momentum that even slowing down the process seems unlikely.

The primary governing body of the EU is the Council of the European Union. Each member nation's government takes a turn as council president for six months; voting on issues is weighted according to size of the country. France, Germany, Italy, and the United Kingdom each have 10 votes, Spain has eight, and so on, for a total of 87 votes.

Overall work of the council is coordinated by the foreign affairs ministers of each country, but negotiations on particular areas, such as agriculture, are handled by the ministers for that field. The council enacts laws proposed by the European Commission, the EU's legal and budgetary advisory.

The commission consists of 20 members, two each appointed from France, Germany, Italy, Spain, and the UK, and one from other member nations. The commission proposes legislation for the council to enact or reject, enforces treaties, and can investigate and take action against companies or countries. It manages the EU budget and negotiates international trade agreements.

Supporting the commission are various advisory and technical bodies staffed by some 15,000 people. A full 3,000 of them translators; the EU transacts business in 11 different languages.

The European Parliament, located in Strasbourg, serves as a public forum. Its 626 members are directly elected to five-year terms on an EU-wide basis by party affiliation rather than nationality. Parliament can veto the budget or fire the commission. Though it cannot enact laws, it has the power to veto the commission's proposals and amend the council's acts.

A court of justice sits in Luxembourg and acts as a supreme court for the EU. Every member nation names one justice to sit on the court. Its decisions overrule those of member states.

The EU is clearly an evolving entity. No one believes that it will remain in its present form. A common currency is a big step

monetary conversions are calculated at 1 euro = 90 cents. Because the exchange rate fluctuates, consider all dollar amounts ballpark figures.)

Standard of Living

The French standard of living is a high one. Education is the largest government expenditure, accounting for 37 percent of the national budget. Minimum wage is about 1,050 euros ($950) per month. The average annual wage

forward, but only 11 of the 15 members entered into the euro system. Another pressure is admission of new nations.

When you look at France today and tomorrow, you must look at it in relation to the EU.

"Far from denying the principle of nationhood, Europe is its extension," Prime Minister Lionel Jospin told the National Assembly in May 2000 as he prepared for France's six-month stint as EU president. "European affairs are no longer foreign affairs, and the European debate is not separate from the national debate. France exists fully in its own right but cannot be separated from Europe."

None of the 15 EU members have yielded their national sovereignty. What they have done through a series of treaties is agree to adopt the same laws and regulations as their neighbors.

This has had huge repercussions in France, most notably in criminal law. The Napoleonic stricture "guilty until proven innocent" has been supplanted by the EU's adoption of "innocent until proven guilty." Less momentous but still the cause of some grumbling, new game laws affect French hunters, adversely they say. EU health and sanitation rules have closed some small businesses and required others to change old practices.

The most celebrated clash between France and the EU so far was the refusal of the French government to lift its ban on the importation of British beef once EU experts deemed the risk of *vache folle* (mad cow disease) was minimal. France wasn't just being ornery: It is the only country in which elected officials can be held criminally liable for their decisions. A former prime minister and his health officials, for instance, were tried in 1999 for allowing blood contaminated with the HIV virus to be dispensed by French blood banks in the 1980s, before they had an effective test for the virus.

On the economic front, due to EU policies French farmers face unwanted imports. Public works bidding has opened up, often to the detriment of French entrepreneurs. And French consumers gnash their teeth while other Europeans pay less for Renaults than they do.

In short, the EU affects nearly everyone and everything in France to some degree. In many respects, global economic and technological changes are producing much of this change; the EU is simply the mechanism by which Europe has chosen to deal with those forces.

Can the current members maintain the economic and political standards already attained? No one really knows. Will the current consensus break down? It's unlikely, but it could fray around the edges. Can those countries applying for membership achieve and maintain the economic and political standards of the current members? No one really knows.

What does seem certain is that the two nations that did so much to rip the continent apart in the past century—France and Germany—are determined to hold it together during this one.

is roughly 20,000 euros ($18,000); the average family saves more than 15 percent of that amount. Professionals earn about 70,000 euros ($63,000) annually. The average French family spends about 200 euros ($180) per year on hygiene and beauty products alone. Here is where the money goes in the average French household—not that different from its American counterpart:

Housing, electricity, heating: 22.3 percent
Food, drink, and tobacco: 17.8 percent
Transportation and communications: 16.7 percent

Health care: 10.3 percent
Household goods and maintenance: 7.3 percent
Leisure and culture: 7.4 percent
Clothing: 5.2 percent
Misc. (restaurants, travel, etc.): 13 percent

Getting Around

Getting around France is easy. Unlike in the United States, where public transportation is a hassle in all but major metro areas, France boasts a plethora of international airports, Europe's most extensive highway system, rapid rail transit both within the country and to destinations throughout Europe, and, in most cities and towns, reliable public transportation.

If flight is your preferred mode of travel, you're in luck in France. Even small cities of 50,000 may have an international airport, although flights may be limited to one other country. Air France, as well as other major airlines, serves regional airports from the Paris hub, usually with several flights daily.

Air travel is relatively expensive, however. For that reason alone, don't overlook the TGV (*Train Grande Vitesse,* or high-speed train). For about one-half the cost of an airline ticket, the TGV will whisk you across the country in five or six hours, at speeds up to 300 kilometers per hour (186 mph). TGV lines run down the Rhône Valley to Marseille and Nice, and traverse the west side of the country to Bordeaux, Biarritz, and Toulouse. TGV lines also connect Paris with London, Brussels, and other major European cities.

Driving is also easy in France. French highways, generally well maintained, fall into three main categories: the limited-access autoroute (*peage,* or toll road), designated by an A before the number; national routes, designated by an N before the number; and departmental roads, with a D before the number.

One of the winding roads that snakes its way through the Languedoc countryside

If you want to move swiftly across country by car, autoroutes are the way to go; the speed limit is 130 kilometers per hour (83 mph) in dry weather. Many drivers exceed the limit and expect slower vehicles to move to the right. Autoroutes are as expensive as they are speedy: You'll pay about 8 cents per kilometer.

The national routes are also good roads, but not limited access. In the past, they were mostly two-lane highways, but are gradually being upgraded where possible to three- or four-lane divided roads. Many of them parallel an autoroute.

Departmental highways vary considerably in width and condition. In thinly populated regions, they are seldom more than two lanes wide. But even so, the main routes, which carry heavy trucks, are well built and maintained. The speed limit on these roads is 90 kph (57 mph). There are two drawbacks to departmental highways: one, tailgating drivers angling for space to pass; the other, the signage or lack thereof.

For example, a departmental road's number may change crossing from one department to another. In rural France, if you don't have a good map you should know the names of the villages along your route rather than rely on highway numbers. Even if the number remains constant, signs may be nonexistent. When they are present, they may indicate only villages a few kilometers up the road, not towns and cities several kilometers away. Drive the back roads of France and sooner or later you'll come to a sign pointing in opposite directions to the same village. Rest assured, both roads will get there eventually.

3 Planning Your Fact-Finding Trip

*L*ots of people fall in love with France the first time they visit. But no one should decide to move there without taking a realistic look at what everyday life in France will be like. The best way to do that is to visit the country and stay where you think you might like to live for as long as you can. At the very least, explore life beyond Paris and the tourist spots. Follow the tips in this chapter to discover for yourself the terrain, climate, and general conditions that appeal to you—don't depend solely on the opinions of others.

Know Yourself

It's time to take an inventory of all the factors—practical, cultural, financial, emotional, geographical—that make you feel at home. For example, climate, terrain, and vegetation all have profound effects on people whether they realize it or not—especially when the familiar supports of culture and acquaintances are abruptly removed. Someone who has spent his or her life on the Midwestern plains, for example, might find the Alps or the Pyrénées a trial; someone from the Rockies might be dismayed by the flatness of the Camargue. Many people find the Mediterranean coast too dry and rocky for their tastes; others find the lush greenery of the Dordogne damp and uninviting. Are you more comfortable in certain landscapes than others?

Similarly, are you an aggressive urbanite, or are you a retiring type who likes it when the sidewalks roll up at dusk? Just as in the United States, daily life in a city in France is far different than life in a small village or the country. If you've always lived in a city, many conveniences you take for granted will be unavailable in a small town. And if you've only dreamed of living on a farm, don't expect the reality to match your dream—although it may still be the life you want.

Consider your lifestyle. Will you be working, studying, or retired? What about your spouse or partner? Think about how you actually like to spend your free time. Is golf a passion, for instance? Many parts of France have no golf courses. Is a day without soap operas, or any American television, a grim one for you? Your favorite programming may not be aired in France. What about fast food? Yes, there are McDonalds in France, but fast food is not a primary staple in this culinary capital. What about reading? Even if you speak French fluently, you may be reluctant to give up recreational

Don't Leave Home Without...

The application process for obtaining a visa will require you to collect certain records, such as birth certificates and marriage licenses. Beyond that, in preparing to move to France, don't forget to gather other important documents, some personal, some professional.

And don't forget to make copies of them and leave them in a trusted location in the United States. Just as aggravating as finding yourself in France without some necessary document is returning to the States only to discover you left your papers in France.

Cover all your bases. Write down an inventory of all your important papers—and make a copy of that, too.

If you or the person usually responsible for the information is incapacitated, God forbid, someone else can find it.

Here is a checklist of the documents you should gather:

- If you own real estate in the United States, collect deeds or mortgage papers, insurance policies, tax records, and guarantees on applicances (water heaters, air conditioners, etc.). In the event of an emergency or the need for repairs, make a list of the service people and building contractors you trust.
- Records of all bank accounts, copies of state and federal tax records, insurance policies, and pension funds. It's probably best to leave stocks with a brokerage, since you may wish to sell or trade them at some point.
- A list of the Social Security numbers, credit card numbers, and passport numbers of all family members.
- Medical records (documenting vaccinations, allergies, eyeglass or contact lens prescriptions, etc.) and a list of the names and phone numbers of your doctors, dentists, optometrists, pharmacists, and other health-care providers.
- An inventory of everything left in storage in the States, including the precise locations. If you or anyone else has to find something, an inventory of numbered boxes detailing the contents of each will be an enormous help.
- Employment and educational records, including awards and letters of recommendation.
- Current addresses and phone numbers of your friends, family members, and business associates. A list of your friends' and relatives' birthdays (and their children's).
- Notarized powers of attorney for you and your spouse or companion.

reading in English, and you can't pop around the corner to pick up a copy of the *New Yorker* or the latest John Grisham paperback in a French village. Are you used to endless selection in supermarkets, year-round? Produce is much more seasonal in France. Apples are available all the time, but not apricots; cherries appear in late spring and vanish by mid-summer.

Life is lived in the details, and you should look closely at your own to see if your preferences can be met in France, or if you can comfortably, willingly adapt.

Talk to Folks

Talk to as many different people as you can who have been in the country. Find out what they liked and disliked about France. Try to meet French people in the United States. Consider hosting a French student, for example, or hire a French au pair. In general, try to establish contacts, so that when you do visit France you will be able to meet people and discuss your ideas and plans with them. The opportunity to hear their viewpoints will be invaluable.

Study Maps

To familiarize yourself with the regions and geography of France, buy good maps and study them. Michelin's are perhaps best known and widely available, but Blay and IGN are also good. A map of the whole country in book format on the scale of 1:200,000 or 1:250,000, with an index, is an excellent place to begin. Such a map will show every commune and even isolated farmhouses; the index will save lots of time no matter where in France you go. Once in the country, you can use it for touring.

Also get a large map of the entire country; it will give you a better sense of proportion—just how far one place is from another, not in kilometers or miles but in relation to places perhaps you already know.

Read

Read up on France. You might start with guidebooks, but remember, most are written by and for foreign tourists, not residents. Among the best are the Michelin Green Guides. Available in English or French, they are packed with maps and good information—historical, geological, and archaeological, as well as practical information about places of interest, transportation, and the like.

From there you can move on to travel literature by authors such as Peter Mayle who have lived in France, fiction set in France, histories of France, and so on.

Once you arrive in France, you'll find more specialized books available. Don't overlook magazines as a source of information on a region or topic. Many fine regional guides in France are published as slick magazines with superb photography and sold on the newsstands rather than in bookstores.

Study French

Even before you visit, consider spending some time studying French. If you move there, you will need to be able to speak at least rudimentary French—after all, you'll be surrounded by French speakers. Knowing some French before you get there will give you a definite advantage. And if you find that French is just not a language you want to speak, France might not be the country you want to live in, either. (See Chapter 4 for information on French language instruction in the United States.)

When you visit France, consider spending your time there studying French. Language classes are conducted throughout the country; finding one that suits your needs in the region that interests you is likely. The instructors may prove helpful and knowledgeable beyond language lessons in the classroom. Part of class may very well be spent discussing the customs of the country and answering students' questions about French life.

Consider Your Family, Relatives, and Friends

It's always easier to make a big change when the people dear to you support your decision. If you're relocating the whole family, how does each member feel about the move? If you have school age children, especially teenagers, how will they adapt? Just because you like the idea of living in a foreign country or a small village doesn't mean your children will. Then again, they might view it as the adventure of a lifetime.

> *... no one should decide to move there without taking a realistic look at what everyday life in France will be like.*

Beyond your immediate family, how about your relatives and friends? It is very common for some relatives and close friends to react to the decision as if it were some sort of personal betrayal. Yes, there are telephones and letters and email, but the fact is, you're considering moving thousands of miles away. It is the emotional experience that will likely determine your eventual satisfaction with the move. While the actual travel time and expense are not much more than many trips within the United States, the psychological separation is far greater.

This is because, although it's relatively easy to keep up with the public events of both societies, it is very difficult to be a participating member of two widely separated communities. Much of the personal minutiae of our lives—who died or divorced or moved away or made a fool of themselves—gets lost. The ephemera of popular culture in the U.S. is not communicated in France. Few Americans know or care about the ephemera of France. Sooner or later you must commit to one country or the other, to decide where you will live and where you will vacation. That is the real challenge—and the reason some relatives and friends may resist your move. Your move will inevitably change some of your personal relationships. Unless you come to terms with that, and understand the enormity of the change you're undertaking, your new life in France may be more frustrating than rewarding.

Visit France

No decision-making process about moving to the country is complete before you've actually visited France. Try to stay as long as possible and live as you would at home. If you've never been outside of Paris, definitely plan on touring the country. France has many faces and finding the countenance that suits you is important. You're an immigrant, not a refugee. You have a choice of where you are going to go, or if you are going to go at all. You may decide that Paris is, after all, where you want to be, but at the same time you'll know more about your adopted country.

There are a few essential items you should take on your fact-finding mission. First, a small calculator, one of those solar-powered, credit-card sized

Collioure, Languedoc-Rousillon

Archie Satterfield

ones. You will be converting dollars to euros and square feet to square meters or vice versa, and adding up various costs wherever you go. It's a handy tool.

Also pack a good French-English dictionary or plan on buying one on arrival. A small paperback version may be nice to carry in the car when sightseeing, but it won't help you write a letter, frame an argument, or provide a context for many of the words you may encounter. Nor will the paper binding stand much use.

Depending on your language ability, a phrase book for travelers such as those published by Berlitz is handy. This type of book condenses a lot of information and vocabulary, packages it in a useable format, and gives a reasonable guide to pronunciation.

Now, start looking around. Tour the country. After you've identified the regions you like, rent a house or an apartment for two weeks or a month and try to fit into the daily life around you. Or try several different regions for a week at a time. Do it more than once and at different times of the year if you can. You may love Paris in the springtime, as countless others have, but not in the winter. Californians, who have been told they live in a Mediterranean climate, may be surprised to find it can and does rain in Languedoc and Provence any month of the year, and that there really are four seasons, not just a wet one and a dry one.

Embarrassing as it may be at first, practice your French. Can people understand you? Do you understand them? These efforts are going to be informative well beyond language ability itself. They will help you gauge how ordinary people respond to you.

Keep an itemized accounting of your expenditures for food and gas and anything else you buy. Spend some time going into stores and looking at prices; make a note of them for your future reference. Are items you would likely purchase if you lived here readily available, or is there a substitute? If the electric meter where you stay is visible, take a reading to see how much electricity you use.

Whether you are moving temporarily or permanently to France, think about renting property. Even for those who intend to buy eventually, a rental affords the opportunity to get to know a city or village before committing to a purchase and also to have the time to find the property that they really want, rather than a hurried compromise.

Time Difference

As you're planning your trip, bear in mind the time difference between France and the United States.

Without taking into account daylight savings, when it's seven in the morning in New York, it's one in the afternoon in Paris. In late March the clocks go forward by one hour; at the end of October they are put back an hour (spring forward, fall back).

Visit real estate offices even if you have no intention of buying at the moment or in the future. Most of them fill their windows with photos and descriptions of property along with the prices. Without even stepping inside the office, you can get an idea about the range of prices for particular types of property and the names of different localities. Before even buying your airline ticket, know that you'll need to budget a minimum of 75,000 euros ($67,500) to purchase a home or apartment. The initial cost may be less, but renovations and furnishings will almost certainly bring the total actual cost at least to that level.

> *Life is lived in the details, and you should look closely at your own to see if your preferences can be met in France, or if you can comfortably, willingly adapt.*

That amount is a minimum almost anywhere in the country for basic housing. In Paris, or Nice, or dozens of other places, it is a down payment; for two hectares of land with a view and a swimming pool, it is not a fraction of a down payment. In this respect, the French are no different from Americans: the nicer homes in the better locations cost more, a lot more than shabby quarters in a rundown neighborhood.

Look at the kind of property you might buy: What would it cost? Are such houses readily available in the area or few and far between? Talk to a salesperson and perhaps visit some of the offerings. When a house is described as livable, are you likely to be satisfied or would you want further renovations and at what cost?

This is the sort of information you need to take back with you for serious planning. Perhaps you will establish rapport with a real estate agent that will prove valuable when you do get serious. On the other hand, you may find agencies to avoid in the future.

For this kind of research, a car is necessary. Both Renault and Peugeot will sell foreigners a new car and buy it back at the end of their stay, with full insurance and roadside assistance. The plans avoid payment of the TVA added to auto rentals and may be less expensive than ordinary rentals, but require a minimum number of days of ownership.

On this score, be aware that distances in France can be deceiving. A journey you anticipate will take an hour becomes one and a half because the route passes through, rather than around, a medium-sized city. Or you get stuck behind a *convoi exceptionelle* (a truck with an oversized load) and can't pass for kilometers. And, while the autoroutes are fast, they are expensive and do not go everywhere. To reach some destinations, your only options will be smaller, slower roads.

So the rational approach is to prepare yourself carefully, consider all your options and weigh the pros and cons of each choice, avoiding all the possible pitfalls. Then do what most people do when suddenly realizing that they are looking at the home of their dreams: Forget all the good advice and follow your heart.

Part II
French Culture

4. Parlez-vous Français?
5. French People and Culture
6. 450,000 Years of History

4 Parlez-vous Français?

Yes, French is difficult, but you'd better learn it anyway. For most of us, learning to speak the language is the most difficult hurdle to cross in living in France.

Undoubtedly, sharing a common language is the primary reason immigrants in any country tend to stick together to form national and ethnic colonies. Some might argue that the Chinatowns, barrios, and ghettos of the United States are the result of prejudice, but the United States is replete with examples of Scandinavians, Germans, and other northern Europeans who are also clustered together and maintain a national identity based on language.

However natural this may be, it presents both a problem and a dilemma for the immigrant. The problem is, there are no great clusters of Americans living in France because relatively few have immigrated here. Moreover, much of the food originally identified as American, such as Coca-Cola, ketchup, hamburgers, breakfast cereal, and even peanut butter, is widely available—another reason why a *quartier* (quarter) never formed.

No matter where you settle, you will find yourself surrounded by French speakers. Radio and television are in French; even most English-language movies are dubbed. While satellite dishes and the Internet make it possible to receive foreign broadcasts, you're not going to get much news about France from other countries.

If the problem is a scarcity of Americans in France, the dilemma is, why move to France if you want to surround yourself with Anglophones?

The perhaps apocryphal tale of the Englishman who retired to France is a case in point. He moved to France only to tell friends back home he was pleased with everything except that there were "too many bloody Frogs about." The story is greeted by many French people with knowing nods.

Language is a powerful force in everyone's life; it shapes our acquisition of knowledge and our relationships with others. That most of us learn a single language as children and then spend years perfecting our skill in it seems to guarantee that a second language will be no snap. The brain is conditioned to one language and the natural paths available when we were children certainly narrow. Wordplay and most humor, emotional responses, and attitudes are all conveyed by language; far more than just gathering information is at stake. Moreover, even if you comprehend the gist of what is being said, understanding nuance requires greater depth. If you don't learn French, you'll miss out on more than you'll ever know.

If You Don't Learn the Language

Even so, the English-only speaker can get by in much of France today, especially in large cities and areas where tourists are common. Most middle-aged and younger French people with even a high school education have studied English for years, along with a third language as well.

> *If you don't learn French, you'll miss out on more than you'll ever know.*

As part of their education, they may also have spent time in England or the United States studying English, and many popular songs today have English lyrics. (Movies and television, however, are virtually all dubbed into French.)

Nonetheless, it is not uncommon to ask a French person if he or she speaks English, be told no, and after proceeding in halting French come to discover the person does speak at least some English, and certainly more than the initial response indicated. Don't take it personally. This is not an attempt to trick you into displaying your feeble French, but merely the understandable hesitancy of any person to converse in a language they're not entirely comfortable with.

Certainly for everyday errands and pleasantries such as discussing the weather, most people will pick up the required French vocabulary quickly enough. Merchants with whom you deal several times a week will soon understand your accent and help you make your purchases. If you patronize the supermarkets, you'll find them no different than in America: All the merchandise is on display and you select what you want off the shelves, without needing to ask for help.

Tutoyer or Not Tutoyer, That Is the Question

One confusing aspect of French is its use of two different forms of "you," the familiar *tu* for friends, children, and pets, and the formal *vous*, used to show respect or to address someone with whom you are not acquainted. To complicate matters, *tu* is only singular, and *vous* is plural as well as respectful. So, even if you were talking to two of your ex-lovers at the same time, you would use *vous*. The practice is confusing even to the French—they have invented the verb *tutoyer* just to talk about the situation.

Many other languages, such as Spanish, follow a similar practice. Even English did in the past—remember "thee" and "thou"? Quakers in America still use these terms today. But since the 19th century, the practice has been little used in English except as a poetic device.

The French themselves appear to be shifting away from it, and few agree on the circumstances under which you switch from *vous* to *tu*. One university professor reported that many of her students address her as *tu* rather than *vous*, something she never would have done even as a graduate student.

No absolute rules apply, but there are times when it is always preferred to use *vous*: in speaking to an official or anyone unknown to you outside of a social situation, and in addressing persons older than yourself, such as your friends' parents or relatives. Certainly, it is the polite way to address shop clerks and repairmen.

You will be safe using *tu* to address pets and children—and anyone who tells you that you may.

Learning French

One common mistake many people make is the assumption that once they have moved to France they will be immersed in the language, and it will come quickly enough. But this fails to take into account that they are often living with someone who speaks French no better than they do themselves.

The inevitable result is that daily discussions occur in the native tongue. Whether you're chatting about the shopping list, buying insurance, going out to eat, or renovating the house, chances are you and your mate will consult and make decisions in a familiar language rather than struggling in French. For one thing, neither of you can make authoritative corrections of the other's mistakes.

French friends and acquaintances will be of some help initially. But the need to make continual corrections wears on both tutor and pupil. Moreover, in a social situation—say at a dinner party of eight—two people with limited language skills will find they are missing most of what is being said even with attentive hosts.

French Instruction in the United States

If you are considering a move to France, even if you haven't determined what to do or where to go once there, you would be wise to begin language study in the United States. There are any number of options, depending on time and location.

One of the best places to begin is your local community college. If it has a French program at all, it will have qualified instructors and a choice of courses ranging from a once-a-week informal conversation class up to university-level five-credit courses. Best of all, it is likely to have an audiovisual language lab that enrolled students can use. Costs of the courses are generally less than the commercial language schools that are hard to find outside of large cities.

On the other hand, some will find the commercial language schools—Berlitz is certainly the best known—a better solution. These schools do only one thing—teach language—and they have to do it well enough to stay in business. Berlitz, for instance, offers specialized instruction and vocabulary for business, as well as more general language courses. Class size will probably be far smaller than that of a community college, the instruction more concentrated.

Moreover, you will find some of them offering short courses—perhaps all day Saturday—covering particular areas of a language. An example of this is the immersion weekends offered by the French American Exchange in the Shenandoah Mountains outside Washington, D.C.

A third possibility is the *Alliance Française*. This is a worldwide organization devoted to the promotion of French language and culture. It has numerous branches in the United States and sponsors language classes. Check the website (www.afusa.org) to find links to individual chapters as well as many French institutions. *Alliance Française* also conducts classes at five different cities throughout France and holds examinations in Paris, delivering internationally recognized certificates of accomplishment for teachers of French. It is a prime contact for anyone interested in France and the French.

Along with formal lessons, consider the possibility of private tutoring. There may be a neighbor, a teacher, or advanced student who can reinforce classroom lessons, explain difficult concepts at greater length, and offer conversation. A tutor's schedule may also be more flexible than that of a school.

French Instruction in France

If you can take the time, there are more than 100 schools teaching French as a foreign language in France. You don't have to be a university undergraduate spending your junior year at the Sorbonne to learn French in France. Many American universities have arrangements with French universities. For example, those who have a basic knowledge of French can enroll in the California state university system for a year of study either in Aix-en-Provence or Paris; university officials put the cost of the year at about $13,000, including transportation. But be forewarned: One middle-aged student reported that when the students in her classes—who were from all over the world—socialized, the language they usually spoke was English because it was common to them all.

There are also private institutions for language in most university towns. Even in rural areas, as long as you are close to a town with a *lycée* (high school) or *college* (middle school), you may find courses offered by qualified individual teachers. These usually vary between 7.50 and 15 euros ($8 and $16) per hour. In one outlying area, a weekly course in French for foreigners was being offered for about 6.50 euros ($7.50) per class, a three-month minimum enrollment required.

Many of these tutors seeking private pupils place a *petite annonce* (classified ad) in one of the many small weekly advertising papers distributed in each region.

The international organization Eurolingua (www.eurolingua.com), which has a French office at Montpellier, offers language-learning vacations in France in which small groups of students spend the morning in class and then have afternoons and weekends to explore the surrounding area. They also offer a program of one-on-one homestays, where the student lives in the tutor's home for a full cultural and linguistic experience. French American Exchange also arranges for study in France. Besides its offices in the United States, Berlitz offers instruction in Paris and Nice.

Many of these schools offer intensive one-week to one-month courses so that language lessons might be combined with a vacation and exploration of a region. The three main associations of these schools offer a wide range of choice of programs.

Villard de Lans, nestled in the Rhône-Alps region

First is the *Association Des Centres Univeritaires d'Etudes Française pour Etrangers*. As the name indicates, these are the university centers for French studies and as such maintain a high cultural level. They also have teaching resources such as language laboratories and multimedia equipment. University credit and diploma programs are offered. For further information, contact ADCUEFE, CIEF/Université Lumière - Lyon 2, 16, quai Claude Bernard, 69365 Lyon cedex 07, Tel: 0/4 78 69 71 35/36, Fax: 0/4 78 69 70 57.

Another group comprises the 30-plus institutions both public and private listed in *Le Petit Guide des Centres de Français langue étrangère*. The guide, updated annually since 1993, inspects the centers it features and includes information about the services offered and cultural activities as well as accommodation and recreation facilities. You can request it by email or by visiting the website. The address is: PETIT GUIDE FLE, Espace universitaire Albert-Camus, 21, avenue du professeur Grasset, 34093 Montpellier cedex 5, Tel.: 0/4 67 91 70 00, Fax: 0/4 67 91 70 01, email: ulys@fle.fr, website: www.fle.fr.

The third association is SOUFFLE, a professional group of 19 organizations that teach French as a foreign language. Established in 1990, its members are diversified in size, status, and style. By-laws of the group call for independent inspections and set requirements for teacher qualifications. Accommodations and associated programs are also monitored. SOUFFLE, BP 133 F-83957 La Garde cedex, tel: 0/4 94 21 20 92, fax: 0/4 94 21 22 17, email: courrier@souffle.asso.fr, website: www.souffle.asso.fr.

Once living in France, you may be eligible for the classes offered by GRETA (*Groupements Etablissements Formation Continue*), an arm of the Ministry of Education devoted to upgrading the skills and knowledge of residents of the country. GRETA operates 31 specialized centers around the country for teaching language, many of them near university cities. However, even in smaller towns, there may be GRETA classes. One GRETA language class included two Americans, a Nigerian, two Vietnamese, a Tunisian, and a Scotswoman, as well as half a dozen French people upgrading their skills.

One problem with the classes not offered in one of the 31 language centers: If you're seeking to improve your ear and conversational skills, you may find the classes too heavily weighted on written grammar in a traditional classroom setting to meet your needs. But they are worth investigating.

Another educational forum that a French-speaking immigrant might find interesting are the various "free" universities that have sprung up largely as antidotes to the rigid French educational system. That system does a good job of educating young people but has largely shut out those who do not follow the narrowly prescribed path to a diploma. Along with such traditional subjects as literature and philosophy, you may also find courses in yoga and art history.

Perhaps the best known is *l'Université inter-âges de Paris-Sorbonne* (Paris-IV, tel: 01-40-46-26-19), where about 8,000 students sign up for courses each year. Registration is by mail (1, rue Victor-Cousin, 75230 Paris Cedex 05). No diplomas are awarded, but then, there are no requirements for admission either.

There are about 50 loosely associated *universités populaires* around France. The largest by far is the Université populaire du Rhin in Alsace. You can contact the *Association des universités populaires de France* (AUPF) at 13, rue des Franciscains, 68100 Mulhouse (tel: 03-89-46-48-48).

Another group of such schools is the *Union française des universités tous âges* (UFTA). These 46 institutions are each linked to an academic university. Originally intended for retired people, they have become increasingly open to wider enrollments. Headquarters for UFTA is

Parlez-vous l'occitan?

For a country that considers itself ethnically homogenous, France is surprisingly diverse linguistically. As in most European countries, many people speak two or more languages, the native tongue and, often, English. But in France, the picture becomes even more complex. For starters, for some the native tongue is not necessarily French. Sure, dialects of *la français* exist, but many French people also speak a distinctly different language within the borders of the country they share. The main ones are listed below.

L'alsacien: Germanic in origin, this language is spoken by about a million people, principally in Alsace and Lorraine.

Le basque: Basque speakers in France, most of them located in the southwest part of the Pyrénées-Atlantique department, number about 100,000. Across the border in Spain, both Basque and Spanish are recognized as official languages, a status denied in France. However, Basque is taught in some schools around Bayonne and in the heavily Basque areas of Labourd, Soule, and Basse-Navarre.

Le breton: Spoken by some 800,000 people, Breton is taught not only in the western part of Brittany but also outside the region in Paris, Rennes, and the department of Loire-Atlantique.

Le catalan: The 260,000 French Catalan speakers are found mostly throughout the department of Pyrénées-Orientales. Like Basque, Catalan enjoys strong support across the border in Spain.

Le corse: Corsican, long considered an Italian dialect, today has about 85,000 speakers. The only minority language to enjoy legal support in France, it is taught in Aix-en-Provence, Marseilles, Nice, and Paris.

L'occitan: Of all the minority tongues of France, Occitan has the largest number of speakers, an estimated seven million. But it is hardly uniform. Heard throughout the South of France, it goes by a variety of names according to the particular region: *provençal, auvergnat, limousin, gascon, languedocien*, etc. These variations are widely taught throughout the South.

Les langues d'oïl: These northern French languages, the speakers of which triumphed linguistically as well as militarily over *les langues d'óc*, have virtually died out. Today, *picard, normand*, and *poitevin* are simply regional forms of French.

L'Evenière, université de Rennes, 1 avenue du Général-Leclerc, 35042 Rennes Cedex (tel: 02-99-63-66-76).

A Word about Accents

The idea that anyone can speak without a trace of an accent is nonsense. Everyone has an accent, and knowledgeable listeners can often pick out your place of birth, or perhaps that of your parents, who may have passed their own inflections on to you. A Scot speaking his native English can be just as difficult for an American to understand as an Asian speaking English as a second language.

The French are no different. They all have accents and will often argue that theirs is the "correct" one. What's correct in the Midi will be scorned in Paris and Alsace and vice versa. A French science teacher who comes from the Toulouse area spent six years teaching in California, where his lack of facility in English made life difficult. His joy at being transferred back to a school in Paris was quickly dampened the first time he went shopping. Here he was, back in France where he would have no trouble saying anything to anyone—and the clerk started mimicking his southern accent! He was crushed.

This is not to say that accents are unimportant. Speaking with an accent so poor or so thick that you can't be understood is not speaking the language. But the rhythm of the words, the phrasing, and the emphasis may be at least as important as the accent. Think of the erudite, well-educated people who have come to the United States and speak with a noticeable accent. Two things are more important than an accent: First, can you be understood, and second, do you have anything to say?

Literature

One of the joys of mastering French is that it enables you to read French literature. For the most part, this body of work is written in modern French. The few notable exceptions include the poetry of troubadours and François Villon and the epic poem "Song of Roland," celebrating one of Charlemagne's knights. Rabelais, whose name became synonymous with ribald humor, contributed *Gargantua and Pantagruel* in the 16th century. The other giant of that century was Michel de Montaigne, whose thoughtful essays could have been written yesterday.

The 17th century was dominated by three playwrights: the neo-classical tragedians Pierre Corneille and Jean Baptiste Racine, and the comic genius Jean Baptiste Molière. Molière's plays are still produced today: *The Miser*, *The Imaginary Invalid*, and *Tartuffe* are three of his better-known works.

The moralistic "Fables" of Jean de la Fontaine from this period are still read today, usually as children's literature. For adults, Madame de Lafayette created the first psychological novel, *La Princess de Clèves*.

Philosophers dominated the 18th century. Two major players were Jean-Jacques Rousseau, whose articulation of romanticism in his *Confessions* and *Social Contract* launched the debates of the next century, and Denis Diderot, the philosopher whose prodigious *l'Encyclopédie* attempted to sum up human knowledge. Voltaire, a playwright and writer but primarily a moral philosopher, spelled out his own cynical view of the human condition in the ironical *Candide*, which remains a staple today. A critic of religious and authoritarian hypocrisy, Voltaire protested against injustice and vanity throughout most of his life.

Another novelist of that century, Pierre Choderlos de Laclos, has also endured. His *Les Liasons Dangereuses* continues to be read and was made into a well-received movie a few years ago starring John Malkovich. It was during this era that the Marquis de Sade detailed his erotic philosophy in several novels including *The Philosopher in the Bedroom*.

Following the Revolution and Napoleon, French literature exploded on the world scene with novelists such as Honoré de Balzac, whose *Comédie Humaine* collected his numerous novels and stories describing French life in the first half of the 19th century. Stendhal's *The Red and the Black*, Gustave Flaubert's *Madame Bovary*, Victor Hugo's *Les Misérables*, and Émile Zola's *Germinal* reach wide audiences both in France and abroad.

Poets Charles Baudelaire, Stéphane Mallarmé, and Arthur Rimbaud likewise influenced their peers in world literary circles. Frédéric Mistral, the 19th-century poet of Provence, wrote in Occitan and did much to popularize that language, spoken widely in southern France. His efforts earned him the Nobel Prize for literature in 1904.

Another early Nobel Prize winner was Anatole France, a novelist and critic of the 19th and early 20th centuries. He became the Voltaire of his day, combining irony and a moral sense to lambast social hypocrisy. He joined Zola's campaign to win justice in the Dreyfus case and was outspokenly anti-clerical in his opposition to dogmatism of any sort. Traditional forms were continued by poets such as Paul Valéry, Paul Claudel, and Guillaume Apollinaire.

Marcel Proust, who died not long after the end of World War I, set a new course for the novel with his monumental *Remembrance of Things Past*. Proust was among those influenced by the prolific philosopher Henri Bergson, who celebrated intuition above formal intellectualism.

Louis-Ferdinand Celine, a doctor as well as a novelist, gained many admirers with his staccato style of writing until his support for German fascism during the war cost him support. Other prose writers who came to prominence in the first half of the century included André Malraux, André Gide, and François Mauriac; the latter two won Nobel Prizes in literature. Both Gide, awarded the prize in 1947, and Mauriac, who won it in 1952, were raised in strict Catholic families; their works often touch on the concepts of sin and sensuality.

Surrealism, with its focus on the subconscious, encompassed both art and literature in the 1920s and '30s; André Breton was one of the founders of the movement. Later in the century, particularly following the devastation of World War II, the philosophy of existentialism came to the fore.

Some of existentialism's best-known French proponents were creative writers as well as philosophers. The Algerian-born Albert Camus was a journalist in the Resistance; his philosophical works and novels such as *The Stranger*, *The Plague*, and *The Fall* won him the Nobel Prize in literature in 1957. Jean-Paul Sartre, who personified the intellectual French Marxist, wrote plays, novels, and philosophical texts. A student of philosophy in Berlin before the war, Sartre not only popularized existentialism among the young but became its chief architect in novels such as *Nausea* and philosophical works such as *Being and Nothingness*. A critic and anti-colonialist, Sartre refused the Nobel Prize in 1964.

Traditional lyric poetry flowed from the pen of Alexis Leger, writing under the name Saint-John Perse, for the first three-quarters of the 20th century. Leger, who pursued a dual career as poet and diplomat, was a bitter enemy of Nazism and spent World War II in the United States. Afterwards he continued his diplomatic career and writing, winning the Nobel Prize for literature in 1960.

Colmar, Alsace

In the theater, important 20th-century playwrights included the poet Paul Caudel and four Jeans—Anouihl, Cocteau, Genet, and Giradoux. Fernando Arrabal, Eugène Ionesco, and a transplanted Irishman, Samuel Beckett, created lasting experimental dramas with the Theater of the Absurd movement. Best known in the United States for his plays *Waiting for Godot* and *Krapp's Last Tape*, Beckett won the Nobel Prize for literature in 1969. The

Archie Satterfield

playwright lived most of his life in Paris and wrote sometimes in French, sometimes in English, doing his own translations. The man who said he preferred "France in war to Ireland in peace" was awarded the Croix de Guerre with a gold star for his work in the French Resistance.

More recently, novelists such as Alain Robbe-Grillet, Nathalie Sarrute, Michel Tournier and Patrick Modiano, Annie Leclerc, Marguerite Duras, and Hélène Cixous have enjoyed critical acclaim.

The last Frenchman to win the Nobel Prize for literature was Claude Simon, in 1985. Simon, who grew up in French Catalonia, fought with the Republicans in the Spanish Civil War. Perhaps his most important novel, *Les Georgiques*, deals with that experience. Simon became well known in the 1950s as a proponent of the *"nouveau roman"* ("new novel"), a narrative technique that ignored many conventions of structure, plot, and character development. Because of his complex style, Simon is considered difficult and remains little known even in France. Others called "new novelists" included Beckett, Robbe-Grillet, and Sarrute, although they were never a cohesive group or true literary school.

5 French People and Culture

French culture is world renowned. Famous for its cuisine, architecture, and celebration of intellectual freedom, France remains one of the most important cultural centers of the world. The French themselves are as individual and diverse as any people anywhere, but some generalizations are possible. For starters, French diplomacy is no myth. The society encourages good manners and you'll find most French people are polite, as well as reserved by American standards. They are proud of their beautiful country and respond warmly to those who appreciate it.

Class

More than two centuries ago, the French Revolution wiped out the feudal distinctions historically made between nobility and commoners. Or did it? Certainly the legal basis for privilege based on class was destroyed. Nonetheless, you need only note the number of public figures today whose names contain *de* or *d'*—denoting noble lineage—for proof that class still matters in France.

A noble title remains a trump card in the game of high society; even today there is a movement to restore the monarchy. Ironically, many of the titles their French carriers wear so proudly originated in some other land. Titled nobility from other European countries ended up in France following the dissolution of monarchies in their own lands. The Rothschild banking family, for instance, whose French branch continues in business today, were made barons by the king of Austria. Add to this situation people who, though not of aristocratic birth, used *de* in their names to indicate their origin. Still others simply fake it—laying claim to a title as a form of self-aggrandizement.

Solidarity and Education

Power and privilege aside, France has always derived its strength from its people rather than its nobility. The French place a high value on *solidarité*, a populist concept of obligation to one another for the good of all. There is even a *ministre de emploi et de la solidarité* (minister of employment and solidarity), one of the most powerful people in the government. This is the ministry that implemented the 35-hour work week and extended full health-care benefits to welfare recipients.

> *Power and privilege aside, France has always derived its strength from its people rather than its nobility.*

Along with *solidarité*, the French place a high premium on education. Indeed, the national budget for education tops 100 billion euros ($90 billion). The robust national educational system, which includes an inexpensive university education to qualifying students, produces articulate and competent citizens. Some 25 percent of France's 60 million people are in school. Two million of them are at university level, where admission depends upon passing *le Bac*, shorthand for the degree granted after passing a national examination at the end of secondary school. *Le Bac* is equivalent to a junior college diploma in the United States.

A highly educated population means a skilled workforce. It also explains the disproportionately high achievements the French have made in various fields of research, as well as the plentiful supply of professionals. For example, one small agricultural village in Languedoc, population 1,500, employs three doctors, three nurses, a dentist, a pharmacist, and a physical therapist.

The Second Sex

When it comes to gender equality in France, you could say that the slogan *"Liberté, égalité, fraternité!"* has been taken literally. Indeed, the French language itself lacks a feminine equivalent of *fraternité*.

In short, despite great strides in economics and politics, French women still face discrimination. They did not get the vote until after World War II, two generations after their American sisters won suffrage with the 19th

Amendment to the U.S. Constitution. But, as if to prove that the vote alone was insufficient, Simone de Beauvoir's *The Second Sex* became a seminal work in the literature of the U.S. women's movement.

Historically, there has been no shortage of strong women in France. The most potent was Jeanne d'Arc, whose courage and leadership changed the course of French history. Yet male descendants have prevailed for centuries. Titles passed to sons or to brothers, not to widows. Even today, unless special provision is made in a will, it is the children, especially the sons, who inherit wealth, not the widow. It is possible for a woman to be put out of the house she shared with her husband in the event of his death.

At the beginning of the new millennium, women lag behind men in all statistical surveys of employment and income. The unemployment rate for women is 35 percent higher than for men, women's salaries one-third lower, and significantly fewer women rise through the ranks, even with equivalent education. Even in traditionally feminine occupations, women are overwhelmingly workers, not managers. The French use the same term as Americans to describe the situation: *plafond de verre* (glass ceiling).

In politics, women fare better. Once given the vote, women won political office. By the 1980s, France had appointed a woman prime minister, Edith Cresson. The head of President Jacques Chirac's *Rassemblement pour la Republique* (RPR) party in 2000 was a woman, Michèle Alliot-Marie. One of the most powerful ministers in the government at the same time was Martine Aubry, *ministre de emploi et de la solidarité*.

France has embarked on a path of legislated equality. A new law requires political parties to field candidates comprising equal numbers of men and women. In the mayoral elections of March 2001, 20 percent of the candidates were women. Another new law requires employers to negotiate on equal employment for women, just as they must negotiate wages and working hours.

Just as in the United States, unequal treatment continues at home. A woman may work at a job as many hours as her mate, but she's still expected to keep house and take care of the children. The *école maternelle* (day care) may look after young children while a mother is at work during the day, but laundry, cooking, and cleaning as well as childcare are still seen as "women's work" in most households.

Gender discrimination also plays a part in France's race and ethnicity problems. For example, some French Muslims continue cultural practices that have long been banned in the West, such as female circumcision and forced marriage. Islam is the country's fastest-growing religion. French Muslims, largely of North African descent but also black African and Turkish, number about two million.

While female circumcision is relatively rare, forced marriage is not. An estimated 10,000 to 20,000 young women are married against their wishes by parental arrangements. The women, who were born in France and have lived there all their lives, are forced as teenagers to decide between fleeing their homes or marrying men they've never met. Older brothers or other family members often help enforce the parents' wishes, so the women have nowhere to turn unless they are willing to denounce their family to authorities. It is a difficult decision.

The Ethnic Mix

The rights of Muslim women are only part of the ethnic conflict in France. As a group, the French of North African descent have become a target for the Far Right in France. The *Front National*, led by the anti-Semitic Jean-Marie Le Pen, has captured up to 15 percent of the vote in some elections by campaigning against "immigrants" in general. The party is particularly strong along the Côte d'Azur.

With slogans such as "French first," the National Front has tried to cloak its racism as patriotism. But the so-called immigrants are French citizens, some of them second- and third-generation. The grandparents of some fought or worked for the French in Algeria until that country won its independence in 1962.

The truth is, France is a nation of immigrants and has been throughout recorded history. Mediterranean ports such as Nice and Marseille began as

---

French Character

The French national character was tellingly revealed when, in the 18th century, the country was introduced to the humble potato. Despite its potential for feeding a growing population, this tuber from the New World found little popular acceptance.

This resistance dismayed one Antoine Augustin Parmentier, a pharmacist and agronomist. He felt the potato would be a valuable addition to the nation's diet, especially in the event of failures of other crops such as wheat.

After making many presentations to the court, Parmentier finally received permission in 1786 from Louis XVI to plant about 50 acres of potatoes in Neuilly—in a vacant field generally regarded as infertile. The potatoes flourished, but still Parmentier could not persuade people to eat them.

Finally, he hit upon a solution: Hire local police to guard the field—but only in the daytime. His hope was that people would sneak into the field at night, dig up some of the new delicacy, and plant it on their own land. The experiment proved a great success. Parmentier then advised other large landowners to plant a nice big field of potatoes—and forbid anyone from entering. Within a generation, the potato became a staple of the French diet.

The contrast between Parmentier's decidedly French experiment and that of Frederick II of Prussia could not be more striking: Frederick sent his troops in to force the peasants to plant potatoes. Is it any wonder that the one nation gave us the Statue of Liberty and the other, fascism?

Greek trading posts. Romans, Germanic tribes, and Scandinavians all emigrated to France. Often they came as invaders, but, over generations, they have become French.

Nor have the Pyrénées been any ethnic barrier in the south. The Basques live on both sides of the border, as do the Catalans. Today, the European Union views the Barcelona-Toulouse axis as an economic unit, just as it was centuries before. In 1886, one million foreigners lived among France's total population of 40 million. By 1930, this figure had swelled to three million, many of them workers recruited from North Africa.

After World War II, France continued to recruit foreign labor, from North Africa, Portugal, and Eastern Europe. By 2000, among the nation's total population of 60 million, four million foreigners lived in France, one-third of them naturalized citizens, one-third of them other Europeans—Portuguese, Spanish, Italians, and others. Americans accounted for a minuscule fraction. In 1998, France issued just 20,252 long-stay visas to North and South Americans combined, about half them for students or stays under six months.

Nevertheless, the French perceive themselves as a homogenous country—if you're not French, you're foreign. The American notion that everyone except the Indians came from somewhere else, and the chief distinction is the number of generations your family has been on the continent, is to the French, well, foreign. *Integration* (assimilation) is a very important concept in France.

Those who are "outsiders" in some way, not fully assimilated, can meet prejudice. In some cases, it may be nothing more than a rude clerk, but in others, prejudice can take the form of school segregation, refusal of housing—exactly the sort of discrimination people of color have faced in the United States. But it is not only skin color that can set you apart: It can also be your accent or your inability to speak the language.

Even some university graduates with advanced degrees fail to be hired when their ethnic heritage becomes known. Parents find their children segregated when moving from nursery school to primary school, or from primary to middle school, whether in Paris or in the provinces. A government-sponsored survey in late 1999 found seven out of 10 French citizens consider themselves more or less racist and said there were too many people of non-European origin in the country. When many of the *"sans-papiers"* (people without proper visas) were given a chance to regularize their situations in 1997, it was learned that many of them were legally entitled to be in France but had been denied processing by xenophobic bureaucrats.

Not surprisingly, racial and ethnic tension sometimes erupts on the streets: a bomb on the Paris metro a few years ago killed several people, and graffiti scrawled on public edifices is a problem in urban France just as it is in the United States.

But there is reason to hope. In the same survey that revealed French xenophobia, 81 percent of the respondents said they objected to the practice of refusing hire to a qualified foreigner, and solid majorities said the same about discrimination in housing or public facilities. The government, both right and left, seems determined to combat the problem. When five provincial council presidents sought to keep their seats by currying favor with the National Front, they were expelled from their parties. And health insurance coverage for welfare recipients was increased from 80 to 100 percent.

France deals with its social problems the way any democracy must: through discussion and debate, education and legislation. Despite a history of political instability, the country has made continued social and economic progress. There is nothing to suggest this will not continue in the future.

Workers United

Labor and farmers are strong in France. They make their needs known to the politicians at the public's expense, usually enjoying widespread support. No other nation has the reputation France has for strikes and demonstrations. Travelers find flights cancelled, commuters can't get to work, the mail doesn't get delivered, garbage piles up, and autoroutes are blocked by angry farmers dumping produce.

France is organized; its workers, farmers, teachers, and civil servants all have *syndicats* (unions) to look after their interests. When a factory closes, or a corporation faces bankruptcy or a takeover, or farmers are told to accept lower prices for their produce, union representatives arrive on the scene to demand that jobs not be lost or living standards lowered.

Three large *syndicats* dominate the labor movement. The *Confederation Générale du Travail* (CGT) was for years dominated by the French Communist party. In recent years this relationship has begun to break down, and the CGT no longer automatically supports positions the party takes. *Force Ouvière*, the second *syndicat,* grew out of schism in the CGT after World War II. Membership of each is estimated at 700,000. The third major *syndicat*, the *Confederation Française et Démocratique du Travail*, began as a Christian alternative to a Communist union but dropped the religious affiliation in the 1960s.

As for representation of farmers, rivaling the three large industrial unions in size is the *Fédération nationale des syndicats d'exploitants agricoles*. In France, the largest agricultural producer in Europe, agriculture continues to engage a sizeable—though shrinking—percentage of the French population. Even though farming no longer employs so many people, the younger generation is not far removed from the land and allegiances remain strong.

In the United States, weak labor law enforcement, anti-union legislation, and lack of organization over the decades have resulted in a population generally acquiescent and docile. Not so in France, and French politicians ignore this at their peril. Perhaps this is why the French are such accomplished diplomats: When displeased, the people take to the streets and create a crisis officials must resolve by compromise.

When the right swept to victory in the National Assembly in 1993, followed by the election in 1995 of President Jacques Chirac, they enjoyed a large majority. But the policies of Prime Minister Alain Juppé—including a two percent increase in the value-added tax (TVA) and resumption of nuclear testing—proved so unpopular that a series of strikes through the winter and spring of 1997 brought the Socialists back to power by summer. The point is not one of left versus right—voters obviously supported the right or they would not have elected Chirac—but of the electorate's readiness to impose its will upon its government.

Cuisine and Culture

Given people's attachment to the land, the major economic role agriculture has played throughout the nation's history, and French people's penchant for intellectual analysis, the French mastery of cuisine is no surprise.

It is a mastery that can border on obsession. The French preoccupation with the quality of food, its style of preparation, and fine distinctions related to smell and taste and service and consumption are well known. The film *La Grande Bouffe* (*bouffe* is roughly equivalent to "pig out"), about a group of men who gather in a hideaway to eat themselves to death, could only be French. There are classes for young children to educate their palates and university-level "centers of taste" on campuses. The Michelin brothers had barely begun producing tires when they launched their famed restaurant guide, *Le*

A Sunday's empty sidestreet in the town of St. Emilion in the Aquitane

Abercrombie and Kent

Guide Rouge, which celebrated its centennial in 2000. To the French, *le bon goût* (good taste) is just as important as *le bon mot* (clever word).

The nation also prides itself on its artistic achievements. Although they never equaled the Italian masters, French artists established themselves in the Middle Ages and the Renaissance. Until the 19th century, French painting, sculpture, and music, while often high-caliber, tended to be formal in structure and content. But that all changed with the Impressionists; eventually, their influence extended worldwide.

Initially rejected by the French establishment, the Impressionists were especially interested in the play of light and color upon the landscape. To capture what they perceived, they threw out the formal rules that had guided French art through the first half of the century. Moreover, they refused to consider the traditional subject matter of mythology and history. Instead they painted shimmering, vibrant landscapes and subjects engaged in ordinary activities. Major Impressionists were Claude Monet, Pierre Auguste Renoir, and Camille Pissaro. Others who joined the movement or painted in the same spirit included Paul Cézanne, Edouard Manet, and Edgar Degas.

> The French preoccupation with the quality of food, its style of preparation, and fine distinctions related to smell and taste and service and consumption are well known.

The name of the movement itself came from a painting of Monet's called "Impression: Sunrise"—which a journalist ridiculed. The artists themselves decided that the term in fact described perfectly what they hoped to do in their work—to capture the impression of the moment.

Impressionism as an aesthetic found its way into sculpture in the work of Auguste Rodin and in the music of Claude Debussy, Hector Berlioz, Camille Saint-Saëns, and Maurice Ravel, among others. Later painters who were not part of the original movement but continued it as post-Impressionists were Toulouse-Lautrec, Henri Matisse, Georges Seurat, and Paul Gauguin.

Pablo Picasso, arguably the most influential artist of the 20th century, was not French by birth, but he lived and worked most of his life in France. Beginning around 1907, he and Georges Braque created the next wave in art, cubism. This angular style of painting that fragmented its subject matter was pursued by others such as Marcel Duchamps and Fernand Léger.

With the advent of cubism, "modern art" was launched, and today anything goes.

A Day of Rest

Like to shop on Sunday? Unless it's window-shopping, you won't do it in France. Most commercial activity takes place between Monday morning and Saturday evening. Many businesses will close Saturday afternoon and reopen Monday after lunch. Other offices may be open Monday through Friday and closed on the weekend. There is no overall rule, but there is very little chance you can spend Sundays shopping for clothes, gardening materials, hardware, or auto parts. Shopping malls and supermarkets are shuttered.

Food shops are sometimes open on Sunday mornings. Grocery stores, butcher shops, and produce markets may open or not, depending on individual owners' preferences. Bakeries more traditionally are open. Many towns and cities have a farmers' market on Sunday, however. Restaurants often close after the Sunday noon meal and do not reopen until Tuesday noon. Service stations usually close, although some have installed pumps you can operate with a credit card even when the station is closed.

It's a given that almost everyone, unless they are in the hotel-restaurant business or are some kind of emergency personnel, will have Sundays off. Amateur sports teams can get together to play—and all the players' friends can come to the game. Saturday night dances and wedding receptions can last until daybreak because no one has to go to work.

> *In short, Sunday remains a genuine day of rest for most of France, a time to relax and enjoy family time.*

In short, Sunday remains a genuine day of rest for most of France, a time to relax and enjoy family time. After the traditional big noon meal, people go for walks or rides in the country, visit friends, take naps, or watch the local soccer or rugby team play.

This takes some getting used to for many Americans in France. After all, most Americans take for granted their 24-hour supermarkets, drug stores, and gas stations, their fast-food joints and building supply stores open 16 to 18 hours a day seven days a week. And no matter how welcome the idea of one day sans shopping, you never know when you might need to run to the store for a quart of milk, a bag of charcoal, or more nails to finish a do-it-yourself project.

Yet most of us readily adapt to—in fact, yearn for—a more measured pace of life in which work is just one component, necessary but no more important than family life, recreation, or cultural experiences. The French way of life tends to be a harmonious one; that is, the different aspects blend and fit together as does French society as a whole. Those who seek a less frenetic way of life, who don't care about shopping for groceries (or anything else) at midnight, who enjoy being in sync with those around them, will find France a delight.

You could call it an orchestrated way of life with Custom & Tradition waving a small baton to keep everyone together. The strikes and demonstrations that often as not disrupt that harmony are some of the musicians telling the conductor he missed a beat or has been neglecting them; they create a certain amount of dissonance as a means of getting everyone's attention, but only to restore harmony.

French Attitudes Towards Americans

Although France and the United States have long enjoyed friendly diplomatic relations, the French do not appreciate what they view as American arrogance. For example, the U.S. government's efforts to flood Europe with bananas grown in Central America, genetically modified grains, and hormone-laden meat while maintaining its own barriers to European products has not escaped notice by the general population. Farmers trashing a McDonald's under construction were greeted sympathetically and grabbed national headlines.

At the same time, the popularity of so many things American—*Coca Cola*, Hollywood films, logo-bearing sportswear, and, yes, even *MacDo's*—mitigates against any ill will. After all, the United States is a very popular

Integration

One Sunday after our big noon meal, my wife and I took a stroll through the village. We came upon an elderly woman also out for a walk, enjoying the pleasant day. After we exchanged comments about the weather, she asked where we were from and what we were doing in the village. When we explained that we had moved to open a *chambres d'hôtes*, she replied candidly that she would prefer to see French people moving into the village. But she quickly added that it was better to have foreigners move in than to see the town slowly die as young people left to find work and the elderly passed away.

Her attitude sums up how many French feel about foreigners: better someone than no one. Last century's migration from farms to city around the globe has also affected France. *Desertification,* as the French call the process that empties the countryside, threatens many rural villages, poking holes in the social fabric, holes that foreigners may fill.

In many country villages even in the South of France, between 10 and 25 percent of the houses are vacant; another 15 to 50 percent are second homes. In many cases, adult children keep the parents' home after inheriting it, returning several times a year to spend vacations with friends and perhaps prepare to retire there. When vacationers are in town, the population in these villages may double. But the overall diminishing of the population has hit village merchants hard: Fewer residents means less business, less business means fewer shops, and finally the town itself can no longer attract new residents.

Americans settling in these small villages face a couple of hurdles. The first is the language barrier. You have to be able to communicate with the people you meet, and, unless you wish to limit yourself to English speakers, that means understanding French.

The second hurdle, accepting a new way of life, is not so clear-cut. Customs and prac-

vacation destination for the French. A joke that made the rounds a few years ago illustrates the view of America as a land of vast abundance:

A Frenchman vacationing in Texas goes out to eat one evening. At the restaurant he asks for a beer and is served a two-quart pitcher. Then he orders a steak and is brought a 32-ounce T-bone. After finishing the meal, he asks directions to the restroom and is told it's out the back door and straight ahead. As he exits the door, the power fails and all the lights go out. The poor fellow stumbles in the dark and falls into the swimming pool.

He cries out in a panic, "Don't flush! Don't flush!"

Jokes aside, most French people feel genuine admiration for the United States. Beginning with the Declaration of Independence and continuing through the most recent technological achievements, the French appreciate American accomplishments. And the helping hand the United States has extended militarily and economically to France has not been forgotten.

These historical ties are widely recognized, but life is lived person to person. On the human level, anyone who considers moving to France sooner or later must ask himself or herself, "Do I belong here?" The answer to this question may well depend on how you are received in France, and that, of course, depends on how you treat the French.

---

tices you may initially find quaint or amusing can become frustrating when you live with them on a daily basis. Feel like grabbing a snack at 5 P.M.? Forget it, the restaurants don't open until 7:30. Like to shop on Sunday? Not in France. Have a hankering for Italian or Chinese or Indian food? It's a long drive to Paris. Enjoy sleeping late every morning? You might be awakened at 9 A.M. by a loud-speaker system announcing the sale of corsets by some traveling merchant. And just because a store stocked an item yesterday doesn't mean it will be available next week or next month.

If you can adjust your expectations, you'll enjoy many advantages from this way of life. After all, that's why the French live the way they do. For starters, the slow pace allows you to slow down. If shops are closed between noon and 2 P.M., you can savor your lunch rather than hastily run errands. (The "HR" you'll see in classified ads stands for *"heures repas,"* or mealtime. Everyone understands it to mean, time out from noon to 2 P.M. and 6 to 8 P.M.) If businesses close at a reasonable hour, there is no graveyard shift to staff. The result is a family-oriented, more cohesive society. The expectation that most people keep the same schedule extends to mealtimes as well. Yet nothing prevents anyone from painting their house on the weekend, or gardening, or doing chores. It's a happy medium between those old puritanical "blue laws" that forbade any activity on Sunday and the helter-skelter, round-the-clock frenzy one finds in the United States.

The French have organized their society to suit themselves, just as Americans have done. Those who can't adapt to the lifestyle differences will remain forever in the category of those who "love France but hate the French." And they probably shouldn't live here. If a relaxed pace that allows for life's simple pleasures appeals, perhaps you should.

In my experience, the French are a polite, rather formal people and they expect the same from others. Remember, French has been the language of diplomacy for centuries, and the desire to smooth over conflict is ingrained in the culture. Even so, familiarity often stops at the front door. Once the ice is broken, however, the French respond with warmth and feeling; an invitation to a family gathering should be considered an honor.

Of course, there are cultural differences. Many Americans, particularly women, are likely to find the macho bias of French society, even politely cloaked as it often is, disagreeable at times. On the flip side, Americans used to efficiency in the marketplace may be perceived as brusque by French merchants accustomed to chatting while ringing up a sale. Yes, it takes longer, but isn't making a human connection worth it?

Here's a litmus test of sorts: What would you do if you ordered a cup of coffee *with* dessert in a restaurant, only to have it served after you've cleaned your plate? This is the norm in France. If you're likely to be exasperated by this custom and make a fuss, France might not be the place for you. If you take this and other differences in stride, even delight in them, rest assured, you'll have no difficulty making friends in France.

6 450,000 Years of History

Humans settled in what is today France nearly a half a million years ago; immigrants are nothing new.

The history of France is long. Human remains 450,000 years old were found near Tautavel, a small wine-growing village not far from the Mediterranean in the department of the Pyrénées-Orientales. Among the oldest remains ever found in Europe, they reveal little beyond the physical appearance of the young, sturdy, 1.65-meter adult.

Fast forward 420,000-plus years: Artists employing sophisticated techniques and materials covered the walls of caves around France with pictures of animals we still find breathtakingly beautiful. Of this culture, little is known beyond the implements they left behind. But their artwork alone is enough to inspire use of the word "civilization."

The 2,500-year recorded history of France is a bloody one, a history of invasion and conquest, of battles won and lost, of heroism and intrigue and the slow forging of a nation. The two great leaders Charlemagne and Napoleon, a millennium apart, brought most of Europe under the French flag. Before and after both of their reigns, the borders of France ebbed and flowed with tide of history.

Roman Rule

The concept of France was born long before the nation. The Romans, following the Mediterranean trade routes of the Phoenicians and Greeks, found the land across the sea to the west quite hospitable, even welcoming. Roman soldiers were rewarded for faithful service with land around Narbonne—the Roman capital, well established by 118 B.C.—60 years before Julius Caesar began his conquest of Gaul.

The Gaul of Caesar's great campaigns was in the north, including Belgium and much of the Netherlands. Caesar pushed his barbarian enemies across the Rhine, a river Napoleon would centuries later proclaim France's "natural boundary." Roman legions quickly moved north up the Rhône River, establishing a garrison at Vienne and soon after built the city of Lyon as their capital in Provence.

Whatever its faults, Rome provided the barbarian tribes of Western Europe with discipline, law, and education. Roman rule could be harsh, but it also introduced an unmatched standard of civilization. When imperial Rome moved east to Constantinople, the Pax Romana failed and Europe descended into the Dark Ages.

Charlemagne and the Church

Christianity eventually replaced Roman rule. When Clovis, king of the Franks, converted in 493 to marry the Burgundian princess Clotilda, he not

The Palace du Pape in Avignon

only extended his kingdom, he gained a powerful ally in the Roman church. When Pepin the Short, father of Charlemagne, was anointed by Pope Stephen II, he established the principle of rule by "divine right"—the belief that the king ruled by God's will and opposition to him was sacrilege. Thus the church blessed the wars in which the anointed king engaged.

Charlemagne—Charles the Great—ruled for nearly half a century, extending the boundaries of his kingdom until it included virtually all of Western Europe, except for parts of Italy, Spain, and the British Isles. In fact, his court was not even within the borders of today's France; it was in Aix-la-Chapelle, or Aachen, as the Germans call their Rhineland city today.

But Charlemagne did more than gain ground. He re-established the rule of law, at least for his lifetime, and granted land to the church for the monasteries that fostered learning throughout Europe. His rule contributed greatly to the widespread establishment of feudalism, ending the Dark Ages and initiating the Middle Ages. Charlemagne divided his vast empire into counties, ruled by a count, with a viscount as a deputy. Soon these positions became hereditary; the lands on the frontier of the kingdom were called *marches* and the military rulers became *marquis*.

A Powerful Aristocracy

Just before Charlemagne's death, he crowned his son Louis king. But Louis was no Charlemagne and gradually compromises were made, dividing the royal authority and fragmenting the empire. As a result, powerful aristocrats who controlled large areas such as Normandy, Toulouse, and Burgundy were able to act independently and oppose the king on occasion.

The tension between the powerful noblemen who controlled vast, rich regions such as Burgundy, Normandy, and Gascony and the king in Paris to whom they owed little more than nominal allegiance shaped much of French history until the revolution. The Capetian dynasty that ruled France through the Middle Ages actually had little control beyond the Île-de-France region around Paris. After all, it was not Philip I, king of France, who conquered England in 1066, but William II, duke of Normandy.

Tension between the crown and the church also grew during this period. The church itself was often in need of reform, yet with so many churchmen from noble families and the church holdings so extensive, there were always political as well as religious ramifications to any change. Kings and noblemen could defy popes, and the bishops whom they named supported them. (Indeed, since it was the eldest sons who inherited the titles, younger brothers often went into the church as a career. Thus many prelates were actually members of noble families and the interests of the monarchy coincided with their own.)

So when Pope Urban II called in 1095 for a crusade to seize Palestine from Muslim rule, it gave church and state a chance to unite in common cause for mutual benefit. The crusaders were doing God's work looting and seizing territory; younger sons from noble families who had little hope of inheritance swelled the ranks. By 1100 Europeans—especially the French—were in control in the Near East.

Consolidating Royal Power

The 13th century saw the consolidation of French royal power within much of the territory of today's France. France even elected cardinal Clement V pope and installed him and several successors at Avignon in 1307, holding the papacy a virtual prisoner for 70 years. The 14th century

Les Cathares

Throughout much of the Midi, between Toulouse and the Mediterranean, you'll see signs announcing, "*Vous êtes en pays Cathares*" ("You are in Cathars country"). Even those with a working knowledge of French history may be puzzled by the reference. Who are the Cathars? To the 13th-century northern French Catholics, they were Albigensian heretics, dissenters from Albi who challenged Roman Catholic authority. They were slaughtered by the thousands in a Catholic attempt to gain control of the region.

The purported heresy—dating to debates by some of the earliest Christians and appearing in various regions throughout Europe and Asia Minor—began as a denial of the Trinity doctrine promulgated by Rome. It gradually evolved into a sketchy challenge to Catholic ecclesiastical authority. In an era of clerical corruption and great church wealth, the Cathars preached asceticism. They believed that the material world, the world of flesh, was evil, created by the Devil. God's world was the spiritual one, reached only after death. Accordingly, they denied the humanity of Christ and the transubstantiation of bread and wine into Christ's body and blood during Mass—two big theological heresies.

The Cathars' beliefs were particularly strong in the south, brought there by the Visigoths when they ruled the region after Roman authority crumbled in the 4th century. Over the years, some people stubbornly refused to give up these beliefs, regardless of what some group of bishops might say. And the corruption of the clergy gave plenty of ammunition to those who believed in the intrinsic evil of the flesh.

The success of the crusades in conquering the Near East inspired both French clergy and nobles to consider the possibility of a similar venture in the south, where a complex political situation prevailed. The count of Toulouse and his vassals, though nominally liege to the king of France, were both independent and attracted to Aragon, the kingdom in the east of what is now Spain that also controlled Provence. Moreover, within recent memory Eleanor of Aquitaine had shown how weak was the French grip on Toulouse and Languedoc after her divorce from Louis VII brought so much of what is now western France under English rule.

In 1210, with the blessing of Pope Innocent III, Simon de Montfort and Abbot Arnaud Amaury, the papal legate, led an army south. Their first conquest was the

brought the transition from the Middle Ages to the Renaissance and the Hundred Years' War with England.

The war lasted *more* than 100 years. The conventional dates are 1337 to 1453, but the seeds were sown with the Norman Conquest in 1066 and England did not give up Calais until 1558. The war started, as did so many then, over the right of succession to the throne; it swept down through the decades involving one king after another. The Hundred Years' War saw no decisive battle, and the plague took a greater toll than the war itself during some years.

After nearly a century of struggle, the war gave France its most enduring heroine, *Jeanne d'Arc,* who did more than anyone to finally end the fighting. Joan of Arc stepped onto the stage of history in 1428, prepared to put the dauphin Charles on the French throne and push the English back across the Channel.

---

city of Beziers, near the Mediterranean south of Montpellier. When thousands of civilians took sanctuary in the cathedral, and the crusaders suspected heretics were among them, the abbot gave the order: "Burn them all; God will know his own." Several thousand died in this first engagement, which set the tone for the next few decades of on-again, off-again warfare. In feudal times, armies generally fought for about six weeks in the summer and then returned home.

The crusaders moved southwest, conquering where they could and leaving islands of resistance in place for later. Many Catholics as well as Cathars suffered the fate of those in the Beziers cathedral. When one southern abbot whose orthodox beliefs were beyond question complained that his family was being deprived of its lands without cause, his abbey and lands were given over to a northern cleric, who ruled in absentia.

Carcassonne was captured after Viscount Roger Trencavel met the crusaders under a flag of truce. They seized him and he died in prison. In another instance, when a village fell to De Montfort, he killed all but 50 of the men. Forty-nine of them he blinded and the 50th he left with one eye to lead the band to the next village to urge surrender.

De Montfort was finally killed in 1218 as he besieged Toulouse, but his son took command and the war went on for several more years. Despite the eventual capitulation of Count Raymond VII of Toulouse in 1229, resistance continued for years in fortified castles set atop rocky crags in the foothills of the Pyrénées. The ruins of these castles— Queribus, Peyrepetuse, Puylaurens, Puivert, and Montsegur, where more than 200 people were burned to death—are important tourist attractions today.

To root out the heresy after the military conquest, Pope Gregory IX ordered the first Inquisition to be conducted by the Dominican friars, whose founder had been instrumental in arousing church action against the Cathars. One of the most zealous inquisitors, Bishop Jacques Fournier, later became Pope Benedict XII.

While the beliefs of the Cathars eventually disappeared from the pages of history, southern resistance to northern authority, both ecclesiastical and civil, remained alive. It was in this region that Protestantism flourished in France centuries later and where many of the revolutionaries of the 18th and 19th centuries were born.

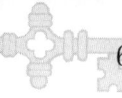

Joan succeeded with her first goal; she broke the siege of Orléans and Charles was crowned at Reims. After the coronation, Joan continued to fight with the army, but was wounded in 1430 and captured by the Burgundians, who sold her to their English allies. The English put her on trial as a heretic in Rouen, where she was convicted, condemned, and burned at the stake in 1431. She had placed Charles on the throne, but he did nothing to save her.

Renaissance and Reformation

Despite his rocky start, Charles VII surrounded himself with wise counselors and, after reconciling with Burgundy in 1435, pushed the English out of France by mid-century. But he ruled an impoverished land devastated and depopulated by war and disease. It was left to his son Louis XI, his successor Louis XII, and then Francis I to rebuild the ravished land and deliver France into the Renaissance.

The 16th century was not destined to be peaceful, however, for it brought the Protestant Reformation. Religious differences served as a new excuse for war—this time civil war that divided families, stifled dissent, and encouraged atrocities on both sides in the name of the Lord. Jean Calvin fled Paris for Geneva, where he established a theocracy and accepted French Protestants, many of whom later returned to France as missionaries.

Efforts at peacemaking, such as Charles IX's amnesty for Protestants in 1560, failed to quell the sectarian struggles that sporadically flared up, often as mob violence or assassinations rather that full-scale war. When Henry III, the last Valois king, died in 1589, Henry of Navarre, a Bourbon, claimed the throne as Henry IV.

Henry had been a Huguenot but as king he returned to Catholicism, supposedly saying, "Paris is worth a mass." He issued the Edict of Nantes in 1598, offering protection for Protestants, and maintained an uneasy truce between the factions until his assassination by a Catholic in 1610.

The religious battles continued sporadically until mid-century. By 1620, Cardinal Richelieu had begun his devious and largely successful efforts to bring a measure of order, if not peace, to European politics. Richelieu established the principle of a balance of power, shifting alliances with nations while keeping France's interests in the fore. These policies were followed by his successors and continued to shape Europe until the revolution.

Intellectual Flowering

The last century and a half of the French monarchy was dominated by the reign of Louis XIV, the Sun King. This era became "the glory that was

France," as it has been romantically called. It was a glorious era because of the intellectual flowering that took place in so many fields—philosophy, the arts, architecture, mathematics, and science. Descartes and Pascal, Corneille and Molière, Mansart and Le Nôtre, Lully and Rameau, and scores of other through the decades advanced education and the arts throughout France and the world. Once established, this intellectual and artistic ferment developed its own momentum for more than two centuries, regardless of political and economic conditions.

This was also the point at which Paris and France became nearly synonymous terms. Louis concentrated power in the court; nobles from the provinces who desired something from the king were obliged to leave their homes and go to court to secure it, often a months-long process during which their estates might be neglected. And the process was as complicated as it was expensive: The court was noted for intrigue and favoritism.

Louis himself was a complex figure. His reign began in 1643 when he was five years old. He grew to epitomize the absolute monarch—this was the man who conceived of the 10,000-room château at Versailles as a fitting residence for a king. He worked hard and well for France. A patron of the arts, he also built a professional army, outfitting it handsomely to fight his almost continuous wars with Holland or England or the Holy Roman Empire.

In the days of Louis XIV, the courtyard surrounding this fountain was filled with courtiers, not tourists.

Leo de Wys

The Sun King Shines

Early in his reign, Louis arrested a powerful but corrupt superintendent of finances and took over the job himself, closely supervising the work of his able aide Colbert. He fostered economic development, increased trade, and colonial expansion; tax reform brought in more revenue. A staunch Catholic and supporter of the church, he nonetheless had numerous mistresses; the very symbol of a royal monarch, he secretly married a commoner when his queen, Marie Thérèse, died in 1683.

During the latter part of his reign, which ended in 1715, the Sun King lost much of his shine. By arrogant acts such as revoking the Edict of Nantes in 1685 and renewing persecution of the Huguenots, he aroused sentiment against him. The continuous wars and European intrigues drained the treasury; in the end France lost much of its hard-won territory in the New World and the region of Lorraine at home. Despite his accomplishments and devotion to France, it is easy to see that Louis' reign laid the foundation for the 75 years of ferment that led to the revolution.

Louis XIV's great-grandson succeeded him as king—also at age five. Neither Louis XV nor his grandson, who became Louis XVI, showed much talent for government. Neither of them could even govern the extravagances of their wives and mistresses. As the century wore on, taxes multiplied and food grew scarce. The Seven Years' War was lost in 1763. Reform was blocked at every turn by one faction or another unwilling to compromise. When revolution finally came in 1789, it seemed inevitable.

Monolithic statues at the Filitosa Archaeological site on Corsica

"Liberté, Egalité, Fraternité!"

To sum up the French Revolution: It was bloody awful. It was chaotic and despotic—and absolutely necessary. The centuries of serfdom and slavery, of kneeling to whatever fool happened to be born to privilege and power or whatever murderous baron could scheme his way there, were not easily erased.

The revolution proceeded from the formation of the National Assembly in 1789 to Napoleon's seizure of power in 1799. The storming of the Bastille was followed by an uprising in the countryside and the cry of *"Liberté, égalité, fraternité!"* echoed throughout France, not just in Paris. Over the next two years, the National Assembly hammered out a constitution that included the king. But when Louis XVI tried unsuccessfully to flee the country that year, the European monarchies threatened France and diplomatic relations grew strained. September 1792 saw a slaughter of political prisoners as prisons were opened and the inmates massacred.

> *To sum up the French Revolution: It was bloody awful.*

The Republic was proclaimed and the king tried, convicted of conspiracy, and executed in 1793. This was the year of the Terror—when anyone even accused of treason was assumed to be guilty and executed. In Paris, 20,000 people were guillotined, twice that number in the provinces. Eventually, the tables turned and the radicals themselves were executed.

Napoleon's Rise and Fall

The conservative Directory that next held power failed to find answers to the economic problems and protests continued. When a young artillery officer used cannon to break up one of these riots, the Directory admired his tactics and gave him control of the army in Italy in 1796. Napoleon Bonaparte did well, even conquering Egypt.

But alarmed by his independence, the Directory ordered him to return to Paris. Napoleon complied, but only to overthrow the Directory at gunpoint. The lower house of the National Assembly, presided over by Bonaparte's brother Lucien, then declared him First Consul of the republic.

Napoleon quickly ended the revolution and set about reconstructing France in his own image. He talked of republicanism and the rights of man and freedom, but he acted like any other despot, ruling ruthlessly. With France in hand, he set about to do the same for the rest of Europe, declaring himself emperor in 1804.

On the continent, Napoleon appeared unstoppable. But the British owned the seas, and finally Bonaparte overreached himself, invading Moscow for no gain and losing half a million men in the process. When his enemy's army entered Paris in 1814, Napoleon abdicated and accepted exile to Elba, a small Mediterranean island. The brother of Louis XVI was crowned Louis XVII and the monarchy was restored.

From Monarchy to Empire to Republic—and Back Again

But only temporarily, for Napoleon returned from exile to muted French cheers and soon was on the march again. This time the British stopped him at Waterloo and took him under guard to St. Helena, a small English island in the Atlantic, where he remained until his death.

During the century between Napoleon and World War I, France seemed rudderless, caught in any current that came along. Louis XVII gave the country limited prosperity during 10 years of cautious rule. He was followed by Charles X, who tried to turn back the clock a century. Charles quickly abdicated in the face of a popular uprising in 1830 in favor of Louis Philipe, the duke of Orléans.

Louis Philipe walked a tightrope trying to balance the various factions, more or less successfully until 1848, when a popular uprising forced him to abdicate and established the Second Republic. It decided France should have a president; the electorate chose Louis Napoleon Bonaparte, nephew of the emperor.

Louis Napoleon bided his time until 1851, when the National Assembly tried to take away the vote from three million people. He arrested the leaders and shut the assembly indefinitely. He then submitted his action to a vote, which he won. A year later, he declared himself Emperor Napoleon III.

Diplomatic Defeats

The Second Empire began in rigid conservatism and steadily liberalized. In its 18 years of existence, industrialization sped up, financial institutions were established, and economic expansion was supported. Tariffs were reduced and trade encouraged; unions and strikes were legalized. Political opponents were given amnesty and the political process opened up.

Where Napoleon III fared less well was in his foreign policy. He tried to install Prince Maximilian von Habsburg as emperor of Mexico without lasting success. He gained Nice and Savoy for France but failed to unify Italy.

But it was the Franco-Prussian war in 1870 that proved the real disaster and cost him his throne. It was a war that Napoleon III did not want, but Otto von Bismarck did. The ruthless Prussian prime minister had his way, manipulating public opinion so that the war cry sounded as loudly in Paris as it did in Berlin. Napoleon himself led French troops in battle and was captured. When word reached Paris, the radicals gained control of the assembly, declared a republic, and formed a provisional government.

The Third Republic

The new government negotiated peace at a heavy price, giving up Alsace and Lorraine and five billion francs in indemnities. This sad beginning set the tone for public life over the next 50 years. The various factions that had fought so bitterly over the past century—radicals, monarchists, socialists, conservatives, communists, Catholics and anti-clerics, bourgeoisie, peasants, and the nobility—didn't let up.

Scandal was rampant—including one of the worst in French history, one that still stirs emotions today. The Dreyfus affair nearly split France apart. In 1896, the only Jew on the general staff, Capt. Alfred Dreyfus, was arrested for selling military secrets to the Germans. Anti-Semitism was so rabid among the aristocratic Catholics who composed France's officer corps that he was tried and convicted on forged evidence and sent to Devil's Island.

It took a decade of bitter controversy to exonerate Dreyfus and restore him to his post. But this was a blot on the face of France that is remembered today.

Cultural Ferment

The ugliness of public life during this era was fortunately balanced by great beauty. It was during the Third Republic that artists began to eschew the conventional for the original. Edouard Manet, Claude Monet, Henri Toulouse-Lautrec, Pierre-Auguste Renoir, Paul Gauguin, Camille Pissaro, Paul Cézanne, Henri Matisse, Edgar Degas—a seemingly endless list of artists flourished during this time. So did musicians such as Georges Bizet, Maurice Ravel, and Claude Debussy; and scientists such as Louis Pasteur, Marie Curie, and the mathematician Henri Poincaré.

In stark contrast to this cultural flowering, World War I hit with little warning. The 1914 assassination of Austria's Archduke Franz Ferdinand in Sarajevo triggered a network of alliances and that set half of Europe at the throats of the other half. France bore the brunt of the war since most of the fighting took place within its borders. Trench warfare produced terrible losses; many soldiers who survived blamed the tactics of the generals as much as the war itself.

France suffered 1.3 million dead and another three million wounded, of whom nearly one million were crippled. An entire generation of young men was lost. In villages all over France stand memorials bearing the names of a dozen or more dead. Often the same last names will appear—brothers and cousins.

Jour-J, le Débarquement, and After

Unquestionably, Normandy was the scene of the fiercest fighting American troops encountered in France during World War II. The day the Allied troops arrived, June 6, 1944, is known as *Jour-J* to the French; the invasion itself, *le Débarquement*.

The first three beaches chosen for the invasion—Sword, Juno, and Gold—ran from the mouth of the Orne River west, where British forces landed, to Bayeux. From Bayeux west to St-Mère-Eglise were Omaha and Utah, where the Americans came ashore. The beaches here are narrow strips of sand backed by steep cliffs, like so much of the coast along the English Channel.

More than two months of vicious combat, including tanks, heavy artillery shelling, and aerial bombardments, devastated many cities and towns. However, the reconstruction effort after the war was extraordinary. While scars remain, many parts of this pastoral countryside appear untouched after two generations of healing.

After spending the first week securing their beachhead, the Americans attacked westward across the Cotentin peninsula to the whaling port of Barneville. The invaders then turned north to take the great port of Cherbourg, critical to maintaining supply lines to the advancing armies, on June 26.

Bayeux was the first city liberated in France, on June 7. Caen fell to British attack on July 9. St. Lô, nearly 40 kilometers (25 miles) southwest of Bayeux, was liberated July 25. This was a difficult part of the battle. Troops had to contend with the *bocage* land ("war of the hedges") quartered by dense rows of apple and pear trees, and roads too narrow for armor and cannon. St. Lô was almost totally destroyed in the war, but rebuilt with charm and today a town of 22,000.

Once past St. Lô the countryside opens up, allowing the tanks to speed ahead, bypassing pockets of German resistance, and to encircle them. Countances, today a pleasant town of 10,000 noted for its jazz festival every May, fell on July 28. Granville and Avranches, opposite Mont St.-Michel, followed on July 31.

On August 1, Gen. George Patton took command of the newly formed 3rd Army and swept into Brittany, taking Rennes on August 4. He then turned east to Orléans and Chartres.

Meanwhile, the British forces moved south from Caen making slow progress. With American successes to the west and British and Canadian pressure coming from the north, the Germans decided to counterattack. On August 6, German tanks moved west, intending to cut off Patton's 3rd Army at Avranches. The American 1st Army met them at Mortain, today a village of 2,500 at the mouth of a narrow valley and the western tip of the *Parc Régional de Normandie*.

A week of heavy fighting followed but the Germans were unable to break through. On August 12, they began a retreat eastward. They were too late. French forces that had taken Le Mans on August 9 sped north and captured Alençon on August 12. A day later they were outside Argentan, cutting off the road to Paris.

Canadian forces entered Falaise on August 17 and pushed forward, connecting with the Americans on August 19. The Germans were caught between the two forces, and on August 21, 1944, the Battle of Normandy ended.

War and Depression

The loss of life was matched by the economic devastation. Over the four years, inflation had skyrocketed 400 percent and the national debt had multiplied by five times. (It was World War I that turned the United States from a debtor nation into a creditor.) The French were determined to make the Germans pay reparations, which unwittingly contributed to the rise of fascism. By the mid-'20s, the economy began to revive and enjoyed full prosperity by 1928—just in time for the Great Depression.

The Depression affected France just as it did other nations: unemployment on a massive scale, falling production, a rising deficit, and no real solutions in sight. Economic gloom paralleled Hitler's rise to power and the rearming of Germany. When war struck again in 1939, it was a thoroughly demoralized France that reacted.

When Germany launched the blitzkrieg in the spring of 1940, France surrendered in less than three months. The Third Republic crumbled. Germany occupied Paris, the north of France, and the Atlantic coast; France was reduced to the agricultural, thinly populated Massif Central, Midi, and Provence. The country's new capital at Vichy was chosen because the resort area had sufficient hotel rooms to house the new government.

The Vichy Government

Marshal Philippe Pétain, a World War I hero, headed the new regime. Little more than a puppet of the Germans, the Vichy government gave the extreme right wing what it had been demanding for decades: It was authoritarian, anti-Semitic, and clerical. Dissidents and Jews were rounded up and sent east, either as slave labor or to the concentration camps. By 1944, Germany was in full control, with troops stationed in the south, executing Resistance figures when they could.

But Vichy did not represent all of France. The other France came to be represented by General Charles de Gaulle, an abrasive, autocratic, and talented soldier who escaped to England and did not surrender. The Vichy government called him a traitor and sentenced him to death. De Gaulle offered the Allies a French component for their propaganda and a conduit to French Resistance groups, who only reluctantly agreed to accept the haughty general as their symbolic leader. Without De Gaulle, France's postwar role in NATO and the United Nations would have been far less prominent.

The Allies' successful invasion of Normandy on June 6, 1944, was quickly followed by the liberation of Paris in late August. May 8, 1945, is officially recognized as Liberation Day in France, a national holiday.

De Gaulle established a provisional government—giving women the vote for the first time—and brought some order out of the chaos left behind by the Nazi occupation. The destruction of property was actually greater than in World War I. A new constitution was drawn up, based on the old one, and the Fourth Republic was born.

Colonial Crises and the Cold War

The Fourth Republic was never equal to the postwar stresses of anti-colonialism and the Cold War. The coalition governments of the Fourth Republic lasted an average of six months; it seemed that any constructive attempt to resolve a problem angered one faction or another, which would then withdraw and topple the government. Numerous crises beleaguered the government, the greatest ones centering on French colonies in Indo-China, North Africa, and the Near East.

Indo-China was the first to break free from colonial rule, in 1954, but not without a bitter war. The lengthy siege of Dien Bien Phu by the Vietminh broke the French will to continue the costly war. Tunisia and Morocco followed. Algeria was another story.

An Algerian nationalist group had been waging a guerilla war against the French for years. To counter them, France installed a heavy military presence, one augmented by troops pulled out of Indo-China. Tough, embittered, and extremely right wing, they were determined to hold Algeria by any means—torture was commonplace. When the government in Paris talked about withdrawal in 1958, the military began planning a coup d'état.

De Gaulle Rewrites the Constitution

De Gaulle refused to go along with them. Instead, the National Assembly gave De Gaulle six months of power to rule by decree. He rewrote the constitution, thus giving France a strong presidency. De Gaulle himself was elected to the post and his party gained a plurality in the parliament. The disgruntled army officers organized their coup but were unable to persuade their troops to follow. Instead, the officers formed a terrorist group, the OAS (Secret Army Organization), even attempting an assassination of De Gaulle. They failed. De Gaulle crushed the OAS and in 1962 recognized Algerian independence.

The postwar years were not all bad for France. Marshall Plan aid helped revive industrial production. It was during this period that France took the first steps toward forming the European Union. In 1951, France, West Germany, Italy, Belgium, Holland, and Luxembourg formed the European Coal and Steel Community. In 1957, these nations signed the Treaty of Rome to establish the Common Market. De Gaulle's government introduced economic as well as political reforms resulting in a five-percent annual increase in the Gross National Product between 1958 and 1967.

De Gaulle's exit from the stage of public life was most unusual. Following a massive general strike that brought the nation to a standstill in May and June of 1968, De Gaulle's party won a big majority in parliament. Industrial wage increased, and university reforms were soon instituted. De Gaulle then decided to introduce some governmental reforms by way of a national referendum. When the referendum lost, De Gaulle walked away without resigning or explanation. He went home and continued writing his memoirs, almost as if the 1958 call to return to public life had been little more than an interlude in a busy afternoon.

Mitterand and the European Union

After De Gaulle, the right wing retained the presidency for more than a decade until François Mitterand's Socialists swept into power in 1981. Mitterand served two seven-year terms as president, and more than once the right gained control of the National Assembly, but *"cohabitation"*—when the president and the prime minister are on opposite sides of the political fence—has worked. Fears that the situation would usher in the instability of the past have not been realized.

During the past 25 years, the various governments of France persevered

The garden in front of Monet's house in Giverny, where he spent his last days

Archie Satterfield

in their commitment to a European Union. Valerie Giscard d'Estaing, as finance minister and later president, was instrumental in establishing a framework for the common currency, now a fact of life in Europe. Mitterand saw to the acceptance of the Treaty of Maastricht, which opened the borders of the EU nations.

> As the recession of the 1990s waned, France faced the new millennium with stability and confidence.

President Jacques Chirac, who followed Mitterand in office, began his term with a legislative majority, but after raising taxes, resuming nuclear tests, and failing to lower unemployment, he was forced into *cohabitation* with the government of Socialist Prime Minister Lionel Jospin, his most likely opponent in the presidential election slated for 2002.

The New Millennium

As the recession of the 1990s waned, France faced the new millennium with stability and confidence. Unemployment declined in 2000, the economy continued to grow without excessive inflation, and consumer confidence remained robust. Moreover, the nation finally climbed aboard the Internet business bandwagon as more firms turned to e-commerce to sell and purchase products.

The EU took the first step in unifying the currencies of most of the member nations—fixing the rate of exchange—and the euro was launched successfully in the financial world. What remains is the release of actual euro coins and bills, scheduled for January 1, 2002. The swift withdrawal of national currencies, including the franc, will follow.

The greatest challenge for France in the coming years may well be this economic unification, coupled with the EU's increasing control of much national policy. The nation's leaders on both the right and the left have been at the forefront of efforts to unite the continent. There is no sign of this ending.

Part III
Daily Life

7. Keeping in Touch
8. Money Matters
9. Staying Healthy
10. Getting Around

7 Keeping in Touch

The industrialized world is wired, and France is an integral part of it. Aside from the language barrier, you'll find it no more difficult to communicate in France—both within its boundaries and beyond—than you do in the United States. Forget the horror stories you may have heard about French phones and service. Vast improvements have been made in both. From email to *la poste* (mail), you'll find it easy to stay in touch while you're in France.

Telephone

THE BASICS
One of the first appliances to get when you arrive is a telephone. You have the choice of renting one from the phone company or buying your own. If you bring one from the United States, be prepared to find an adapter because the French system does not use the familiar little clear plastic jacks. Instead they have a much larger plug about two inches long. Adapters are simply the French plug with a little hole in the bottom for the American-style jack. They are inexpensive and can be purchased at your local electronics shop.

Cell phones are readily available and widespread in France, just as they are in the U.S. In fact, there is at least one cell phone for every three people. Cell phone numbers begin with 06 everywhere in the country. There are pitfalls to avoid however. First is to make sure that the phone will work where you want to use it. Despite what the phone companies say about their coverage, a village need not be very remote for the cell phone to be useless inside a house, or even in the street outside. The second, related pitfall is that once you sign the contract for one of these phones, you have it for 12 months and the monthly service charge will be deducted from your bank account regardless of use.

Whereas Americans are used to dialing just seven digits to reach a friend or business associate, you'll dial 10 in France. In 1998, the country was divided into five areas with two-digit area codes tacked on to the traditional eight-digit phone numbers. Paris is 01, the Mediterranean coast 04, the northeast 03, the southwest 05, and the northwest 02. When calling from outside the country, you use the country code, 33, and drop the initial 0. Inside the country, you must dial the 0, even within the area.

TELEPHONE SERVICE

Many people have heard horror stories about phone service in France, or remember when businesses commonly used teletypes for communications because the phones were so unreliable. A hangover from those times, most businesses today have a separate fax (*telecopie*) number as well as a phone number.

Nor do you have to go to a *tabac* (a shop or bar-café where *cigarets* are sold) to get a *jeton* (token) every time you want to use a public phone. Those days are gone. Instead, *tabacs* sell phone cards—the size of a credit card and good for a certain number of message units. These are used in many public phones. Some public phones will also accept credit cards such as Visa or MasterCard, and a few still take coins.

Today, the French telephone system is the equal of any, with call-waiting, call-transfer, and all the other extras that phone companies like to tack on. France Telecom, the national phone company, was separated from the postal service some years ago. More recently, it was privatized. To remain competitive, it dropped its rates and continued reduced rates during off-peak hours, such as evenings and weekends. Basic phone service costs about 15 euros ($13.50) per month; additional services cost extra. Subscribers are also charged for each phone call, even if it is next door or across the street.

Despite recent lowerings of French long-distance phone rates, for transcontinental calls you may want to subscribe to one of several services that operate from U.S.-based computers. Here's how it works: You dial a U.S. number, connects with a computer, and hang up. The computer locks onto the French phone number and calls back—at a cheaper U.S. rate. You then answer the return call and dial a U.S. number, or a number in any other country and wait for the party to answer.

THE MINITEL

An unfamiliar, and very handy, aspect of French telephony is a device called the Minitel, a specialized computer and modem that accesses phone company data banks. In effect, the Minitel is like a directory for the entire country and very handy if you're looking a number in a distant city. France Telecom rents them to its subscribers. There are various models, some that include faxes and/or answering machines, but all have a keyboard and a screen and plug into the phone line. They look like small computer monitors.

To use a Minitel, you tap a couple of buttons to make a connection. Then you type any of various four-digit numbers—3611, for example, brings up a screen with blanks for name, type of business, town, and address. Fill in the blanks for last name and town and you get a list of everyone by that name in that town, along with their phone numbers and addresses. Fill in the town and a type of business, an electrician, for instance, and you get all the electricians. If there are none, the Minitel offers the possibility of selecting nearby towns for the search. The first three minutes of such a search are free.

Other Minitel services cost from the moment you enter the code, as little as 15 euro cents but up to 1.35 euros per minute, depending on the particular service. But the cost is usually less than the alternative. For instance, in less than five minutes, you can look up a train schedule, make a reservation, and order a ticket delivered to your home. Compare that to the time and cost involved in going to the depot, buying a ticket, and returning home.

> *From email to* la poste *(mail), you'll find it easy to stay in touch while you're in France.*

Another benefit to using the Minitel, consumer organizations that test appliances and other products make their results available through the device as well as in their magazines. For newcomers furnishing a home and facing an array of unfamiliar brands and models, this can be a real boon. Chances are you will not have had an opportunity to collect articles in previous issues of *60 Millions* or *Que Chosir*, two such organizations that publish monthly magazines similar to *Consumer Reports*.

As handy as it is, the Minitel is losing ground to Le Kiosque, software you can download from the Internet (www.lekiosque.fr) that performs the same functions. In effect, Le Kiosque allows any PC to do what a Minitel does, but with a faster modem and no monthly rental charge.

Computers and the Internet

Although France is behind the U.S. in the use of home computers, they are gaining wider acceptance. By the spring of 2000, more than six million people were online in France. For email alone—remaining in touch with family and friends in the U.S.—a computer is worthwhile. The six- to nine-hour time difference between France and the U.S. makes phone calls inconvenient in either direction. Nothing strains a relationship like answering the phone at 4 a.m. to hear someone say they just called to chat. And with telephony software improving all the time, you can use the Internet to make inexpensive calls as well.

French *domaines* (Web designations such as .com, .org, and .edu in the United States) are often designated by .fr, but .com is just as common. Fnac (pronounced fuh-NAK), a major French retailer, offers the Internet Service Provider Mageos.com, for instance.

The system of Internet Service Providers (*fournisseur d'accès à Internet*; the French acronym is FAI) in France is a bit different than that in the U.S. because of the telephone rate structure that charges for every call. Because FAIs are generally located in Paris and a few other large cities, using the Internet meant a long-distance call for users outside of those areas. To minimize costs and encourage use, the national FAIs began using numbers with the prefix 08. Now you connect for the price of a local call. (The 08 prefix can be an 800 number with no charge attached; in most cases, however, it is the equivalent of a 900 number and you are charged by the minute at varying rates.)

France Telecom itself is a major FAI, owning the provider Wanadoo. Compuserve was for years a good choice for anyone who wanted to use the same email address in both the U.S. and France and perhaps other countries. America On Line is also present in France. Other FAIs include Club-

Internet Service Providers (FAIs)

Below are listed the major Internet Service Providers in France, their telephone numbers, and website addresses.

1. Wanadoo
   0 801 105 105
   www.wanadoo.fr

2. Infonie
   0 803 825 825
   www.infonie.fr

3. Club-Internet
   0 155 454 647
   www.club-internet.fr

4. AOL
   0 169 199 450
   www.aol.fr

5. Freesbee
   0 805 025 025
   www.freesbee.fr

6. Liberty Surf
   0 836 688 656
   www.libertysurf.fr

7. Freesurf
   0 825 807 806
   www.freesurf.fr

8. World Online
   0 836 698 484
   www.worldonline.fr

9. Mageos.com
   0 825 099 109
   www.mageos.com

10. Compuserve
    0 321 134 949
    www.compuserve.fr

Internet and Infonie. Some FAIs such as Lokace Online, Free, and Freesurf, along with the Dutch FAI, World Online, do not charge a monthly fee, but you still pay for the phone call.

Internet portals and search engines such as Yahoo, Microsoft, and Alta Vista have French connections. There are also French search engines such as Nomade.

La Poste (mail)

Mail service in France is generally good, certainly comparable to that in the States, although somewhat more expensive. A first-class letter costs about half a euro (45 cents) anywhere in the European Union; to North America, the price is about two-thirds of a euro (59 cents). *La Poste* offers such familiar services as *poste restant* (general delivery), *Chronopost* (express mail), *lettres recommandées* (registered letters), and money orders. Of course, mark your airmail letters "*par avion*." Just as in the States, the post office sells a limited selection of boxes for mailing packages. In recent years, Federal Express and DHL have both established themselves in France, opening up an era of competitiveness.

One big difference between French and American post offices is that *La Poste* offers banking services. You can open a checking or savings account at the post office, a great convenience if you happen to live in a village without a bank.

As for receiving mail and packages from outside of France, be aware that shippers are required to list the value of the package's contents. This is duly noted by Customs officials. The moral: Don't expect to avoid paying the 19.6 percent TVA by ordering merchandise from the United States. Your goods will be be delivered, followed in short order by a bill for the tax due.

Television

The opposite of the situation in the States, much of French television is public. Owners of television pay an annual tax of about 100 euros ($90) to help underwrite this programming. Public channels also sell advertising to support themselves, just as private channels do. In this respect, the major difference between the two seems to be that the public channels do not interrupt movies with commercials, while the private channels run a single "intermission" to broadcast a number of commercials.

The two public television channels serving the general public are France 2 and France 3. France 2 is the flagship, with correspondents in the major world capitals and full coverage of international events. Its programming is the same throughout the country throughout the day.

More limited in worldwide coverage, France 3 concentrates on France. Its programming changes depending on the region, with telecasts from 13 locations around the country. Some two dozen news bureaus attached to different stations often work with the local press to cover stories of less than national interest. Part of France 3's programming also includes material in regional languages.

Both channels broadcast syndicated shows, movies, and re-runs from around the world, all dubbed into French. However, they also include prime-time discussions of serious subjects, major sporting events such as the Tour de France bicycle race, and the French Open tennis tournament.

Two other public channels play a lesser role in French television, sharing Channel 5 on the dial—*La Cinquième* from 3 a.m. to 7 p.m. and *Arte*, a French-German collaborative effort, the remaining hours. *La Cinquième* runs many of the shows that are staples of public TV programming in the United States—language lessons, nature shows, and documentaries on foreign countries along with panel discussions of issues and interesting old movies.

Arte often uses its prime time to explore a particular theme during an entire evening. For example, it might open with a documentary on a topic such as suicide, show a feature film involving suicide, then move to a round-table discussion of the issue, and end the evening with one or two more documentaries. It also repeats films at different times during the week.

Perhaps the most popular television station in France is privately owned TF1, at least during prime time, which begins just before 9 p.m. Both France 2 and TF1 conclude their evening newscasts about 8:45 and follow with about 10 minutes of commercials before launching into the evening's entertainment. TF1 often garners 25 to 40 percent of the audience, although it's programming is not unlike that of France 2 and 3 with feature films, reportage, made-for-TV movies, sports, and music shows.

One curious difference between French and American television: Feature films—those that have appeared in the theaters—may not be shown on Wednesday or Saturday nights. The first is the traditional night films open at a theater, the second the favorite night for dates and entertainment. The policy stemmed from the French audiovisual council's efforts to support the French movie industry. The irony is that the most popular films being shown in French theaters these days are not French, but American-made.

The second private channel is M6, aimed at a younger audience. It carries little news, lots of syndicated shows about teenagers—"*Buffy contre les vampires*" has been a Saturday night mainstay—music videos, and telefilms.

France's one pay-TV channel, Canal +, is available throughout the country. It requires a decoder to receive most of its programming, heavy on movies and sports.

Cable television was slow to arrive in France and today exists primarily in the large cities and nearby suburbs. About six million homes get a total of 20 cable networks. A small satellite dish, however, will bring in many of the staples of cable TV, such as CNN, MTV and the Disney Channel.

Radio

French radio is a national affair, with a handful of networks, public and private, covering the country. Puzzling to many is where to find them on the dial. The same program will appear at one frequency in Paris and another in Strasbourg and yet a third in Lyon. (See Appendix for frequencies.)

Radio France is the overall name for the various publicly financed radio networks: France Inter, France Info, France Musique, France Culture, and Radio Bleue. There is also a public network that offers regional programming, its broadcasts differing from area to area. Three big private radio networks broadcast on both AM and FM: Europe 1, RTL, and RMC. Local radio programs are offered in the private sector by networks NRJ, Europe 2, Fun Radio, and Nostalgie.

Newspapers and Magazines

The first newspaper to appear on the streets of Paris was *La Gazette* in 1631. It began a lively tradition that continues today. French newspapers are very different from American papers in that they do not contain anywhere near the volume of advertising. Many are tabloid size and thin, 32 to 48 pages perhaps. The two-pound Sunday editions laden with color sections, pre-printed advertising, and supermarket coupons are unknown here.

Le Monde, one of the most respected of the handful of national dailies, prints a combined Sunday-Monday edition, for instance. Its nod to U.S. journalistic practices is to include a 40-page tabloid section listing radio and television programming for the coming week following its much smaller news section. *Le Monde* also publishes separate, specialized periodicals that are sold independently, such as *Le Monde Diplomatique*. Other national papers include *Le Figaro*, *Liberation*, and *Le Parisien/Aujourd'hui*.

The small town daily papers common in so many U.S. cities, papers with circulations of 10,000 to 30,000 covering one or two counties, is not known here. Instead, regional dailies cover particular areas of France with lots of editions. The different editions permit coverage of numerous villages and their very local news: births and marriages, photos of an athletic team of 12-year-olds lined up in a row, an amateur theatrical group presenting a performance, six-year-olds in costume going to a party.

Reading Matters

When it comes to English-language periodicals in France, the choices are few and often far between.

For a daily newspaper, the obvious choice is the *International Herald Tribune* (www.iht.com). It is owned and supported by the *New York Times* and *Washington Post* and has the news services of both papers available to it.

The *Herald Trib* is familiar. It has sports pages that include baseball, financial pages listing the U.S. exchanges, and familiar columnists like William Safire and Thomas Friedman. It even runs comic strips such as "Calvin and Hobbes," "Doonesbury," and the "Wizard of Id."

The paper is now printed in Toulouse and Marseille, so even in the South of France it is available and timely. Home delivery is offered in Paris, Lyon, Marseille, Reims, Lille, Aix-en-Provence, and Strasbourg. Mail subscriptions may arrive the same day much of the country.

But it is the **International** *Herald Tribune*, after all, and a good portion of the news—a typical edition is 20 pages—concerns the Middle East and Asia rather than the United States.

Additionally, there are European editions of various American publications like the *Wall Street Journal*, *USA Today*, *Time*, and *Newsweek*, but they are not widely available on newsstands. You will find them in large cities, however.

British papers are more easily obtained, often at train stations and at newsstands in towns where tourists are common. These include the *Times*, the *Financial Times*, and the *Guardian*, rather than the popular tabloids.

One English-language magazine that is very helpful in Paris is *FUSAC—France USA Contacts* (www.fusac.fr). Published twice monthly, with a press run of about 60,000, *FUSAC* is distributed free in Paris. It's not news but all advertising—mostly classified ads for jobs, apartments, furnishings, personals, and the like. If you're in Paris and feel a need to orient yourself or make contact with other Americans, this publication can be helpful. It is a source of used household goods and information about the general Anglophone entertainment scene—many of its advertisers cater to U.K., Irish, and Dutch clientele, rather than strictly Americans.

A magazine published 10 times a year in England, *Living France* (www.livingfrance.com) is devoted entirely to expats in France. It contains feature stories about various regions of France, personality interviews, advice columns, and extensive advertisement of property for sale.

An English-language newspaper published monthly in France is *The News* (www.french-news.com). Based in Perigueux, it serves a rural, British audience. Unfortunately, the website uses the difficult-to-access Adobe Acrobat format for its pages, limiting usefulness. An annual subscription costs 18.29 euros ($16.50).

In the end though, the French press does a better job of covering France than anyone else. And for those who crave local U.S. news, accessing an American paper via the Internet will probably be the most satisfactory option.

For books, there are English-language lending libraries in some cities. Paris has one, as do Toulouse and Montpellier. And most larger cities have an English-language bookstore, or at least a foreign-language section in a larger store.

In the Midi, the best source of used English-language books is the tiny village of Montolieu. Located in the Montagne Noir between Carcassonne and Toulouse, Montolieu decided more than a decade ago to become a "book village" as a means of boosting its sagging economy. The strategy seems to be working, with more than a dozen shops, including Booth Books and the English Book Store, and Sunday book markets to draw sellers who lack a permanent site.

Magazines are also an important part of the French press. *Paris Match*, the provocative color weekly, combines *People*-style celebrity coverage with reportage as serious as anything appearing in the *New York Times'* Sunday magazine. Most French magazines are aimed at specific audiences. *L'Express*, *Le Point*, and *Nouvel Observateur* are popular news magazines. Both *Time* and *Newsweek* publish European editions. *Elle* and *Marie Claire* cater to women.

One type of publication in France is quite different from its American counterpart. *Bandes dessinées* (comic books) are a serious art form in France. There are many for children, of course, but many others boast historical or adult themes and story lines. Comic book artists such as Hugo Pratt are considered cultural figures in France. Many of the books are published in hardcover in large formats. Among the better known series are Asterix, about Gaul in Roman times, and Tin-Tin, an adventurous young reporter.

8 Money Matters

Surprise, surprise, you'll probably spend very few francs in France—they're being phased out to make way for the euro, the new currency of the European Union. But no matter what currency you exchange your dollars for, be prepared to spend a lot of them. France isn't cheap. But, just as in the United States, you generally get what you pay for, and then some.

From Francs to Euros

The franc is an endangered species soon to become extinct. The euro is taking over. On January 1, 2002, France and the 10 other EU member nations that agreed to adopt the common currency will begin circulating the new coins and bills. Until then, to the general public the euro is little more than an abstract number—6.55957. That's the number of francs that equal one euro. Conversely, one franc equals 15 euro cents.

The other countries adopting the euro are Germany, Austria, Belgium, Spain, Finland, Italy, Ireland, Luxembourg, the Netherlands, and Portugal. Each of their currencies was calculated in relation to the others and a conversion rate to euros fixed for each. Thus, a German mark is worth 51 euro cents, a Dutch florin is worth 45 euro cents, while a Spanish peseta is worth 0.6 euro cents.

For two months, both bills and coins in francs, centimes, euros, and cents

The Euro

The symbol of the euro resembles an "E" or a rather shallow "C" with two horizontal bars through the middle. Both the new euro bills and coins will be colorful affairs, and the bills will come in different sizes depending on denomination, just as franc notes do now. The EU will print an initial 12.7 billion euro bills in seven denominations—500, 200, 100, 50, 20, 10, and 5 euros.

Although the theme of the bills' design is European architectural heritage, the images are symbolic rather than representative of any actual structure or monument. The front side of the bills displays windows and gateways, symbolic of openness and cooperation in the European Union. The back side depicts different bridges, connoting communication among European nations, and between Europe and the rest of the world.

As for the coins, 70 billion will be struck in denominations of 2 euros and 1 euro, and of 50 cents, 20 cents, 10 cents, 5 cents, 2 cents, and 1 cent. (Each euro will be divided into 100 cents.) The faces of the coins will be uniform, the backs bearing designs representing individual countries, so national symbols will not disappear entirely from the monetary system. But no matter the design or the country it symbolizes, euro coins and bills will be legal tender in all 11 EU member nations.

Distribution of 2.5 billion euro bills and 10.1 billion coins to French banks and post offices begins in the fall of 2001. By the middle of December, the French will be able to buy a "euro kit" of 40 different bills and coins for 100 francs to familiarize themselves with the new money.

Beginning January 1, 2002, individuals will be able to exchange francs for euros at the banks. As merchants deposit their receipts, the banks will retire the francs, giving out euros.

After February 28, 2002, the franc will no longer be legal tender, but may be exchanged for euros. The Bank of France will exchange coins for the next year and bills for 10 years.

If you use plastic more than cash, don't be surprised by the appearance of French credit cards. Rather than the magnetic strip that contains the account information, a *puce* (chip) is embedded in the face of the card that the merchants' machines read.

will circulate. (The euro will be divided into 100 parts called cents, not centimes.) Merchants will accept either currency during that period. However, all checks and credit card payments will be only in euros. At the end of February 2002, the francs and centimes will no longer be accepted as legal tender.

The speed and finality of this procedure may surprise Americans, who are used to circulating and spending new and old bills interchangeably. However, during the past decade France changed the appearance of all of its bills and some coins to prevent forgeries and used exactly the same method as the one used to introduce the euro.

Conversion to the euro will have a profound psychological effect on the French: Nothing will drive home the fact that the franc no longer exists as money than a merchant's refusal to accept it. The changeover to the euro is revolutionary for the entire European Union, far more so than the ending of border checks. After all, the border check was little more than a formality if a traveler's papers were in order. They did not hinder movement among the various EU member countries.

In contrast, the euro will have far-reaching consequences. First, while the different currencies in Europe hindered economic growth, the euro opens up vast opportunities for it. For example, Europe might have been a potential market of 300 million, but what business could cultivate it when producers were unable to predict the costs of their materials from one nation to another? Before the euro, 11 different currencies seesawed in value—not just in Europe but vis-à-vis the United States and Japan as well—every day in response to elections, strikes, scandals, employment statistics, and inflation. The euro can and does fluctuate in relation to the dollar, the yen, and the pound (the United Kingdom refused to join the currency pact), but the franc, florin, lira, and mark no longer fluctuate in relation to one another.

The euro also stabilizes economic exchange. For example, if a German supermarket chain agrees in April to buy wine in October from a French producer for 10 francs per liter, it knows that wine will cost exactly 2.97 marks per liter. If a French hardware distributor buys electric heaters from an Italian manufacturer for 77,450.80 lira apiece, it knows each heater will cost 262.38 francs. And after January 1, 2002, that wine will cost 1.52 euros and the heaters 40 euros apiece.

> *The changeover to the euro is revolutionary for the entire European Union, far more so than the ending of border checks.*

It is the euro that makes Europe a unified market and a global economic power. Its advent is comparable to the enormous change the United States made when it scrapped the Articles of Confederation for the Constitution. Many areas of multinational government were not at issue among the European nations; postal service, transportation, and, since World War II, defense all were settled through treaties of cooperation. But lack of a single currency remained a stumbling block that has now been removed.

To make the single currency work, participating nations had to align their economies and work to keep them in alignment. This meant controlling inflation and insuring price stability. By 1998, inflation in the euro nations was under two percent.

Because unemployment remained high, the creation of jobs and lowering government deficits through economic development rather than taxation became important goals. Structural reform and discipline were also required in national budgets to prevent the factors that traditionally created discrepancies in exchange rates. This meant balanced budgets and government deficits within a three percent limit. The EU created a central bank to oversee the individual nations' central banks.

These reforms have not come easily, and few have been fully realized. Nonetheless, they seem well rooted. When the Socialists came to power in

France in 1997 and later the Democratic Socialists in Germany, leaders of both parties vowed to continue along the path of European unity. They, in fact, have done so.

What remains to be seen is whether the members can maintain their political will in face of greater adversity. Through most of the 1990s, the price of oil declined and unemployment remained high, two conditions that helped keep inflation below the two percent level. But following the fixing of the euro conversion rates, two developments occurred: The exchange rates between the euro and the dollar (1: $1.17 in January 1999) and the euro and the yen fell further than expected, and the price of oil skyrocketed.

By the summer of 2000, the euro was worth about 90 cents. Initially, EU economists showed little concern; the weak euro, they said, would ensure the competitiveness of European products on the world market and stimulate recovery from the recession. But with the price of oil tied to the dollar, a weak euro lacked purchasing power and thus inflationary pressures began to increase. As the head of the Bundesbank once remarked, inflation has something in common with toothpaste: It's easy to get out of the tube, but once out, very difficult to put back.

Aside from the threat of inflation, the euro and the economic umbrella it represents has also produced political stress. For one thing, any nation's currency is symbolic of its history and identity. (Indeed, the UK's reluctance to give up its own coins and bills is one of the main reasons it has refused to join the euro system.) To give up a national currency is a serious step away from nationalism.

Beyond the symbolic, political stress has been caused by member nations' need to adopt fiscal and budgetary policies that would produce the statistics that allowed them into the club, so to speak. Government spending had to be curbed, inflation limited, publicly-owned shares of corporations divested, and so on. In many European countries, these economic strictures required political action that governing bodies and their constituencies found not only distasteful, but contrary to long-held philosophies. Yet, despite more than a half century of increasing unification and individual member nations' fears of eroding identity, the European Union remains a collection of sovereign nations, each capable of taking some drastic step in a different direction.

Cost of Living

One caveat: Don't move to France to reduce your cost of living. Budget item by budget item, French prices equal or exceed their counterparts in the United States, if only because of the 19.6 percent value-added tax (TVA) added to labor as well as materials. Even insurance is taxed in this way.

Even without the TVA, many items are more expensive, such as gasoline, offsetting whatever items might cost less.

Yet you will almost certainly lead a different style of life in France than in the United States. These differences can simultaneously lower some of your expenses while enhancing your quality of life. It's not really paradoxical when you consider what drives up the cost of living in the States.

Take commuting, for example. At roughly $2 per gallon, gas is cheap in America; in France it will run you close to $4 per gallon (4.5 euros). But cars are larger and distances greater in the States: a commuter driving an SUV 30 miles or more each way to work averaging 20 miles per gallon will spend at least $6. In France, 20 kilometers is considered a long commute; driven in an average French sedan, it costs about 2.2 euros ($2). What's more, there are far fewer two- or three-car families in France. Even so, the cost of operating a car in France is estimated at about 6,000 euros ($5,400) per year.

Along with gas, food is more expensive pound for pound in France than in the States. But many French people grow fruits and vegetables for their own consumption, increasing their quality of life while cutting down on their food bills. Indeed, the backyard vegetable garden now so rare in America is part of life in France. Even in villages where the houses are built one on top of the other, residents trek to the edge of town to tend gardens on small patches of ground they rent or own.

Housing is comparable to what you'll pay in the States, with some exceptions. Your housing costs will depend, of course, on where you live and what you live in. French houses and apartments, especially older ones, are typically smaller than you'd find in the States. Even in new construction, two- or three-bedroom/one-bath houses are common. Yards are often diminutive compared to those on American suburban lots. But what you sacrifice in square footage, you gain in savings.

Not surprisingly, you'll find the most expensive housing in Paris and its suburbs. If you hail from a pricey city like San Francisco, you won't be shocked at all, and other parts of France may seem like bargains to you. But if you're from Maryland or suburban Atlanta or Houston, where homes fetch far less than they do in California, you'll find housing costs in France either comparable or more expensive. Moreover, prices are rising—more than 11 percent in 1999, according to one study.

In the provinces (generally understood to mean everywhere but Paris), you can find a decent home for less than $100,000. Whether it's your dream home or not is another question. Prices in the provinces are increasing, both in and around the larger cities offering employment opportunities and

Budgeting in France

Beware, "sticker shock" may strike when you start pricing everyday items in France. After you calculate it just cost you $40 for 11 gallons of gas, you'll realize this is no cut-rate country. Goods and services, including insurance policies and utility bills, come with a whopping 19.6 percent value-added tax. Believe it or not, the French regard a trip to the United States as a chance to buy merchandise at bargain prices.

France is a wealthy country. Its work force is well educated and well paid, with a strong sense of social responsibility. It maintains its infrastructure and preserves its *patrimoine* (national heritage), reflecting 2,000 years of historical development. None of this comes cheap, and the French are willing to pay the price (even though they may grumble about it). Inflation continues low, averaging around two percent; unemployment remains high, above 10 percent, but has been slowly decreasing for the past year. During the 1990s, many common expenses—auto repairs, restaurant meals, personal services—increased at almost twice the rate of inflation, largely due to rising wages and higher taxes.

But rest assured, you don't have to be a millionaire, or even close to one, to live in France. You can buy and furnish a comfortable three- or four-bedroom house for $100,000. Cars cost about what they do in the United States. And although gas prices are higher, you probably won't use as much fuel because you won't drive so far.

Good thing, too, for gas prices reached record highs in the summer of 2000 due to a tripling of the cost of crude oil. Both gasoline and diesel fuel increased at least a franc a liter over the previous year's prices. Even the most ambitious plans to cut fuel taxes seemed unlikely to return prices to pre-jump levels.

Fortunately, medical costs are far less expensive than in the States—a visit to the doctor costs about $20. Electricity averages about 11 cents per kilowatt hour. Since most of France's electricity is produced by its nuclear plants, the oil crisis will have little effect on this rate.

Household and yard help costs about 7 or 8 euros ($6 or $7) per hour, a reasonable rate that enables many working French women to hire someone to clean their houses. Although domestic workers often prefer to be paid in cash (for obvious reasons), you can also use a *cheque service*. It works like this: With special checks obtained from your bank, you pay the employee the agreed-upon rate. When the employee deposits the check in his or her account, the bank deducts the amount due for Social Security tax from your account. At

in the countryside, where both French and foreign buyers are driving up the values of the more desirable properties.

Outfitting your home in France will probably cost more than it does in the States. Major appliances are more expensive in France. Side-by-side refrigerators (the style is called *"americain"* in France) can cost 2,775 euros ($2,500). Smaller refrigerator/freezers, measured in liters rather than cubic feet, cost 550 to 900 euros ($500 to $800). Brand-name washing machines cost between 550 and 1,100 euros ($500 and $1,000). Television prices have declined in the last decade, but for brand names you'll still pay more than in the States. An ordinary hair dryer may cost as much as 33 euros ($30).

Likewise, clothing and household linens are more expensive. Although list prices of such items as name-brand running shoes, jeans, and bedding

the end of the year, you may deduct the entire amount from your taxable income. If you are not earning income in France, you of course don't need the deduction.

Here is a reasonable monthly budget for a couple in a two-bedroom house or three-bedroom apartment.

Expense	Cost in Euros
Rent:	800 ($720)
Food & household supplies:	300 ($270)
Utilities:	100 ($90)
Auto (fuel, insurance, & depreciation):	600 ($540)
Health insurance:	350 ($315)
Clothing:	200 ($180)
Recreation:	200 ($180)
Total:	**2,550 ($2,295)**

These categories are averages—for example, a house in a rural village may rent for 400 euros ($360) per month rather than 800 euros ($720) in a city. If you buy a house outright, you'll strike that expense from your monthly budget. Heating bills increase the colder the region and the larger the house.

One point to bear in mind if you buy or rent an unfurnished house or apartment: You'll bear the large, one-time expense of appliances and furniture. Budget a minimum of 20,000 euros ($18,000) for this, possibly more, depending on your tastes and the size of your bank account.

Look at the categories and consider where you might want to splurge or, conversely, economize. Perhaps 200 euros ($180) per month for clothing is insufficient for a fashion plate like you. Perhaps it's too much if you're the type who delights in trips to *"le frip,"* as the French call used clothing markets, where you can pick up a nearly new sweater for about 6 euros ($5.40). You may choose to economize even further by waiting for the annual August sales. If like to you eat out several times a week (and you may be tempted to do so in this culinary capital), you may want to budget more for food per month. If you're a gardener, like so many French, you may opt to "grow your own" and cut down on your food bills.

You may find some of the monthly bills you pay in the States have vanished: no cable TV perhaps, no daily newspaper subscription or membership at a gym, no gardener because now you do it all yourself. The monthly income that France requires for the long-stay visa will let you live quite comfortably in most parts of the country. The luxuries you allow yourself and the ways you economize will finally determine just how you live.

may be comparable, you'll seldom find the sales, markdowns, and discounts so common in the United States.

Utility prices are more difficult to compare with those in the States because they vary widely in both countries. Telephone service, for one, is more expensive in France. You'll pay a monthly charge plus a fee for every call. Water rates vary, but have generally risen in recent years to pay for new sewage treatment plants. Electricity rates vary according to time of day, but users pay a flat monthly fee based on the size of their service, plus usage at 10 euro cents per kilowatt-hour, reduced to about six euro cents per KWH during hours of low demand, TVA included.

So, what *is* cheaper? Wine—as long as you don't demand classified growths from Bordeaux châteaux. Some foods are also real bargains. You can buy a fresh baguette for less than a dollar and treat yourself to a delicious croissant for about 50 cents. A dab of fresh goat cheese costs about a buck, and fresh oysters in the shell, about 3.5 euros ($3) a baker's dozen. And you can savor an excellent five-course meal at a nice restaurant for about 22 euros ($20).

Banking

Banks in France are not much different from their American counterparts. They offer credit and debit cards, checking and savings accounts, safety deposit boxes, and personal, business, and property loans. They also make change and sell insurance.

Even without a long-stay visa, Americans owning property in France can open checking accounts that permit them to transfer funds from home and pay bills in France. In many cases, bills such as insurance and electricity may be paid by direct deduction from the account. In other instances, you send along to a creditor a *releve d'identité bancaire*, or RIB, several of which are included in each book of checks, filling out the date and amount. For many Americans living in France, the greatest difficulty paying bills is spelling the amounts in French.

> *Keeping tabs on your American bank account is easy via the Internet.*

In general, French banking rules are stricter than those in the States. Writing a check without sufficient funds is grounds for termination of the account, and other banks may refuse to open a new account for those who have done so. Also, you can't cash a check outside of a bank or cash a third-party check; checks made out to a person must be deposited in his or her bank account. Nor can you post-date a check. A merchant selling something by installments will demand a check for each payment, dated the day it is written and only to be deposited when the payment is due.

One similarity between American and French banks: neither likes to loan money without security. If your assets are outside of France, borrowing from a bank may be difficult. The process for borrowing money is just like it is in the United States, but with tighter limits. If you are seeking a personal loan, you must have the income necessary to make the payments and still have enough to live on.

If you desire a loan to buy property, expect to come up with a down payment of 30 to 40 percent and to repay it in 10 years or less to get the best rates. Thirty-year mortgages are not unheard of anymore in France, but the norm is 15 to 20 years. For the French themselves, a variety of special financing arrangements complement the traditional mortgage. These allow young couples to buy a home. However, they usually are tied to employment or savings previously accrued.

Many Americans coming to France will need no more than a checking account. To have obtained a long-stay visa, you will have to have shown sufficient income to live on without working while in France. If you are eligible to work or open a business in France, you'll be in a better position to borrow within the country, if necessary.

The large French banks—such as Crédit Lyonnaise, Société Générale, BNP (Banque Nationale de Paris), and Banque Populaire—have branches in most cities. However, Crédit Agricole is more likely to have branches in villages and may be more convenient for that reason. Another option is *La Poste*. In France, as in other European countries, the post office functions as a bank, offering checking and savings accounts.

When the national currencies disappear in 2002, foreign banks are likely to make inroads in France, and vice versa. A certain amount of fusion and consolidation has already taken place in French banking, a trend likely to continue. Since all check and credit card transactions will be in euros, there will be no difference between a German or Dutch check and a French one.

If you are retired or living off income in the United States, you should probably keep your American bank account and simply transfer funds into a French checking account as needed. Wire transfers are often expensive, however. One solution is to increase the daily limit on an ATM card attached to the U.S. account to $1,000 or more. This will allow you to withdraw about 1,100 euros per week. For larger sums, such as for the purchase of property, international firms that specialize in currency trading, such as American Foreign Exchange (www.Afex.com), will write a check drawn on a French bank for a fee.

Keeping tabs on your American bank account is easy via the Internet. Many U.S. banks maintain websites that allow you to review your account's activity. In the past, such sites have not permitted electronic banking from Europe; however, considering the growth of e-commerce, this may change. If it doesn't, you can make payments and handle other financial arrangements the old-fashioned way—through the mail.

Taxes

The French generally consider taxes to be an onerous burden—and certainly they are heavier than in the United States. American taxpayers, despite all their complaints, pay less in taxes than the French.

The beginning is the 19.6 percent value-added tax, or TVA in French. It works like a sales tax, but unlike a tax on retail sales of merchandise, it is added to labor and less tangible products and services such as insurance. Each time someone transforms something for sale—adds value to it—the tax is imposed. And it is the consumer who pays; businesses deduct the TVA they pay from the TVA they add to their products and services.

The extent to which the TVA helps finance the French government may be easily seen in the budget for the year 2000. While income tax revenue brought in 51.5 billion euros ($46.3 billion), revenue from the TVA was more than double that—103.9 billion euros ($93.5 billion). This is out of net total receipts of 236.5 billion euros ($212.8 billion).

Nonetheless, there is movement to lower the TVA. In 1999, the TVA charged for home improvements and renovations was lowered to 5.5 percent. In April 2000, the overall TVA was lowered by one percent, from 20.6 to 19.6 percent. Small businesses now may opt for a system of taxation that bypasses the bookkeeping involved with collection and payment of the TVA; medium-sized ones grossing up to 762,000 euros ($685,800) may also choose a simplified reporting and payment system.

In addition to the TVA, the French pay property taxes. Their rates vary according to the locale and are updated annually for inflation. Property taxes come in two different levies: *taxe foncière* (property tax) and *taxe d'habitation*, the tax owed each January 1 by the person occupying the property, either the tenant or the owner, even if the latter has another residence. The criterion is that the property is habitable; the owner of a barn without a roof or of a house without electricity would not be expected to pay this tax. When property is sold, these taxes may be prorated, although this may be negotiated.

Then there are the taxes on the money you make. People earning an income in France are required to pay income tax, capital gains tax, and sometimes, wealth tax. Probably the most critical factor in all of these taxes is your domicile, or principal residence. The wealth tax is levied on the worldwide holdings of anyone domiciled in France—one of the reasons some of France's wealthiest citizens have moved out of the country. Not only is their wealth taxed, but those in the highest income bracket are taxed at 54 percent.

All of these taxes can add up. If you're planning to move to France, examine your situation carefully to see how you will be affected. Although U.S. citizens can exclude up to $78,000 of income earned in France in 2001 and up to $80,000 in 2002, the Internal Revenue Service imposes certain tests, one of which is physical presence in the country for 330 days of the year. Meeting this test may mean that you are subject to French taxes. However, for the non-resident (that is, the person not domiciled in France) only the income earned in France is subject to taxation, at a lower rate than the resident pays. The amount withheld from a non-resident's earnings is regarded as satisfying his or her tax liability whereas the resident is taxed on worldwide earnings.

Americans not working or operating a business in France, especially retirees, are probably better remaining domiciled in the United States. For one thing, retirees can take advantage of Medicare when in the States, thus cutting down on the amount of health insurance they carry. What's more, you're familiar with the U.S. system; at the point of retirement, you know pretty well how it works and what to expect. You don't need the aggravation and uncertainty of a new and different tax system, at least as complicated and arbitrary as its American corollary, and surely more so navigated in a foreign language.

Social Security

France's Social Security system differs from that in the States in several significant ways. First of all, it is not uniform; various occupations have different plans. Farmers, salaried employees, craftspeople, shopkeepers, and civil servants all participate in different plans. Yet the system is by no means chaotic. It's been compared to a set of Russian dolls, the kind that look alike but come in graduated sizes, one fitting inside the other.

The French system is facing a major influx of new retirees. Until recently, it has taken in about 110,000 new pensioners a year. Starting in 2006, as baby boomers retire, that number will more than double, to 250,000. Furthermore, these folks will live longer on the average than their predecessors, putting a further strain on the funds. The demographics are staggering: Today there are 10 active workers for every four retirees; by 2040 the ratio is expected to be 10 workers for every seven pensioners.

The strategies for solving this problem are limited. The U.S. solution has been to increase the age of retirement. Others include higher taxes on wages, financing from another source, higher wages, and, of course, diminished benefits.

The important thing for Americans to know is that France and the United States have a treaty covering Social Security as well as taxation. This treaty allows citizens from both nations to work in either country, pay into either system according to their employment and when eligible to retire, and receive credit for their total number of years. Years of work in one country will not be lost in the other. Nor will you have to pay into both systems. Again, depending on the situation, you will be eligible—and required—to pay into one or the other but not both.

Those who have paid into Social Security in both countries may be eligible for benefits from one or both countries. If you meet the basic requirement for either country, that country will pay you. The United States will begin reduced payments at age 62; France will begin payments at age 60. Those who do not have enough time in either country alone may qualify by combining their credits from both countries.

The system is somewhat complicated, but France will compute benefits based on French credits alone and then on French and prorated U.S. credits and pay whichever is greater. The U.S. may reduce your benefits if you are receiving some from France, so it is wise to determine the various options before making a decision.

One thing the treaty does not include is health care. The American Social Security system will not extend Medicare benefits outside the United States. Retired Americans with Medicare coverage who are stricken outside the country cannot be treated under Medicare except on home turf. Say you're on a two-week vacation abroad and you have a heart attack. You may have paid thousands of dollars into Social Security and Medicare, but you will not be reimbursed one cent by Medicare for any treatment you receive in a foreign country.

9 Staying Healthy

Health care in France is generally good. Doctors are plentiful and hospitals well staffed and located around the country. Remarkably, many doctors still make house calls. Privately employed nurses visit patients in their homes to administer medication or give care. Health care is generally less expensive than it is the States (although medication may cost more). On the downside, Medicare won't help you much in France.

Know Your Health Status

Before planning a move to France, you'd be wise to get a thorough medical check-up. If you discover some health problem, you may prefer to resolve it before leaving the States—not because the French health-care system is poor, but because you may be more comfortable being treated by a doctor and system you know. What's more, you'll be in familiar surroundings, with friends and family on hand to lend support. Pay a visit to the optometrist and dentist before your move as well. Women should also have a thorough gynecological examination.

The documentation of any conditions you may have will help whatever health practitioners you may consult in France. With up-to-date knowledge and, one hopes, a clean bill of health, you can undertake your move with confidence.

You and the French Health-Care System

Americans who come to France to live but not to work (retirees and those on sabbatical, for example) must provide for their own insurance and show proof of it before obtaining a residency permit. If you are salaried or self-employed, you and your family will be covered by the French health-care system, which is part of Social Security. (The exceptions are Americans sent to France by their companies for periods of less than five years who arrange to continue their American health insurance while in France.) French citizens are covered from birth.

The Price of Good Health

Health care in France is inexpensive compared to that in the United States. Whereas a visit to a physician in the States can set you back $100 or more, a trip to the doctor in France costs only about $20.

Most physician and dentist fees are fixed by agreement with the Social Security system. For these 54,000 general practitioners, the fee for an office consultation is 17.53 euros ($15.75). The fee rises to 19.06 euros ($17) on Sundays and 25.15 euros ($22.65) at night. House calls (yes, some doctors still make them) cost an extra 3.81 euros ($3.40), except in Paris, Lyon, and Marseille, where the charge is 5.34 euros ($4.80). If the patient is in another town, there is a mileage charge as well. Specialists are reimbursed at the rate of 22.07 euros ($19.85) per office consultation.

In some rural regions, doctors take turns being on call on weekends so there is always a doctor available. And when a doctor goes on vacation, he or she makes sure another physician is available as a replacement.

The nation's 1,300 midwives receive 152.50 euros ($137) for assisting at a birth, 167.75 euros ($150) to deliver twins.

Some 99 percent of France's 37,000 dentists work under this fee system also, charging 16.77 euros ($15) for an office visit. Sunday consultations and emergencies cost 19.06 euros ($17), 25.15 euros ($22.60) for night calls. A specialist charges 22.07 euros ($19.85) for an office visit. Specific procedures are charged according to a coefficient multiplied times 15.50 francs. For teeth cleaning, the coefficient is 10, so the charge is 155 francs, or 23.63 euros ($21.25). A crown costs 107.48 euros ($96).

The price of a hospital stay varies by region and depends on the nature of the stay. For instance, a pediatrics or cardiology patient might be charged 500 euros ($450) per day, an orthopedic surgery patient 700 euros ($630) per day. Intensive care costs about 1,400 euros ($1,260) per day.

Prescription medicine can be expensive. Few non-prescription medicines are available outside of pharmacies. "Parapharmacies" have started to spring up in the *hypermarché* malls, but they sell mostly cosmetics and vitamin pills rather than medicine.

Prices of over-the-counter remedies are comparable to that in the States. (The ones below are for the largest containers available.) At pharmacies, a box of 30 aspirin tablets, 500 mg. each, costs about 2.40 euros ($2). A box of 12 Pepcidac pills, a brand-name anti-acid, goes for about 5.26 euros ($4.50). In a large chain supermarket, vitamin C, 500 mg. in size, runs 2.90 euros ($2.60) for 24 tablets. A bottle of multivitamin pills, containing A, B complex, C, D, and E plus iron and calcium, costs 3.81 euros ($3.40). And you'll pay about 6.07 euros ($5.50) for a 12-ounce bottle of saline solution for contact lenses.

The French health-care system is universal. Effective Jan. 1, 2000, full health care was extended to any legal resident of France. At that time, insurance covering 100 percent of medical costs was extended to the poorest 10 percent of the population—those receiving general welfare assistance (RMI, as it is called in France), and those with monthly incomes below 534 euros ($480). The total annual price tag for the system is 1.37 billion euros ($1.23 billion).

The coverage all French citizens have is called the *régime obligatoire*. It covers 65 percent of the costs of doctors' visits and medication and all of the costs of hospitalization. Some salaried people buy complementary insurance to cover the balance of medical costs, visits to specialists, and better dental and eye care.

Self-employed individuals also must enroll in the system and pay for their own coverage. For a self-employed couple with minimal income, the *régime obligatoire* amounts to about 625 euros ($560) per year. (The exact amount varies according to income.) For the same couple, complementary coverage for 100 percent of the balance of care costs 1,100 euros ($990) per year. Plans that provide less coverage but more than the *régime obligatoire*, and plans that pay more than 100 percent of some charges, are also available at lesser and greater costs.

Under the French health-care system, every medical intervention has a set fee. For instance, a visit to a general practitioner costs 17.53 euros ($15.75). The *Caisse Primaire d'Assurance Maladie* (CPAM) pays 80 percent of that amount and complementary insurance covers the balance. Fees for a specialist such as a cardiologist are higher, 22.87 euros ($18); CPAM pays 18.30 euros ($16.50) and the complementary insurance pays the balance.

Although most doctors are in the system, it's wise to check first. Some physicians and private clinics do not agree to this schedule of fees. A doctor is free to decide to participate in the system or not. If a doctor has not signed an agreement with the health-care system, his or her fees will be reimbursed at a much lower rate and the patient must pay the balance. Additionally, some doctors are approved to charge fees beyond the normal ones, and some complementary insurance policies cover this extra charge.

Providing for Your Own Insurance

For those Americans who must provide their own insurance, there are a number of companies that offer health coverage for expatriates and others who will be out of the country for extended periods, such as students studying abroad.

Aetna, for instance, offers plans with a variety of options—deductibles of $250 or $500, 80 percent or 100 percent of hospitalization costs, annual exams, etc. Provision may also be made for return to the United States to receive care. The cost varies with the options and the age of the insured.

In the spring of 2000, for example, coverage with a $250 deductible for a single person under 30 was about $100 per month. For those 10, 20, 30, and 40 years older, the price increased to $1,550, $1,950 $2,550, and $3,740, respectively.

For couples in the same five age brackets, the amounts were $2,500, $3,150, $3,956, $5,166 ,and $7,744, respectively. For a family, the amounts were $3,904, $4,892, $5,740, $6,650, and $11,310, respectively. For those who chose a $500 deductible for the same plan, the rates were about nine percent less. Taking a a $5,000 deductible reduces the rates by about 50 percent. The age of the oldest person insured by the policy determines the rate.

Annual cost of dental coverage that could be taken only in conjunction with a medical plan was $198 to $638 for an individual in the five age groups, $369 to $1,190 for couples, and $588 to $1,896 for families, again depending on the age of the oldest person.

Remember that policies such as Aetna's are for coverage worldwide, including countries and regions where standard Western health care is not easily found. They are more likely the types of policies that multinational corporations purchase for executives and their families sent to Third World countries. Other plans are tailored specifically to France, noted below, and are less expensive even for the older age brackets.

Among other firms that offer insurance to expatriates are the policies sold by MultiNational Underwriters, Inc. (www.ushealthplans.com), of Indianapolis, Ind. Like Aetna, they have plans that cover persons who may wish to receive care in the United States as well as abroad. Their rates are lower, but do not cover everything that the Aetna plans do. They are broken into five-year age increments rather than 10-year.

For instance, a man between age 20 and 30 would pay $928 to $1,023 for one plan that includes care in the United States and $529 to $583 for a plan that does not. A woman in the same age bracket would pay $1,522 to $1,675 or $732 to $806 for the same coverage. (At 55, beyond childbearing age, the rates equalize and after that women's rates are less than men's.)

Expats may also obtain health insurance from two well-known French companies, Axa and Gan, offered by the *Association Internationale de Prévoyance Sociale* (www.expatsante.com). The AIPS coverage will pay for 100 percent of the cost of care under the French system. Annual rates per person are approximately as follows: Children under 18, 833 euros ($750); 18 to 29 year olds, 1,143 euros (about $1,300); 30 to 39 year olds, 1,257 euros ($1,130); 40 to 49 year olds, 1,438 euros ($1,300); and 50 to 65 year olds, 1,990 euros ($1,790).

The AIPS coverage is good for an annual maximum of 228,693 euros (about $205,825). It also includes dental work and eye care. If the insured must return to the country of origin because of a serious accident or illness, the policy also covers that.

Retired Americans considering a move to France should know that

Medicare will not cover them outside the country. However, most people have a supplementary policy covering the 20 percent of their U.S. health-care bills that Medicare does not cover. These supplementary policies often cover 80 percent of the cost of health care when the policy holder is traveling outside the United States. Some expatriates take advantage of this by purchasing minimal policies qualifying for a long-stay visa and relying on the supplementary policy to cover 80 percent of their health-care costs as "travelers," if necessary.

If you choose this option, you'll need to maintain an address in the United States, even if fictional—perhaps your children or another trusted relative will let you "use" theirs. Or you may choose to return to the United States periodically, where you'll be on solid legal ground to make use of Medicare and your supplementary health care policies.

On the whole, you should not regard a move to France any differently than you would a move from Minneapolis to Phoenix or from Philadelphia to Denver. Wherever you go and whatever your age, you need to find health practitioners in whom you have confidence and whom you are going to have to pay for their services. Maintaining a long-distance relationship may seem like a great way to save money—until you actually need immediate care.

Pharmaceuticals and Remedies

In France, you won't find the wide selection of inexpensive over-the-counter pharmaceutical products available in large quantities that we take for granted in the States. Bottles of 1,000, whether vitamins or aspirins, are rare. Even hygiene products such as toothpaste usually come in smaller containers than you see in America. The wide array of cold and headache remedies, cough drops and syrups, allergy relievers and the rest of the acres of patent nostrums you find in any American drug store or supermarket are scarce in France. To be sure, over-the-counter drugs and remedies are available in France, but the multiplicity of brands and sizes of containers is minimal.

In contrast to the United States, in France homeopathic remedies are widely available at pharmacies, and their prescription and purchase may be included in health plans.

Hospitals

France has more than half a million hospital beds, about nine for every 1,000 persons, fewer than the number in United States, but above the

European average. In recent years, the number of hospital beds has dropped slightly—about two-thirds are public and one-third private—but hospital stays have shortened, so the capability to care for patients has not been sacrificed.

In the last decade, hospital reforms have also tried to better coordinate service and facilities in any given region to avoid duplication and conserve resources. The hospitals in France employ about 150,000 doctors of various types and pharmacists; these are in addition to doctors in private practice who also admit and care for patients in the hospitals as necessary. About 950,000 nonprofessionals also work in the hospitals of France.

University hospitals are huge institutions. The one in Toulouse, for instance, has about 2,500 beds. Patients are transported in from a wide region for various treatments and procedures. The advantage is that the professors and their students see large numbers of patients with a particular ailment or. Such a hospital may perform dozens of angiograms and angioplasties per week, and the physicians are completely familiar with all aspects of the operation. Furthermore, posts at these hospitals are generally prized and sought by the physicians themselves.

Smoking

Smoking remains a public health issue in France, where tobacco has long been grown and the production of cigarettes overseen by the government as an important source of revenue. More than a quarter of the population aged 15 and over are smokers, with men outnumbering women 32 to 22 percent except among the young, where the rate for both sexes is 22 percent. Smoking is also a class issue: 44 percent of the unemployed say they are smokers, while only 32 percent of those working do.

France has passed laws concerning smoking in public places, and the general population is well informed of the health hazards. The story is told of the minister who was asked why his government, realizing the toll that tobacco took in health costs, did not do more to reduce smoking in the country.

"Ah," he replied, "those costs belong to my successors. The costs of reduced consumption and therefore less tax collected, those costs are mine."

The Environment

Environmentally, France is different from the United States and other industrialized nations. Dirty air and polluted water, and industrial and agricultural wastes all pose problems in some regions. Perhaps the biggest concern involves the nuclear waste generated by the plants that produce about 75 percent of the country's electricity. Even if the government were inclined to shut these plants—and it is not—disposing of the radioactive material would still be a problem.

Nearly 800 tons of radioactive waste are stockpiled at La Hague, far enough from Cherbourg for safety but too close for comfort. New shipments are taken to the Aube near Troyes. There are also tons of slightly radioactive wastes at various uranium mining sites in France. Despite the weak radiation this material generates, its mass represents a health hazard.

Nuclear Power

France is a nuclear power both in the military and civilian sense. Shortly after President Jacques Chirac came to power, he authorized a series of nuclear weapons tests in the Pacific, surprising the people of France and angering nations around the globe.

Chirac was following in the footsteps of President Charles de Gaulle, who pulled away from NATO and gave France nuclear weapons independent of the United States.

Beginning in the 1970s, France also initiated construction of a series of nuclear power plants to generate electricity. Those plants—an investment of nearly one trillion francs—now produce about 80 percent of France's electrical power. To a country with no gas or oil of its own, the economic advantage is tremendous. The plants also allow France to export energy to other countries worth about three billion euros ($2.7 billion) annually.

The environmental consequences of France's nuclear power are mixed. The country's emission of greenhouse gases is impressively low compared to other Western nations that use oil, gas, or coal to generate electricity. But nuclear waste disposal remains as great a problem in France as in any nuclear country in the world. The dump at La Hague, near Cherbourg, was filled to capacity and closed by 1995. A new one near Troyes still has plenty of room, but the potential for disaster remains.

The tremendous 1999 storm that slammed into the French west coast revealed nuclear power plants' vulnerability to disaster. Two of the four reactors at Blayais, near Bordeaux, were shut down for four months after storm waters swept into the plants. Authorities responded by raising the dike around the plant by a meter and taking other steps to secure the facilities. The scare resulted in a re-examination of the rest of France's plants; seven others were found deficient. Environmental groups have called for France to abandon nuclear power but with no apparent affect.

Here is a list of the departments and communes where *Electricité de France* nuclear sites are located.

Departments — Communes
Ain (01) — Bugey
Ardèche (07) — Cruas
Ardennes (08) — Chooz
Aube (10) — Nogent-sur-Seine
Cher (18) — Belleville-sur-Loire, Chinon
Drôme (26) — Tricastin
Gard (30) — Marcoule
Gironde (33) — Blayais
Isère (38) — Creys-Malville, Saint-Alban
Loir-et-Cher (41) — St. Laurent-des-Eaux
Loiret (45) — Dampierre
Manche (50) — Flamanville
Moselle (57) — Cattenom
Nord (59) — Gravelines
Haut-Rhin (68) — Fessenheim
Seine-Maritime (76) — Paluel, Penly
Tarn-et-Garonne (82) — Golfech
Vienne (86) — Civaux

In June 2000, the national commission charged with studying how France handles its radioactive waste assailed the lack of action in assuring the secure disposal of the waste. It recommended not only more research on improving disposal methods but also far stricter surveillance of what has already been stockpiled.

The parallels between the nuclear waste problem in France and the United States are striking. Both countries have produced it as part of their nuclear energy programs and neither nation has been able to find a way to detoxify it. Both have adopted the disposal method: Collect it in an isolated spot and encase it in material that will shield the public from its harmful effects. Despite assurances of careful maintenance by the governments of both nations, leaks have occurred at sites. Prudence dictates avoiding them. Fortunately, that's easy to do in both countries.

Maintaining high quality drinking water is also a challenge. In limited areas, pesticides and nitrates from agriculture have degraded underground water supplies. As contaminated sources are identified, their use is halted. In the heavily agricultural region of Midi-Pyrénées, for instance, while only 7,300 people had water that frequently showed more than 50 milligrams per liter, another 150,700 had water that tested between 40 and 50 mg./l. (Adults normally consume more than 100 mg. of nitrates daily in solid food.)

Phosphates are another contaminant, largely from laundry soap. This problem has fallen by 30 percent since 1990 though, as detergent manufacturers have changed their formulas.

Another problem, found throughout the country, is bacterial contamination. So many small villages have relied historically on sources of water that are not treated and seldom tested. In the department of the Aude, for instance, which is largely rural, some 13 percent of the water samples tested in 1999 failed to meet one or more the 62 separate water purity standards. The vast majority of these failures occurred in villages in which total population is less than 10 percent of the entire department. The cities and villages where most people live had good records.

Testing of the water supply has become more rigorous and frequent in the last decade, with new standards applied in 1989. This is the key to better water and has done much to clean up the supply. After all, the purpose of the testing is to control any problems that occur. As a result, water bills have risen considerably in the past decade—from nine francs per cubic meter in 1990 to 15 francs per cubic meter in 1997—often to help pay for new sewage plants. The average annual water bill is about 300 euros ($270) today.

Air pollution consists of all the ingredients of smog: oxides of nitrogen, sulphur dioxide, carbon monoxide, hydrocarbons, and ozone. The internal combustion engine is responsible for much of it, and asthma and other respiratory problems are a major health problem, especially in and around Paris.

As with water pollution, testing has become increasingly rigorous. The number of air pollution measuring stations jumped from 1,150 in 1994 to 1,950 by 1998. In times of peak pollution, authorities will order some drivers off the roads, based on license plate numbers and certificates of cleaner-running motors. Outside of Paris and the immediate surrounding area, this is not a factor to consider.

France produces nearly 650 million tons of solid waste and household garbage annually. The average Parisian was responsible for about 500 kilos while the rest of the country averaged about 350 kilos per person. Recycling is most successful with glass; more than three-fifths goes back. Other products have much lower returns—a little more than one-third of the paper, a quarter of the batteries and one-fifth of the plastic. About half of the paper products are made from recycled material.

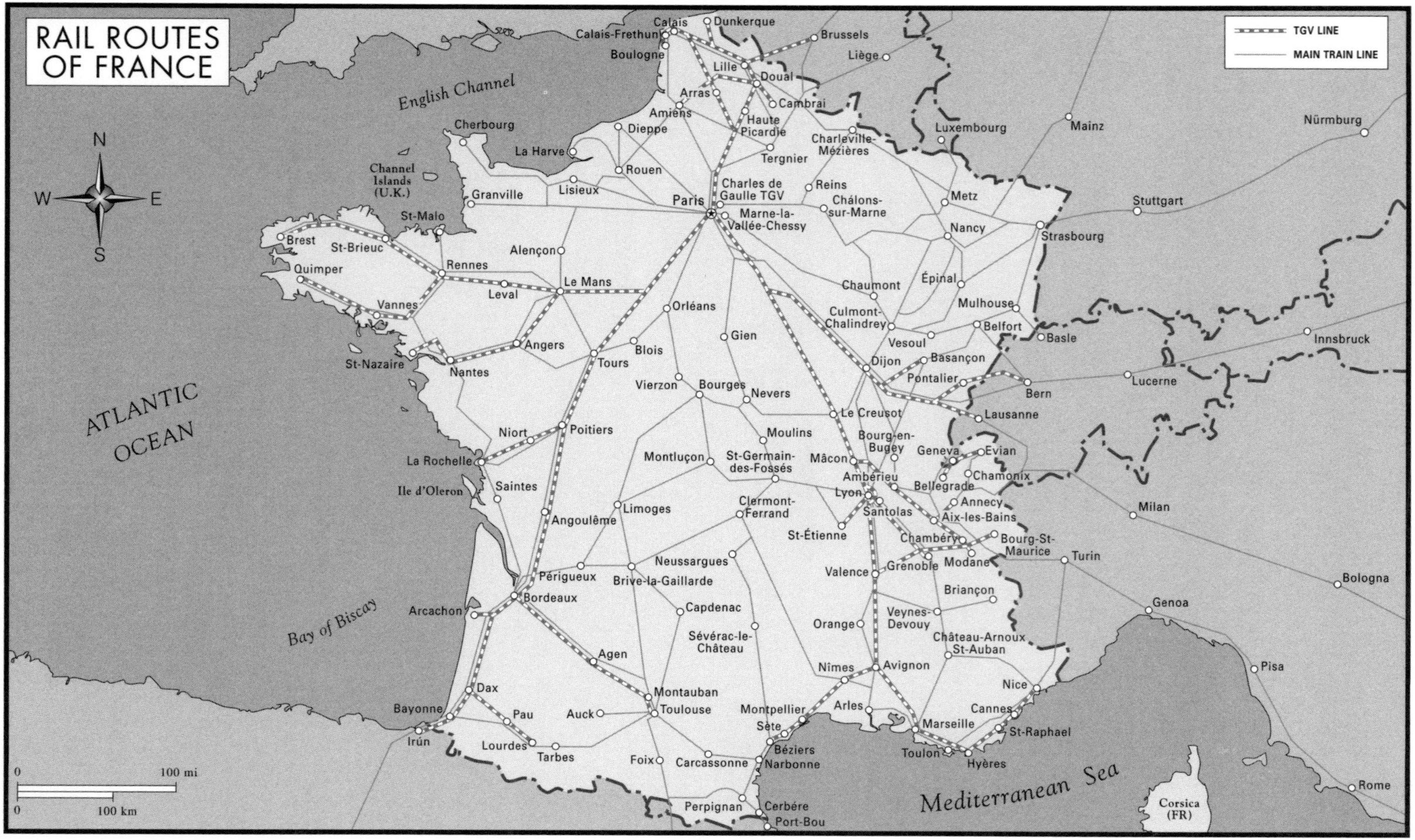
RAIL ROUTES OF FRANCE
TGV LINE
MAIN TRAIN LINE
N
E
S
W
English Channel
ATLANTIC OCEAN
Bay of Biscay
Mediterranean Sea
Channel Islands (U.K.)
Corsica (FR)
0
100 mi
0
100 km
Calais
Dunkerque
Calais-Frethun
Boulogne
Brussels
Liège
Lille
Douai
Arras
Cambrai
Amiens
Haute Picardie
Dieppe
Cherbourg
La Harve
Rouen
Tergnier
Charleville-Mézières
Luxembourg
Mainz
Nürmburg
Granville
Lisieux
Charles de Gaulle TGV
Reins
Paris
Marne-la-Vallée-Chessy
Châlons-sur-Marne
Metz
Stuttgart
St-Malo
Brest
St-Brieuc
Alençon
Nancy
Strasbourg
Rennes
Quimper
Le Mans
Leval
Chaumont
Épinal
Vannes
Orléans
Mulhouse
Culmont-Chalindrey
Belfort
Basle
Innsbruck
Angers
Gien
Vesoul
St-Nazaire
Nantes
Tours
Blois
Dijon
Basançon
Pontalier
Bern
Lucerne
Vierzon
Bourges
Nevers
Lausanne
Le Creusot
Niort
Poitiers
Moulins
Bourg-en-Bugey
Geneva
Evian
La Rochelle
Montluçon
St-Germain-des-Fossés
Mâcon
Chamonix
Ambérieu
Bellegrade
Ile d'Oleron
Saintes
Lyon
Annecy
Clermont-Ferrand
Santolas
Aix-les-Bains
Milan
Limoges
Angoulême
St-Étienne
Chambéry
Bourg-St-Maurice
Neussargues
Grenoble
Modane
Turin
Valence
Périgueux
Brive-la-Gaillarde
Bordeaux
Briançon
Bologna
Capdenac
Arcachon
Genoa
Veynes-Devouy
Orange
Sévérac-le-Château
Château-Arnoux St-Auban
Agen
Nîmes
Avignon
Pisa
Dax
Nice
Montauban
Bayonne
Auck
Toulouse
Montpellier
Arles
Pau
Cannes
Sète
Marseille
St-Raphael
Irún
Lourdes
Tarbes
Béziers
Toulon
Hyères
Foix
Carcassonne
Narbonne
Rome
Perpignan
Cerbére
Port-Bou

10 Getting Around

In the past, you could say of French transportation that "all roads lead to Paris." But during the 1990s, that truism began to give way, although that city remains a transportation hub in France. Today, you can climb off a 747 in the morning at Charles de Gaulle airport, catch a high-speed train to Lyon, and arrive in time for a nap before dinner without ever entering Paris. The same is true of automotive travel. While in the past roads inevitably took you through the most congested areas, today's limited-access highways skirt Paris and other cities. And while Paris remains the hub for French and American air travel, other European carriers use their own countries as hubs, flying into various provincial French airports from Amsterdam, London, Brussels, and Frankfort, among other cities. In short, fast trains, regional airports, and good roads make travel easy in France, although not inexpensive.

Trains

Trains in France are operated by the *Société Nationale Chemins de Fer Français*, or SNCF, as it is usually called. The emphasis today is on passenger trains, as freight traffic has slowly diminished over the years with less call for rail transport of coal, iron, and oil. For two decades now, SNCF has been building up its fleet of high-speed TGVs, *Trains à Grande Vitesse*, increasing their number and extending the tracks and roadbeds that permit them to clip along at 270 kilometers per hour (167 mph) to top speeds of 350 kph (217 mph). These trains account for more than 25 percent of all passenger service in the country. Competition from both air travel and the automobile has meant that train travel has grown more slowly than it might have otherwise.

These fast, luxurious trains link London with Paris, Brussels, Geneva, and the rest of the continent via the "Chunnel," the tunnel constructed under the English Channel for just that purpose. Such a train travels the 1,200 kilometers (744 miles) from Lille to Nice, for instance, in 10 hours. Connecting trains make the trip down the Rhône Valley to Marseille or Montpellier even faster. Another line leaving Paris passes not far from Orly airport headed toward Tours, Bordeaux, and Spain. The 600 kilometers (372 miles) from Paris to Bordeaux takes about three hours on the TGV.

The high-speed trains not only crisscross France but extend throughout western Europe, often rivaling airplanes for speed and ease of travel. While someone on a tight business schedule is more likely to fly from Toulouse to Paris in the morning and return in the evening, many travelers find the five- to six-hour trip by train in a spacious car with wide seats to be quick and comfortable. For some routes, the TGV has made the overnight sleeper train a relic of the past.

SNCF has a complicated fare schedule that involves discounts for large families, frequent travelers, annual vacations, children and seniors, students and apprentices, advance reservations, and other factors. Often a limited number of discounted seats is available, and discounts are not available on every train at every time. The various discounts run from about 25 to 50 percent, so they are worth seeking out.

For those who enjoy train travel, the two plans of greatest interest are the *Grand Voyageur*, available to everyone, and the senior card. The Grand Voyageur is similar to the frequent-flyer airline plans: It costs 15.25 euros ($13.75) to join for three years, then you earn credit towards free tickets with the tickets you buy. This includes not only France but most European countries. Each franc spent gives you at least one point; various promotions give double points. You must accumulate 16,000 points before qualifying for free tickets or other benefits.

To be eligible for the senior card, you must be 60 years or older. It costs 44.20 euros per year (about $40), but entitles the holder to a 50 percent fare reduction in France and at least 25 percent in other European countries. It also confers other benefits: a discount on baggage service, car rentals from Avis, and a reduction of 30.49 euros ($27.50) from the cost of transporting your car by train.

Here is a comparison of different fares (as of fall of 2000) for the three-hour trip from Paris to Bordeaux. All prices are for second class, since on the TGV, there is little significant difference between first and second class.

Full fare: 53.68 euros ($48)
Senior card: 26.68 euros ($24)
30-day advance purchase: 26.68 euros ($24)
8-day advance purchase: 35.06 euros ($31)

Suffice it to say that a full-fare first-class ticket will cost between 8 and 14 euro cents (7 and 12 cents) per kilometer; second class costs about two-thirds the price of first class. The price per kilometer drops as the distance increases. Reservations are required for the TGV and optional on other trains. From the Paris hub, the TGVs leave with great frequency, making most French destinations less than an eight-hour trip.

Since passenger service is the majority of its business today, SNCF does a lot to attract customers. Families, for instance, can get their own compartments, complete with nearby changing table and bottle warmer for babies. Arrangements can made for the care of children between four and 13 years old traveling alone during school vacations. Baggage can be picked up at your residence and dropped off at your destination. Travelers in wheelchairs are accommodated. Even pets are allowed as long as they do not bother nearby passengers.

Buses

With such an excellent rail system, long-distance bus service is rare in France. However, most cities have bus systems, and secondary systems

In general, cars in France (and the rest of Europe) are much smaller than those in the United States.

serve the environs and small villages. These often double as both a commercial passenger vehicle and the local school bus. You might see commuters riding on the same bus with school children being transported to a middle school in another village, and older students headed to the *lycée* (high school) in the city.

While helpful, these buses are quite limited. Generally, they run from a particular group of villages to a hub city in the morning and back from that city to the same villages in the afternoon—getting the pupils to school before 9 a.m. and returning in the late afternoon to take them home. So, in most cases you cannot make a connection to go elsewhere. Mostly these buses are valuable for a trip from a village to the nearest train depot—but not on Sundays or holidays, when they remain in the garage.

Death-defying Drivers

That French traffic can be a killer. Especially on those long weekends.

In May 2000, after two very deadly holiday weekends, Easter and May Day, Transport Minister Jean-Claude Gayssot vowed to stop the carnage on French highways.

During the four-day Easter weekend, 90 people were killed and 2,119 injured on the highways of France. On the May 1 weekend, the number increased to 98.

That was an increase in Easter fatalities of 14 percent from 1999, another four-day weekend when 79 were killed. Comparing the May 1 weekend fatalities to 1998, another four-day May 1 weekend, they were up 15 percent.

For comparison, the United States counted 393 fatalities on the four-day 1998 Memorial Day weekend. Considering that the U.S. population is nearly 4.5 times as great and a smaller percentage of the French are drivers, the French carnage is impressive.

Part of the problem is the French attitude toward driving and traffic laws. In a survey taken in May 2000, some 93 percent of French drivers rated themselves as very good drivers who obeyed the law. However, they revealed in the same poll that:

Half of them routinely exceed the speed limit on the highway and one-third do so in towns.

About two-thirds of them did not know the penalties for running a red light (fine of 760 euros/$684 and suspension of license up to three years), drunk driving (maximum of two years in prison, a fine of 4,500 euros/$4,050 and suspension of license for five years), or speeding (fines from 400 to 1,500 euros/$360 to $1,350 and suspension of license for three years).

In a 1997 survey, one-third of French drivers said everyone should be free to decide how much he or she could drink before getting behind the wheel.

Gayssot warned that serious offenders lose their licenses for two months and the most grievous face a fine of 1,500 euros ($1,350) plus jail time. He also launched an extensive public education campaign, the effect of which remains to be seen.

Nonetheless, terrible as the figures are, the French do seem to be making some progress in curbing highway fatalities.

Back in 1990, on a six-day Easter holiday, the toll hit 171; the following two years it was 142 and 149, respectively. As bad as that seems, one can go back to 1972 when 163 were killed on a three-day Easter holiday.

Automobiles

The question of whether or not to own a car in France depends on personal preference and where you live. Certainly, an auto is not a necessity in Paris; for many it would be nothing more than an expensive nuisance. On the other hand, if you plan to live in a small village and eager to get to know the countryside and take frequent trips, a car may be very desirable.

Despite good public transit, the convenience of the automobile is not to be denied, and commuting is becoming more and more common. While the number of air and rail passengers has risen only slightly in recent years, travel by private automobile has nearly doubled since 1980, as has the number of vehicles on the road. France now has one car for every two persons, well behind Italy but above the European average. (The United States has one vehicle for every 1.3 persons.)

Requirements and Rules of the Road

Your American driver's license will be recognized in France as long as it is valid. French driver's licenses are issued for life and require a physical examination along with a test on laws of the road. If you become a permanent resident, your American license can simply be exchanged for a French one, without going through the various examinations.

Driver's licenses and vehicle registration are handled by the *préfecture* of the department in which you live. (There is no department of motor vehicles in France.) The last two numbers on French license plates designate the department in which the vehicle is registered. The plate stays with the car as long as it remains registered in the department even if ownership changes hands.

Just as you would in the States, make sure you have your license on you when you drive. If you happen to be stopped by a *gendarme* (police officer) and can't produce it, you could be arrested on the spot. For the same reason, you should always carry two documents in your car: the *"carte grise,"* as the gray title is called (no pink slips here), and proof of insurance. Rather than patrol highways as they do in the States, French police set up roadblocks to stop motorists. They will demand to see these two documents, along with an operator's permit, and the absence of any of them can mean immediate arrest. Moreover, upon discovery of a safety violation, such as bald tires or burned-out headlights, they may forbid you to drive the vehicle until the repairs are made. Best to keep your papers in order, and your car in good shape.

French rules of the road vary little from those in the United States. The French drive on the right side, stop at stop signs, pass on the left, and generally follow the same practices American drivers do. Two notable exceptions are that you cannot turn right after stopping for a red light, and at intersections without signals or signs, you yield to the driver on the right. This can be disconcerting when you are on a through road and a driver suddenly pulls out from a side road because he has the right of way.

Another practice that unsettles many American motorists in France is the propensity of French drivers for tailgating. However dangerous, it is often the only way a motorist can get in position to pass slower vehicles on a two-lane road. Leaving a safe distance between yourself and the car ahead becomes an invitation to the motorist behind to zip between the two of you.

Probably the biggest problem American motorists in France will face is a familiar one: congestion. The American experience is being replicated in France. As more people turn to the automobile as their primary transportation, the roads become overcrowded; as the highway system expands, so does the number of vehicles, and the congestion continues. Consider the truck traffic alone coming from Spain into France. In 1995, 11,000 trucks trundled in daily; by 2000 there were 15,000. Authorities predict that figure will double by 2015.

The Highway System

Fortuately, French roads are generally excellent, well maintained with appropriate signage. They exist in a hierachical system with A roads, denoting autoroutes, at the top, followed by N, or national routes, and D or departmental highways. The autoroutes are limited-access toll roads that make regional travel fast and comfortable, though expensive: Tolls hover around 8 euro cents per kilometer. And at legal speeds of 130 kph (80 mph), the extra fuel burned at $1 or so per liter also adds to the cost.

Most of the autoroutes have been built since the mid-1960s by private companies that raised the necessary capital for their construction. Radiating from Paris, the four-, six- or eight-lane divided highways connect most of the larger French cities. Bypassing towns and most cities, they often provide scenic routes through the countryside. Slower traffic should keep to the right on autoroutes, a sometimes difficult proposition since trucks are limited to 90 kph (55 mph) on these roads and often clog that lane. However, with the legal limit of 130 kph (80 mph) often little more than a convenient fiction for impatient drivers, it doesn't do to dawdle in the faster lanes.

Autoroutes are also an important link in the whole European Union transit scheme, since goods from other European countries must often pass through France to reach their eventual destination: produce from Spain to Germany, and electric appliances from Italy to England, for instance.

Heavy trucks, which now carry more than half of all freight in France, are required to use the autoroutes unless making local deliveries. The tolls they pay help with the upkeep of the autoroutes, and their absence on other roads lessens the maintenance necessary and eases traffic.

National routes often parallel the autoroutes. Although some are divided highways, they are not limited access and may go through the center of towns. On divided national routes the speed limit is 110 kph (68 mph). On two- or three-lane routes, the limit is 90 kph (55 mph) in the country, but lower in towns and cities.

Departmental (county) routes vary widely. Most of them are two-lane roads of greatly differing widths—anything from lanes generous enough to accommodate the largest 18-wheelers with room to spare to country lanes barely wider than a single car.

Don't Get Taken for a Ride

Used car dealers don't have the best reputation in the United States (something lower than a snake and more crooked than a pig's tail).

This is not the case in France. Although there is always some possibility of chicanery (or, more likely, simply failure to notice a defect), you can go to an auto dealer and expect to find cars guaranteed to be in excellent mechanical condition.

The dealer's guarantee in France is somewhat variable depending on the age and condition of the car, but it is usually for three, six, or 12 months and will cover both parts and labor. But even a car five or six years old may merit a one-year guarantee.

Moreover, if the used car you buy is the same make that the dealer sells new, the guarantee will be good anywhere in France and probably in Europe. Some dealers extend this universal guarantee to any car they sell; others will limit to repairs at their own garage if it is another make other than their franchise.

In other words, if you buy a fairly new used Renault from a Renault dealer, you will get one-year guarantee for parts and labor good anywhere in Europe. Not included are parts that are expected to wear such as tires or brake pads. The same goes for other makes as well.

You'll pay a premium for this peace of mind. Dealers routinely sell cars for 800 to 1,000 euros ($720 to $900) above the average selling price on the open market for a similar vehicle.

Buying from an individual is no different than in the U.S., but you will have one advantage: French vehicles more than four years old must undergo an independent inspection every two years and no less than six months of being sold.

This inspection does not guarantee mechanical perfection, but does insure that brakes and steering and other factors such as suspension that might affect the safe operation of the vehicle are in working order.

The difference is this: Buy a car from a dealer and if the starter or alternator or the water pump fails within the time of the guarantee, it will be replaced without cost to you beyond inconvenience. Buy from an individual and you're on your own, although the savings may be worth the risk.

Buying and Maintaining a Car in France

New cars cost more in France than they do in the United States—the difference amounts roughly to the French TVA, the 19.6 percent sales tax. For about 13,500 euros (about $12,000), you get a small, basic vehicle. Another 3,500 to 4,500 euros (about $3,000 to $4,000) will fetch you a larger, more powerful car. Spend 22,250 euros (about $20,000) and you get a full-size sedan. Vans go for a premium, as do luxury models.

Diesel-engine cars, far more prevalent in Europe than in the States, are also more expensive. Diesel fuel is about 20 percent cheaper than gasoline, however, so they may be more economical in the long run. Depending on many factors, the cost of buying and operating a car three years old or less for 10,000 kilometers a year will run between 305 and 915 euros ($275 and $825) per month. These costs will be less, of course, for older vehicles. When you purchase a vehicle, you'll pay a one-time tax and registration fee, but no more as long as you own it.

If you plan to buy a car while in France, pick up the national weekly tabloid, *l'Argus*, for current prices on the various makes of cars sold in France. Classified ads for used cars often refer to *"prix Argus,"* indicating the asking price mirrors what *Argus* states is the price for a similar vehicle.

Part of your auto maintenance will be a required mechanical safety inspection once every two years. Additionally, any car at least four years old must undergo such an inspection within the six months prior to its sale. The seller is obligated to furnish proof of this to the buyer, but is not required to make the repairs. While the inspection is helpful in assessing the steering and suspension, lights and brakes, and emission level, it does not check for other repairs that might be necessary.

Insurance should never be taken off a vehicle because the owner remains liable for any damages, even if the vehicle were stolen when the damage occurred. For this reason, when individuals buy or sell a vehicle, they are careful to ensure that the termination of the seller's policy and the inception of the buyer's coincide.

Car Rental

Renting a car in France is no different from renting one in the United States. All you need is a valid driver's license and money, preferably a credit card. The rental agencies themselves will be familiar to you. Hertz, Avis, and Budget are the big ones in France, with offices in all the cities and airports. Avis has a special relationship with SNCF, the French railroad, that permits you to pick up and return a car at the depot itself, a great convenience given the congestion and one-way streets that often surround depots.

Air Travel

For air travelers, France offers a network of regional international airports along with the great Parisian hub. Given the distances across France and to neighboring European cities, these airports offer great convenience. While the train takes you quickly enough from Paris to London, Brussels, or Geneva, to get to any of those cities from Bordeaux, Nantes, or Nice by rail is a much lengthier proposition, more or less an all-day affair. But day trips to Paris or other European cities from Toulouse, Marseille, or Nice—impossible even with direct connections on the TGV—are easily accomplished by air. Frequent flights are offered throughout the day at prices competitive with train travel. This ease and affordability have contributed to a doubling of air passenger traffic in recent years.

Many of these provincial airports (those outside Paris) also serve to feed passengers to other hubs around Europe for flights to the United States. For instance, you fly Lufthansa to Frankfort, and then to the United States; KLM takes passengers to Amsterdam, Sabena to Brussels, and British Air to London for transfer to U.S. flights. Air France, of course, sends its North America–bound passengers through Paris.

Within France itself, Air France is the dominant airline, offering far more domestic flights than any other airline. For instance, even a small airport like Montpellier sends half a dozen flights to Orly alone before noon.

Air fares change constantly, but Air France maintains a certain number of flights with at least some reduced-fare seats. People 60 years or older, families traveling together, including grandparents with grandchildren, and couples are all likely to find discounts off the regular fares.

Unfortunately for air travel within the country, often as not you must go through Paris to reach another provincial city. So what might be a five-hour train ride involving one transfer becomes almost exactly the same by air. For example, someone traveling from Toulouse to Biarritz by train leaves Toulouse about 10 A.M. and arrives about 3 P.M. with a transfer at Bordeaux. By air, you leave Toulouse at 10:15 for Roissy and catch an 11:55 flight to Biarritz, arriving at 1:10. Add the travel to and from the airports in Toulouse and Biarritz and the time is nearly the same, but the cost is greater.

Part IV
Moving In

11. Making the Move
12. A Roof Over Your Head
13. Prime Living Locations
14. Paris and the Île-de-France
15. The Midi and Languedoc
16. Provence and the Côte d'Azur
17. Normandy and Brittany
18. Burgundy and the Rhône Valley

11 Making the Move

You've finally made the big decision: You're moving to France. Now it's time to roll up your sleeves and get to work. There are many details to take care of before you leave, such as applying for your long-stay visa and deciding what to take with you. Once you arrive in France, you will need to register with the local authorities and set about the process of settling into your new home.

The Long-Stay Visa

Vacationing Americans need no formal visa to enter France. It is assumed—and legally required—that your stay will last no more than three months. But if you plan to remain in France longer, you are required to obtain a long-stay visa. Once in France, you'll take this visa to your local prefecture to obtain a *carte de séjour* (residency permit). It is good for one year and must then be renewed. After three years, you can obtain a permit good for 10 years before it must be renewed.

Applying for a long-stay visa will be your introduction to French bureaucracy. Fortunately, the regulations are clear and the application process has been streamlined in recent years. If your situation fits comfortably within the rules, chances are everything will go quickly and smoothly. Difficulties generally only arise when applicants seek exemptions or exceptions.

At the time of your initial application, you must be in the United States and are not permitted to go to France until the visa is granted. The process, which can take up to two months, may be done by mail, a convenience for those living far from a French consulate (see Appendix for the office nearest you). The application form itself may be downloaded from the consulate website. Children's applications should be filed with the parents'.

The first requirement for a long-stay visa is a passport valid for at least three months beyond the expiration date of the visa. (U.S. passports may be renewed in France via mail to the appropriate American consulate.) Your application packet must include your passport and three photocopies of it, eight copies of the application form, and eight passport photos. Your passport will be returned to you with your visa in it.

In the application packet you must also submit proof of financial independence during your stay amounting to at least $1,800 per month. This can

Keeping Tourists Out, Letting Immigrants In

The anomalies of immigration—along with the contradictions of current regulations—in the European Union are illustrated by the predicament that a couple of newlyweds experienced in the fall of 1999. Michael, an American writer, married Jennifer, a black Trinidadian director of a social work agency, and they came to France on their honeymoon. Both middle-aged, it was a second marriage for both of them.

Jennifer, a university graduate, had been in the United States since she was a teenager and had all the proper papers for residence. She was so comfortable with her American life that she did not think to get a visa for the honeymoon trip. Arriving in Paris with her Trinidad passport at Charles de Gaulle, she was refused entry, separated from Michael who had been passed through already and quickly hustled away. So much for Gallic romance.

The couple was allowed a brief telephone conference. Advised by the airline that Jennifer could be flown to England, which permits entry of Trinidadians, where she could then obtain a visa from the French consulate, they decided to split up, with Michael continuing to their destination. They agreed that Jennifer would call him when she got a visa.

In London, the embassy told her a visa was impossible in less than two weeks. American husband or not, there was nothing they could do for a black woman from Trinidad who wanted to spend her honeymoon in France.

She phoned Michael and told him the situation looked hopeless and she was ready to fly back home. But their French hosts had told Michael that passports were not checked on the TGV from London to Paris and he persuaded Jennifer to try the train. She did and 12 hours later called him and said, "I'm in Montpellier—come pick me up!"

After a week in Languedoc and another week in Paris, the happy couple boarded the plane for home.

Can someone legally enter one country of the European Union but be barred from the others? At this time the answer has to be "technically, yes; practically, no." Logically, it does not seem as if even the technicality can stand. No EU nation has successfully stopped illegal immigration; with the end of border checks within the EU, stopping everyone who can legally enter at least one member nation seems virtually impossible.

include pensions, verified independent income, rent from a house, etc. An alternative to proof of financial independence would be a notarized declaration from someone in France, such as a family member, that he or she will provide for your support and can prove sufficient income to accomplish that.

The application also requires an address where you will stay in France. If with family or friends, submit a letter from them so stating along with a certified copy of their identification. Otherwise, include a copy of the deed or lease, or the promise of one, on your residence in France.

You'll need to include three additional documents. If both you and your spouse are applying for long-stay visas, submit a copy of your marriage license. Proof of health insurance is also required. Finally, France won't grant you a long-stay visa if you are a criminal; obtain a certification from your local police department that you're not a convicted felon and there are no warrants out for your arrest.

Lastly, include a stamped return envelope for your documents and a money order or certified check for about $100 (the exact amount varies with the exchange rate; French authorities will tell you the exact fee). Once you have started the application process for the long-stay visa, do not plan to go to France until it has been issued. It will not be sent to you in France.

> *Travelers should pack an ample supply of patience, curiosity, and desire to participate in their adopted culture.*

If you have been hired to work in France, there are additional steps to take. First, submit a draft of your work contract to the appropriate French consulate. At the same time, your employer in France—even if it is simply a branch of a U.S. firm—will need to apply to the local employment office for recruitment of a foreign worker. The application is processed and sent to the *Office des Migrations Internationales* (OMI), which then instructs the consulate in the United States to order you to have a physical examination. Then the visa is granted. For senior corporate managers, approval by the employment office is only a formality; for other employees, justification is necessary and approval may depend on the particular skills of the individual and the rate of unemployment in France.

After arriving in France, take your visa and medical exam results to the prefecture of the department in which you live to obtain the *carte de séjour*. It is good for one year and renewable annually; after the third year, you may apply for a residency permit good for 10 years.

Student Visas and Special Cases

There are other long-stay visas that apply in particular cases. These include the student visa, the au-pair visa and one for researchers.

Students staying between three and six months should get a temporary long-stay visa. This is valid for multiple entries into France and does not require the holder to obtain a residency permit. Students staying over six months, however, get a visa that allows them to enter France one time and is valid for three months. During that three-month period, the student must register at the prefecture to obtain a student residency card.

The first type of student visa is much less complicated than a long-stay visa, and it is possible to have it issued in one day if applying in person. To apply, submit the original plus one copy of the following documents:

- A passport valid for at least for three months beyond the last day of stay in France
- The application form, filled out completely and signed
- The *pré-inscription* (letter of admission) to the school or university you'll be attending in France; note that this institution must be one accredited by the Ministry of Education
- Proof of sufficient funds while you reside in France, such as a notarized letter from your parents stating that they will provide you with at least $600 per month in France, a letter from your bank stating you have a sufficient balance to withdraw at least $600 per month, or a letter from the institution granting you a fellowship or a student loan. (This $600 amount could be reduced if you can present a letter from a host verifying that your lodging will be free of charge.)
- Also include two recent passport-size photographs.

If the student's stay will be less than six months, proof of health insurance will be required with the application. Students under 28 years old who stay longer than six months will be required to join the French student health-care system. Students older than 28 must provide their own insurance.

Students under 18 years old will also need notarized authorization from both parents indicating who will be guardian of the minor and a statement from the host family in France accepting responsibility. Processing the application will take at least six weeks.

Graduate students granted teaching assistantships at a French university follow a similar procedure but will need the original and one copy of their letter of appointment and their acceptance by the cultural department of the embassy. Professors and researchers should submit all the necessary documents from the institute where they will work along with three copies.

Applicants for an au pair visa must be between 17 and 30 years old. They should submit two long-stay visa application forms, two photographs, the original and one copy of the au pair contract (obtained by the family in France), and a letter of admission from a language school.

What to Bring, What to Leave Behind

HOUSEHOLD GOODS

Depending on the circumstances of your move, you may want to leave many of your belongings behind. Intercontinental moves of household goods can be very expensive. One company quoted a price of between $5,000 and $5,500 to ship a 2,200-pound container from San Francisco to Paris. For a heavier container, up to 11,000 pounds, the price was between $7,000 and $8,000. These prices are not prohibitive for large quantities of furnishings, but unless you have an employer who is paying for the move, it is better to sell much of what you have in the United States.

Be warned, however, this will not be easy. One of the most miserable days of my life was the day we held a garage sale before moving to France. I watched books and pictures and pieces of furniture that were like old friends go out the door, knowing I'd never see them again. But, unless the objects are quite valuable or irreplaceable, it just does not make economic sense to cart them to France.

Besides, compensation for your sacrifice awaits you when you arrive at your new home. For many people, one of the great delights of their initial years in France is traveling about looking for antiques and *brocante*, the French term for used household goods. You can find great deals on grand old armoires, buffets, beds, and tables, and searching for them is a wonderful way to explore the countryside as well as get a glimpse into French life and customs.

Linens are one category of furnishings that should be considered for the move, however. Although U.S. mattresses are measured in inches and

Jobs like this are hard to come by these days.

Abercrombie and Kent

French ones in centimeters, American sheets will fit either. A standard double bed in France is 140 centimeters wide and 190 centimeters long—

What Will You Leave Behind?

Anyone who moves to France, or even just buys property there, should be aware that French inheritance laws differ greatly from those of the United States.

Perhaps the greatest difference is the strong preference given to the deceased's children, whether legitimate, illegitimate, or adopted, over the widow. In fact, the deceased person's parents and brothers and sisters stand to inherit before the widow, who may get nothing at all depending on circumstances.

These are complicated legal questions and everyone would be well advised to call upon his or her local *notaire* for assistance. In the event a French person dies without a will, here is how the law parcels out the estate.

Any child or children of the deceased are first to inherit. An only child would have rights to at least half of the estate, two children to two-thirds of the estate, and three to three-fourths. If the children are not alive, their children—the grandchildren of the deceased—or grandchildren stand to inherit.

Moreover, a French person is not at liberty to ignore his descendants. The law protects their inheritance—they are *héritiers réservataires*. A French person cannot easily leave the children's share to someone else.

Should there be no living descendants, the inheritance would go to the parents of the deceased, if they are alive. Next after them are the deceased's grandparents; an estate would be equally divided between paternal and maternal grandparents.

Assuming the grandparents and great-grandparents are also deceased, the estate would pass to the brothers and/or sisters of the deceased. Next in line would be nephews and nieces and their children. Should there be no grandparents, great-grandparents, brothers or sisters, the uncles and aunts would stand to inherit.

Where does this leave the spouse? The convent was one solution in medieval times. But today the answer could be: out in the cold.

In fact, the situation may not be quite that extreme, because a portion of property acquired by the couple after their marriage may go to the surviving spouse. But even this can pose a financial hardship.

For example, one spouse dies and their two children inherit two-thirds of the deceased's estate, a home appraised at 200,000 euros ($180,000). The children want to sell the inheritance and give the surviving spouse the chance to buy it. Suddenly, the survivor is faced with the need to come up with 133,000 euros ($119,700) to buy it from the children, or sell the house and find somewhere else to live.

For a couple who never married, the situation is even more critical, for the child or children would inherit everything, not just a portion of the community property.

There are ordinary legal remedies to resolve these situations but they must be taken. A will, of course, is one. But there are also tax considerations; taxes must be paid on inheritances. Life insurance and gifts are other ways of transferring property or providing for a spouse.

There are many, many variables involving inheritances and taxes upon a property owner's death in France; one may also inherit debts and the obligation to repay them from one's own pocket. Taking the proper steps well in advance of death may ease financial burdens on those involved as well as prevent familial squabbling.

But Americans moving to France must be aware that they cannot rely upon a will drawn in accord with U.S. law to accomplish this; you must have complied with French law as well, and the two systems differ in important areas.

that's 56 inches by 76 inches—very close to the 54-inch by 76-inch U.S. mattress. The same goes for other standard bed sizes, single, queen and king.

The bed itself, along with box spring and mattress, is a debatable item because of the expense of transporting its bulk and weight. These items are certainly available in France, as is a spring system not seen in the U.S. called *lattes*. Lattes are pieces of wood about 1/4-inch thick and two or three inches wide that span the width of a single bed or half of a double bed. In their simplest form, they bow slightly upward and set in a steel frame. A foam or latex mattress sits on top, and the bow in the *lattes* provides the spring beneath the mattress. In more complex and expensive forms, each end of the *latte* is set on a rubber mount to give it exceptional flexibility. Even the simple ones are quite comfortable. The density of the foam mattress also determines the comfort. At least 12 cm thick foam of a minimum density of 28 kg per cubic meter should be used in such mattresses and 15 cm of 35 kg density foam is certainly preferable.

Pillows in France are sometimes square rather than rectangular, but the familiar rectangular ones are widely available to fit American pillowcases.

Finally, if you were considering bringing your gun, think twice. France's gun laws are much stricter than those in the United States. For starters, you will need to obtain a permit from *Douanes* (Customs) to import arms and ammunition. Of course, automatic weapons are banned.

APPLIANCES AND COMPUTERS

What about those appliances you paid so much for over the years? Sorry—forget them. Your washing machine, refrigerator, stereo, mixer, and power tools won't work in France, which uses a 220-volt electrical system. Your computer, however, may operate on 220 volts, but your printer probably will not.

If you do bring your computer and other technological gadgets with you, be aware that you are likely to encounter one of the largely unspoken rules of the multinational corporation: Just because the manufacturer sells an item in 169 different countries does not mean it's guaranteed in all of them. Have a problem with that modem you bought at CompUSA for your Mac? The help line is a 1-800 number—not a free call from France, and you won't get a replacement sent to you outside the United States, either. Buy a Japanese camera in the United States and just try to get it repaired under warranty in France. The list goes on. You're a U.S. citizen who purchased a product guaranteed for one or two years, then up and moved to another country nine months later. Tough luck. Sales are worldwide; guarantees are not.

> *For the job seeker, the Internet is a great advantage.*

Fortunately, computer prices have come down considerably in France in recent years; the main difference now between French and American prices is the 19.6 percent sales tax you must pay in France. In August 2000, you could buy a 600-MHz. PC with 64 Mo. of RAM and a 10 Go. hard drive and monitor for less than $900. What's more, purchasing a computer in France assures you the guarantee is valid, and you establish a relationship with someone who can later help you when those inevitable computer problems crop up.

Another alternative to purchasing an entirely new system is to go laptop. Active matrix screens and 6 Go. hard drives mean this is probably the only computer you need. One word of caution, however: Get a name brand or you'll have difficulty finding parts. Toshiba, IBM, H-P, Compaq, Dell, and Gateway are all familiar names in France; you will be able to buy hard drives, batteries and power supplies, modems, and even CPUs for them.

Software is a different story. By all means, bring it along. It's expensive to replace and, besides, the help files in French software are in French, remember? If you leave your computer behind, consider bringing at least the hard drive loaded with your software to be installed in a new machine.

One other consideration in talking computers is the keyboard. The French keyboard is different—annoyingly different for those of us trained on the QWERTY version. The advantage is that it includes all the accented characters; the disadvantage is that many of the characters, particularly A, W, and M, are not in their familiar places. (Note that the previous sentence has 27 A's in it—that's 27 times you might have typed Q and had to erase it.) Fortunately, keyboards are light. Bring yours along.

Pets

Perhaps the most difficult thing to leave behind is a pet. Fortunately, you won't need to if you move to France. France recognizes that a properly vaccinated animal is no threat to public health. You may bring up to three dogs and/or cats into France, only one of which may be under six months of age.

To do so, you'll need to present a valid rabies vaccination certificate dated at least 30 days before the move (30 days is the incubation period for rabies) and not more than one year. The second requirement is a letter from a veterinarian who examined the animal not less than 10 days before the move and pronounced it in good health. Only small amounts of pet food, 1 or 2 kilos, may be imported—don't worry, France sells plenty of chow.

Birds and rodents may also be brought into France with a veterinarian's certificate, but you must receive permission from the Ministry of Agriculture as well.

The logistics of transporting your animal friends should be carefully planned. Check with the airline you're using about its fees and particular requirements on cages. Cost generally runs between $100 and $125, although some airlines charge extra for large dogs. Contrary to popular belief, tranquilizing is generally not necessary and may even be harmful to dogs, especially if they wind up sitting somewhere hot for hours. Tranquilized dogs cannot pant—that's how canines "sweat"—and therefore cannot cool themselves.

Once You're in France

REQUIREMENTS
After arriving in France, you may register with the consular section of the U.S. embassy in Paris. There is no requirement for this, but forms are provided and information about your whereabouts will not be released unless you give permission to do so. Passport details will be noted, making it easier to apply for a replacement if your passport is lost or stolen.

Some visas require you to appear at the local prefecture within a specified period of time, as noted above. These include students staying more than six months, who are required to get a student residency card, and those who entered France with an employment contract.

People with a long-stay visa must renew it annually at their prefecture for three years, at which time they may be eligible for a residency permit good for 10 years.

KID STUFF AND RECREATION
Children will have to be registered for school, of course. Placement will be up to school authorities, but parents should take an interest in the child's education. While teachers consider themselves the masters of their classrooms, they also need to know something about their pupils. They may have suggestions about ways parents can help their children become acclimated to a different language, culture, and educational system.

Being involved in your child's schooling is also a good way to meet people. Just before noon and 5 P.M., parents gather outside the school to wait for their children and chat with each other. In small villages, there may only be a primary school. Pupils will be bussed to *college* (middle school) and *lycée* (high school) in larger towns.

Enrolling your child in sports is a good way to help them make friends, but know that sports are separate from education in France. (No, the Sorbonne doesn't field a tennis or a soccer team.) Athletics are organized through the community rather than the schools.

Soccer, volleyball, judo, tennis, and basketball are all popular for both girls and boys. Players are organized by age into leagues. Another popular game is handball. It is played on a court the size of a basketball or tennis court with a goal like that in hockey and a ball the size of a big grapefruit. Teams of players dribble and pass the ball as in basketball and score when they throw the ball into the goal. Once the player with the ball faces the opposing goalie, defense is almost impossible, but it's great exercise running up and down the court.

Rugby, the closest the French come to American football, is popular in the south and usually an exciting game to watch as well as to play. While golf courses remain few and far between, tennis courts are quite common even in small villages, as are community swimming pools.

WORKING IN FRANCE

Forget coming to France and finding work as a grape picker or dishwasher. George Orwell might have been able to do it 70 years ago, but if you've read *Down and Out in London and Paris*, you know it wasn't an easy life even back then.

The French call it *"travail au noir"* ("working black"). It has nothing to do with race and everything to do with paying taxes. Illegal workers don't pay into the Social Security system, nor do their employers. And illegal workers do not pay income tax; many of them are collecting some form of welfare at the time. Others are legitimately employed in a trade—have the skills and insurance already—and do jobs on the side to increase their net income.

> You're moving to France. Now it's time to roll up your sleeves and get to work.

An established member of a community—a native with friends and family and support—may be able to pick up odd jobs of some sort, it is very difficult for a stranger to come into some town and do the same. Many people are willing to turn a blind eye to the activities of a person they grew up with or have lived near for years, but they may regard it as civic duty to denounce a foreigner doing the same thing. For one thing, unemployment ran 12 to 13 percent during the 1990s. In a country with a skilled, well-educated population, there were no good jobs going begging.

Non-payment of taxes is serious. Employers are unwilling to take a chance on someone they do not know—or someone they do know who bears a grudge—keeping quiet. Moreover, there are numerous benefits to the employer to work within the system, such as tax relief, apprentices, and salary subsidies. The result is that while a homeowner might pay the cousin of a friend to paint his house, this sort of gainful employment comes neither easily nor consistently to a foreigner.

Another factor affecting Americans looking for work is the European Union. It extends greater possibilities of working legally in France to English, Irish, Spanish, Portuguese, Belgians, Dutch, Greeks, and other foreigners than it does to Americans. There is a pool of legal foreigners as well as French people who might be looking for work at any given time.

Yet there are Americans working legally in France. Many of them are well-educated people in a technical, though not necessarily high-tech, field.

French salary levels are low compared to American ones, but they offer benefits and stability and a chance to live in France.

Dot.commers can find a welcome, but perhaps not the financial rewards they expect in the United States. With the recession that kept French unemployment so high throughout the '90s coming to an end, perhaps France will experience the same shortage of skilled labor the United States saw and foreign workers will be hired.

For the job seeker, the Internet is a great advantage. Not only can you use it to search for jobs in France, many of the employment sites offer a place to post your curriculum vitae (CV), the term usually used in France rather than resumé. Email also cuts the waiting time for replies.

The American Chamber of Commerce in France (www.amchamfr.org) also publishes a directory of all the U.S. firms that operate in France. It might be used as a source list for sending out applications.

A rather roundabout possibility for gaining employment in France is gaining citizenship in another European Union nation, such as Ireland. It is not necessary to give up your U.S. passport and citizenship when applying for citizenship in another country. And many Americans, either through ancestry or marriage, may be eligible to become citizens of an EU country. As such, they will have immediate access to French employment.

Another possibility to consider is doing a period of professional development in France, called a *stage* in French. It refers to a stint spent refining your knowledge, or learning particular techniques in your field, or just gaining experience under another master. Pay is minimal, perhaps only room and board if that. This is common in cooking and wine-making, for instance, and the *stagiare* is almost certain to benefit upon return to the United States. But it also gives you the experience of seeing what it is like to work in France and may result in contacts that could lead to employment later.

Some of the same sites that offer jobs also post listings for *stages*. They include:

- Emploi Center (www.emploicenter.com), a high-tech site.
- Etudis (www.etudis.com), which allows students to post their resumés online as well as to look at propositions offered by firms.
- Emailjob (www.emailjob.com), which lets you either put your resumé online or receive by email offers that might be of interest.
- Other sites may be found on the various Internet portals such as Yahoo, Excite, MSN, and Nomade.

12 A Roof Over Your Head

Your home in France is your castle. Foreigners have the same rights to rent, buy, and own property as the French themselves. Nationality makes no difference in purchase or rental. Where and how you live is largely up to you—what you can afford and what you can find.

For many expatriates, the search itself is often the most trying part. Often people come to France with a preconceived idea of what they want—a little cottage in the country surrounded by a garden, a spacious city apartment with a view overlooking a park and a smart bistro down the block for morning coffee or before-dinner *aperitifs*. Just the sort of image you have seen in dozens of films.

But then you bump into reality. You find what you want but can't afford it. Or, price is no object but nothing's for sale or rent in your desired location. You may indeed find your dream home or apartment in France—and even be able to afford it—but it's nevertheless wise to have realistic expectations about what's available and how much it will cost, just as you would back in the States.

Housing in France

To begin with, you should familiarize yourself with the ways French housing differs from its American counterpart. Most notable, homes and apartments

Deciphering the Classifieds

Any search for real estate will inevitably lead to the *petites annoncements* (classified ads). A house or apartment may be said to have *carac.* (character), or to be *charm.* (charming), *coq.* (cute), *except.* (exceptional), or *rav.* (delightful). Here is a glossary to help you decode the jargon and abbreviations of this specialized text.

a louer—for rent or lease
asc. (ascenseur)—elevator
a vendre or *AV*—for sale
bal. (balcon)—balcony
boxe—parking place
caution—security deposit
ch. or *chb. (chambre)*—bedroom; a *chambre de bonne* is a maid's room.
chauf. cent. (chauffage centrale)—central heating
com. (commission)—agent's commission
cft. (confort)—conveniences, such as a dishwasher, carpeting, etc.
cour.—courtyard
cuisine eq. (equipée)—major appliances installed
dche. (douche)—shower
et. el. (étage élevé)—upper floor
garçonnière—bachelor's apartment; small studio or room
grenier—attic; room under roof
imm. (immeuble)—building; it may be an *imm. mod.* (modern) or *imm. anc.* (old), an *imm. nf.* (new) or *imm. rec.* (recent).
interméd. (intermédiaire)—agent
jar./jdn. (jardin)—garden
kit.—kitchenette
lux.—luxurious
loyer—the rent
m2 (mètre carré)—square meter, about 10.75 square feet
meublé—furnished
moq. (moquette)—wall-to-wall carpeting
p. (pièce)—rooms, not including bathroom
poss. (possibilité)—possibility of
pr. cpl.—couple preferred
poutres apparentes—beamed ceilings
ref. nf. (refait neuf)—newly remodeled
slle. (salle)—large or formal room; *salle de réception* is a large living room; *salle à manger* is a formal dining room; *salle d'eau* is a room with water (sink, shower, etc.); *salle de bains* is a bathroom.
ss. (sans)—without
stdg. (standing)—classy, fashionable address; *gd. stdg., tr. gd. stdg.* is deluxe
s/ (sur)—on
terr.—terrace
ttc (toutes charges comprises)—all charges included; *chgs. (charges)* means there is a supplementary monthly fee in addition to rent. *Ttc* means, literally, *toutes taxes comprises* and is widely understood in cases such as this to indicate a complete price.
ventes—listings for sale
vide—unfurnished
w.c.—water closet, meaning the toilet is in room separate from bath and sink

tend to be smaller, with fewer rooms and less square footage. Apartment kitchens are often postage-stamp size; appliances are smaller as well. New two-bedroom, one-bath homes are not uncommon in France, yet virtually none are being built in the States any more, where the three-bedroom, two-bath house is almost a minimum.

There are other differences as well. Floors are more likely to be tile than wood or carpeted, heating derives from hot water radiators rather than forced air, and garages are less common—not extraordinary differences, but noticeable. You'd be wise to look at many possibilities so you're able to distinguish differences you can expect from downright substandard housing. True, kitchens may be smaller, but not as small as *this* one. Yes, electrical outlets are not as numerous as they are in American housing, but a room without any is substandard.

For help in finding the right location for you, as well as for getting settled once you decide, visit the *mairie* (mayor's office) of your town. They can provide you with helpful information on public transportation, parking, garbage collection, and recreation facilities and opportunities. This information might help you decide how pleasant or convenient life there might be. The *mairie* is also where you go to register a child for school.

A great source of information about housing in France is *the Agence Nationale pour l'Informations sur le Logement* (ANIL). This agency provides information to the public on various aspects of housing including financing, taxation, and legal matters such as owners' and tenants' rights. The local chapters are also clearinghouses for information about new properties for sale or rent. Check out the ANIL website at www.anil.org.

Renting versus Buying

Several factors will influence your decision of whether to rent or to buy. An important one is location. Renting is far more common in metropolitan areas, where there are few houses but many apartments, than it is in rural areas and small towns. Another is cost. Not only are home prices high in metro areas, the typical 30-year American mortgage is not yet common in France. Seven to 15 years is the norm, requiring larger monthly payments—even people of ample means may be unable to afford to buy a

Like Chartres, Rousillon had its beginnings as a fortified hilltop village.

house or a large apartment in Paris. Renting makes the most sense for those who wish to live amid the city's cosmopolitan splendor.

You may be able to afford your ideal home or apartment, and even find it, only to discover nothing that meets your requirements is for sale when you're ready to buy. In that case, renting makes the most sense. Once established comfortably in a neighborhood, you can wait for the sort of apartment or house you want to come on the market. During your wait, you will enjoy the benefit of becoming knowledgeable about the neighborhood's good and bad points without having made the commitment of a purchase.

> Your home in France is your castle.

In contrast, in rural areas and villages, you will find fewer rentals available. There is a far higher percentage of owner-occupied housing, and apartments are few. Buying a home makes more sense in these locations because you will have a much greater chance of obtaining a suitable residence. In some thinly populated areas, building a new home may be the best solution. The price of new construction may be only slightly more than that of complete renovation, and in the end you will have exactly what you want rather than a compromise made by accepting what is available.

In or near a provincial city, you will probably have the greatest choice of both rentals and homes for sale. In most cases, prices will be more reasonable than in Paris, and you'll find a relatively large stock of both houses and apartments for rent or sale on the market. Especially for those considering retirement in France, these cities may be the ideal locations, and not

The countryside of the Eure-et-Loire département

only for their selection in housing. While proximity to or residence in a medium-sized city will mean higher prices for either purchase or rental, it also means easier access to cultural events and institutions, medical care, and air and rail transportation.

Remember, aside from Paris and Marseilles, France does not have large cities by U.S. standards. Major cities such as Nice, Lyon, and Toulouse are all less than one million population. By choosing carefully, you can find small towns with good services within 20 kilometers (12.4 miles) of most cities. You will also likely find an international airport, TGV service, and fully equipped hospitals in the metropolitan area.

Renting an Apartment

Renting in France is different in some ways from renting in the United States. For one thing, the typical month-to-month agreement for an unfurnished apartment is not the norm. Instead, tenants typically sign a three-year lease for unfurnished property. Furthermore, there are often charges you would not expect in the States. Foremost among these is the *taxe d'habitation* that the tenant, not the owner, must pay. There can also be a variety of maintenance charges. It makes no difference whether you rent an apartment or a house—the rules are the same.

Additionally, in France the tenant must have insurance; a landlord can demand proof of this insurance, and termination of the policy can be grounds for terminating the lease. This insurance protects the proprietor of the building from losses that might be caused by a tenant—fire, water damage, explosions, and so forth. These policies should also provide against damages to third parties such as neighbors. Proof of this insurance should be presented annually to the landlord. Your finances will also be of concern to a landlord. You should be prepared to prove a monthly income at least three times the rent.

> *Renting makes the most sense for those who wish to live amid the city's cosmopolitan splendor.*

In France, unfurnished often means bare walls, ceilings, and floors. Light fixtures, kitchen cabinets, and appliances may all belong to a tenant. (Furnished rentals do include these amenities, of course. What's more, they do not require a written lease and may be occupied for shorter periods.) The lease also describes the parts of the premises for the exclusive use of the tenant and areas that are for communal use.

The rental of an apartment or house may require a large initial outlay of cash, although not so great as a purchase. If the rent were 900 euros per month and the real estate agent handling the rental received a fee of

8 percent of the annual rent and a two-month deposit were required, the total payment would be 900 + 864 + 1,800 = 3,564 euros ($3,207), plus any extra charges that might be involved.

If there are to be increases in rent during the period of the lease, the landlord should specify them. Rents are usually based on last year's rent plus any increase in the cost of construction index, although landlords may be able to justify greater increases following renovations. As in the States, you'll typically pay rent once a month; if you pay it more than three months in advance, a deposit should not be necessary. This is because landlords may not require deposits of more than two months' rent.

When you decide to leave, you should give notice at least three months in advance (many people vacate apartments before the three-year lease is up). Inform the various utilities and services of your departure date. *Electricité de France* (EDF) will read your meter on your last day and forward the bill to your new address. You may also want to make an appointment to have the electricity turned on in your new residence. Follow the same procedure with the telephone company. The post office will forward mail for one year to another address, charging 16.77 euros ($15) to do so. Also let your insurance agent know that you're moving out and change the policy to reflect your new address.

The landlord should go over the premises with you using the *états de lieux* inventory form that was completed when you moved in. This is important in seeking the return of a deposit. If the landlord finds any damage that was done during your stay, he will withhold all or part of the deposit. Deposits must be paid to the tenant within two months after he or she moves out.

After you move, the prefecture needs to be informed of your new address; an electric or telephone bill will serve as proof. The same must be done for automobile registration. If you have moved to a different department, the annual tax will change. Your health insurance must also be changed to your new address and if your bank account has also changed, you should provide the new information.

Buying a Home

Probably most people who have the means to move to France will sooner or later buy a residence. The security of owning your own home, whether a house or an apartment, is quite comforting to most of us. Moreover, for those who leave their native land to settle elsewhere, property ownership makes a definite statement: My home is here. And for those who look at property realistically rather than as speculators intending to get rich off their purchase, French property has been a good investment.

Purchasing a home in France is little different from doing so in the States. You find a property for sale and make an offer. If the offer is accepted, you sign an agreement *(compromis de vente)* and pay a deposit, usually not more than 10 percent of the purchase price. This deposit is a guarantee of good faith and will be forfeited if the buyer reneges on the deal. It is returned if the seller reneges. When the title is cleared, usually within a month or two, and the wishes of the buyer and seller have been met, the final papers are signed and the balance is paid.

However, there are a few twists that can snag a deal. First of all, it is important to know that property sales—even those originating with a real estate agency—go through a *notaire* (notary). The French *notaire* is much more than an American notary public, although he does serve that function among others. While the preliminary agreement may be drawn up by a real estate broker, it is the *notaire* who draws up the deed *(acte authentique de vente)*.

The *notaire* performs two important public functions: He guarantees the title, that is, that the seller has the right to dispose of it; and he collects taxes due on the sale. For this, he receives a not-insignificant percentage fixed on a sliding scale of the purchase price—nine to 12 percent depending on the total price. If a real estate agent's fee—from four to 10 percent—is added, the price can mount and you must take this into consideration.

The *notaire* can also perform a private function, serving as a knowledgeable third party involved in the negotiations and can arbitrate between buyer and seller. Knowing the history of the property, the *notaire* may be in a position to reason with a seller making some questionable demand. Or, he

Maisons de Pays de Caux

You Pay for What You Get

Probably everyone who has dreamed of buying a house in France has heard about some "bargains"—advertised in a magazine or on a website, posted in the window of a real estate office, or overheard in the rosy story of some friend of a friend who picked up an old château for the price of a new car.

Attention! Prudence! The prices quoted in this book have generally been those of large cities; some readers have undoubtedly said to themselves, "You might have to pay those prices in Paris or Manhattan, but surely in some little country town, the French equivalent of Crookston, Minnesota, or Brawley, California, the prices would be much cheaper."

It's true. They will be—but not as much as you might think.

Let's go to Gorron in the *département* of Mayenne. You've never heard of Gorron or Mayenne? Bet you'd never heard of Crookston or Brawley, either, until you read this book.

Gorron, a market town of 3,000, is pretty far from everything except France: 23 kilometers (14.2 miles) from the town of Mayenne, 28 kilometers (17 miles) from Mortain, 17 kilometers (10.5 miles) from Ernee—you get the picture. No national highways pass through Gorron, the *Guide Michelin* found nothing of interest there, and no hotel or restaurant to recommend. It just happens to be a pleasant place to live. It's not quite Normandy, nor Brittany, nor the valley of the Loire—sort of in between—and it's not Provence or the Dordogne, but the houses there are built of stone and your neighbors all speak French.

Maître Jean-Paul Garnier is the *notaire* in Gorron, as his father was before him. Here is what Me. Garnier says property is worth.

In a village 13 kilometers (8 miles) from Gorron, he recently sold a house of 75 square meters (800 square feet) in need of total renovation but with a small garden for 18,300 euros ($16,470)—the price of a new car. But when you add in what "total renovation" means—new wiring and plumbing and insulation and heating and maybe a roof and insulation—that new car becomes a Ferrari instead of a Ford.

What the prospective purchaser must understand when they see an old stone house for sale for a pittance, is that the cost of making it as comfortable as they would like may be greater than the cost of a seemingly much more expensive property.

Renovations of an old house—even a small one—can easily cost 50,000 to 80,000 euros ($45,000 to $72,000). Many old village and country houses have wiring and plumbing that is totally inadequate for a modern home. The conditions you find acceptable for a vacation may be intolerable month after month, especially as the seasons change.

In Gorron itself, Garnier sold a five-room house of 90 square meters (975 square feet) may be able to make clear to the buyer the reasons for the seller's demands. Property sales are anything but unemotional affairs—particularly when the property may have been the seller's lifelong home and the buyer is a foreigner—and a cool-headed arbiter may be the key to a successful purchase.

The other hurdle to clear before a piece of property can change hands is the commune's right of first refusal in any sale. The commune is the basic geographical unit of France, combining the urban planning and zoning powers of both city and county in the United States. Unlike American cities, in which jurisdiction stops at the city limits, the French commune's boundaries extend beyond the limits of the village and take in surrounding countryside; at the boundary begins the territory of another commune. As a result, the land surrounding the town remains under the commune's

in good condition but in need of much decoration with a large garden and *dépendance* (outbuilding, such as a garage or stable) for 76,231 euros ($68,607). That's 850 euros ($765) per square meter.

Larger houses to renovate—225 to 300 square meters—are more difficult to find in the towns, Garnier said, and had no recent examples of sales to quote. He anticipated that such a house would bring a price of 30,000 to 50,000 euros ($27,000 to $45,000) depending on the work that needed to be done. However, not far away in Ceauce, there was a house in excellent condition about 300 square meters on a 2.5 acre lot for sale for 152,500 euros ($137,250). That's 500 euros ($450) per square meter plus the land.

A very nice two-room house in the countryside around Gorron that had been renovated in 1996 on 500 square meters of land sold for 61,000 euros ($54,900). In a village not far away, an old mill with only three rooms but on 2.5 hectares of land (6 acres) was appraised at 107,000 euros ($96,300).

"We have in the region many country houses that need to be renovated. Prices can go from 7,600 euros to 38,000 euros [$6,840 to $34,200], depending on the size of the house, the site and, the general condition," Garnier said.

He cited the example of a little stone house in the country with 1,300 square meters of land that had water and electricity but no heat or septic tank. It was one big room with a fireplace and an attic that could have been converted. It sold for a little over 12,000 euros ($10,800).

In a village a couple of kilometers from Gorron a renovated house well sited on 2.5 hectares sold for about 137,000 euros ($123,300), he said. Near the same village, a country house and a *dépendance* that was well situated on 5,354 square meters of land (about 1.25 acres) but needed renovation including a septic tank, sold for a little more than 38,000 euros ($34,200).

Garnier said that land without any services such as water and electricity sells for about 1.5 euros ($1.35) per square meter. Land with services but otherwise undeveloped is about 7.5 euros ($6.75) per square meter, and land in a development is twice that price. A new house in the vicinity of Gorron with two bedrooms, garage, and garden costs about 61,000 euros ($54,900).

More than the number of rooms, it's the options such as a fireplace or a terrace or veranda that increases the price, he said.

What should interest foreign buyers is that land and a new house in Gorron costs just about what land and a new house in a village in Languedoc or the Midi-Pyrénées would cost. In France today, the cost of materials and of labor is roughly the same everywhere. What changes is the value of the land, and the type and quality of construction.

control. The discrepancy between strict city zoning laws and lax county rules that have permitted so much uncontrolled development surrounding American cities simply does not exist in France.

French law gives the commune an option on all the property within its boundaries. When a bona fide offer is made, the *notaire* presents the offer to the *mairie*, giving the town the two months to buy the property at that same price and use it for some public project.

In most cases, the commune does not exercise its right and the deal proceeds as negotiated. Tenants also have a right to buy a property when it is put up for sale, even if the owner does not intend to sell it until after the lease is up. The rights of tenants to pre-empt a sale extend to farmland as well, where the situation becomes a more complicated legal affair.

Anyone who spends much time looking for property in France is certain to hear tales about paying part of the price under the table with buyer and seller declaring a lesser price to reduce taxes and notary fees. While some of these stories are factual, a foreigner should be especially wary of any such arrangement.

First of all, a low price may result in either the commune or a tenant exercising their right of pre-emption so that you don't get the property after all. Second, you enter your new community known as someone willing to circumvent the law. Third, this practice is illegal and at some point could backfire. Suppose the day after the property becomes yours it is destroyed; is any insurance company going to reimburse you more than the declared purchase price? Exaggerated examples perhaps, but worth consideration.

In France as in the United States, there are private developers who buy land and build on it, selling the houses or apartments even before the work is complete. Agreement to buy such a residence may be done under a reservation contract, with payments spread out as the work is completed.

Building a New Home

An alternative to buying an existing house is to have one built, buying land separately and contracting for the work to be done, just as you would in the States. However, not all land may be built upon. Remember, communes' limits extend to the border of the next commune and development does not occur unrestrained as sometimes happens in the U.S.

Determining whether a piece of land is buildable or if a building might be converted to a residence is easily done at the *mairie*, where you request a *certificate d'urbanisme* for the property. This will be provided without charge and you need not be the property owner to obtain it. However, it is not a building permit; it simply tells you that a particular piece of land can be considered for a building permit.

Building plans will have to be approved by local authorities, and this means a French architect must draw them up. Some builders will have plans on hand or will have them drawn for a specific site for a flat fee. This is probably less expensive than hiring an architect yourself, who will charge a percentage of the total contract for his or her efforts.

However, there is an important consideration: The architect you hire is working for you; the architect the contractor hires is working for him. If you intend to have that professional advice plus oversight of construction that an architect provides, it's certainly wise to select your own. To have someone who knows the locale and climatic conditions and can advise you of advantages and disadvantages of various materials and practices is surely worthwhile.

On the other hand, a contract for a single-family home is a powerful document in France with lots of protections for the client included. The contract with the builder should specify exactly the quality of the materials used in the construction. Since France has national standards for construction, these are well known and easily determined. If you ask at least two builders for a bid, their materials can be compared and each should be able to show examples of their previously constructed properties.

An architect may also take over many of the responsibilities a general contractor would handle in the United States. These include putting the various subcontracts out for bid, selecting craftsmen he knows to be skilled and reliable, and ensuring that the materials used are the ones specified and paid for.

The contract should also contain financial guarantees for completion of the work on time and at the agreed upon price. If the contractor should fail to do so, the guarantor would be responsible for continuing the work. It should also contain a guarantee of perfect completion whereby the contractor agrees to perform any necessary work for a year after delivering the house; a guarantee of good working order that ensures equipment added by the contractor but not constructed by him such as plumbing fixtures and heaters will work for at least two years; and a 10-year guarantee against defects related to the construction.

The contract for building a single-family home is strictly regulated by law in France so that its provisions are easily enforceable. For instance, it includes a schedule of payments to be made as work is completed. The contractor cannot demand payment except as set forth in the following schedule (percentages are cumulative):

The date the contract is signed—5%
The date the building permit is received—10%
The date construction begins—15%
The date the foundation is finished—25%
The date exterior walls are up—40%
The date the roof is in place—60%
The date interior walls and windows are installed—75%
The date plumbing, carpentry, and heating are finished—95%
The date the buyer accepts the house—final 5%.

For those who decide to have a single-family home built, there is a special kind of insurance that should be purchased as part of the contract. Despite the guarantees within the contract, should there be a problem, the homeowner may face a lengthy and perhaps costly process to remedy the situation. This is especially so if a number of years have passed since construction; the builder may have gone out of business, for instance.

The solution is *l'assurance dommages-ouvrage*, insurance against faulty work. This insurance covers necessary repairs for the homeowner and puts the burden of pursuing recovery of damages on the insurance company.

Courts have held that a home is worth substantially less if this insurance was not included in the construction. So if you think you might want to sell your house less than 10 years after construction, you're well advised to consider this insurance even if they have full confidence in the builder.

Two good websites that deal with house construction are www.faire-construire.com and www.maisoninfo.com.

Renovating an Older Home

When it comes to deciding between renovation and new construction, relative overall costs play a small role because there may be little difference between them. Much more important are likely to be factors such as the site, the materials of construction, and availability.

If you simply must have old stone walls, there is no alternative to renovation. When many of those old walls went up three or more centuries ago, there was no electricity and perhaps no running water. Such modern conveniences have to be added.

The decision to renovate an old house is often intensely personal. It may result from a lifelong dream, a challenge, or even just a passing fancy. Any of these are sufficient reason to undertake such a project. Certainly, many foreigners who move to the French countryside rather than the cities come with this idea in mind. But before making the decision, you should consider several points:

- How much of the work will you do yourself? Renovation may involve any or all of the following crafts—masonry, electricity, plumbing, roofing, landscaping, and tiling. Aside from the skills involved and unfamiliar materials, remember that construction work is hard physical labor. Are you up to it?
- Can you stand clutter? Any construction project is going to make a mess for a period of time. If you hire professionals to do it, it will probably take less time than if you do it yourself, less time you have to live in a construction zone.
- Will you be satisfied with the results? An amateur may be able to cover a wall with plaster but never achieve that perfectly flat surface that is desired. In much the same way, you can add electrical circuits or tile a floor only to discover later that you did not do an adequate job due to your inexperience. Know your own abilities or wait until you've gained the needed skill working on lesser jobs.
- Do you have the time to devote to such a project? Whether you do the work yourself or hire it done, renovating an entire house takes time, usually months. Installation of a new roof or even a skylight might be delayed for weeks due to rain, for instance.

- Is your spouse or partner in agreement? Even strong relationships can be stretched to near breaking by either a move to a new country or by a major home remodeling project. To undertake both at the same time when only one of you is enthusiastic about the project is bound to cause problems.

Many old houses in France may be little more than shells by today's construction standards. For instance, they may be wired for electricity, but it is totally inadequate for a home filled with appliances such a washer and dryer, dishwasher, heaters, etc. Plumbing may exist, but again be inadequate both in the size of the water pipes and the number of bathrooms. There may be no insulation or a leaky roof.

Putting all this right in an older house may be more expensive than starting from scratch in new construction. You can buy a new, well-built house in many rural villages for less than 70,000 euros ($63,000). But to live in a new house in a new development is not why many people want to move to France.

One approach is to find an older house that you consider liveable and renovate it while living there. This is certainly feasible. However, it should be noted that you can also have a house built, specifying in the contract that certain jobs will be done by the owner rather than the builder, thus reducing the final cost. In any case, using your own labor may make a particular property affordable if time is not of the essence.

For those who choose to hire the work done, France is full of skilled artisans. One way to proceed is one step at a time. Craftsmen will give a written *devis* (estimate) for a job. It will break down materials and labor. Discuss the project with the craftsman and ask his opinion of your plans. Many people arrive in France ignorant of local construction materials and techniques and he may have other suggestions.

Start with a relatively small job and see if you are satisfied before launching a large project. But remember that the better craftsmen may also be the busiest, so you may have to wait. (Contractors are the same the world over and carefully planned schedules fall apart.) Also, a good electrician may be able to recommend a plumber or mason or vice versa. Anyone who takes pride in his own work is not likely to tarnish his reputation by suggesting a person he knows will do a second-rate job.

> *Purchasing a home in France is little different from doing so in the States.*

In any event, hire licensed tradespeople. They stand behind their work and it will be of a certain standard. (Okay, it's not a perfect world and not all workmanship is equal. But by and large, the person who has to stand or fall on the quality of his work within a community will do a better job than someone supplementing a welfare check with odd jobs.)

Furthermore, the licensed craftsman has his own insurance and pays taxes; you won't be financially responsible if he is injured on the job or liable for unpaid taxes. It is the law that the employer—and that's what a homeowner who hires an unlicensed handyman becomes—must pay Social Security taxes for workers, and French authorities will not ignore this requirement if it is brought to their attention. And one of the licensed, tax-paying craftsmen in town may see that that happens.

Hiring a licensed craftsman provides a side benefit to you as a newcomer in a community. A good craftsman is usually well respected and people value their opinions. Establish a good relationship and you will have made a worthwhile acquaintance. In small villages, these people will be your neighbors; you also want them to be your friends.

If you opt to buy a house in unlivable condition, it may be a good idea to turn to an architect. For one thing, changes to the exterior will require drawings for approval. For another, the architect should be familiar with local craftsmen and know their strengths and weaknesses. Finally, the architect may have a bit more clout in getting them to arrange their work schedules since he represents not only the project at hand but potential future jobs as well.

Perhaps the most important bit of housing advice to give to anyone moving to France is simply, don't get in over your head. No matter how carefully you select a property, the unexpected can occur and you should have the reserves to deal with it. Despite the current rising price of real estate, it may not continue, just as the boom of the '80s peaked and values declined. You cannot be sure that a residence will be worth more tomorrow than it is today, or even that a buyer at today's price can be found tomorrow.

North Sea
Isle of Man (U.K.)
West Frisian Islands
ENGLAND
Amsterdam
NETHERLANDS
GERMANY
BELGIUM
Lille
Nord-Pas-De-Calais
LUXEMBOURG
English Channel
Picardi
La Harva
Upper Normandy
Channel Islands (U.K.)
Lower Normandy
PARIS AND THE ÎLE-DE-FRANCE
Paris
Ile-De-France
Alsace
Strasbourg
Lorraine
NORMANDY AND BRITTANY
Chartres
Champagne-Ardenne
Brittany
Orléans
Pays De La Loire
Centre
Nantes
Burgandy
Franche-Comté
ATLANTIC OCEAN
FRANCE
SWITZERLAND
BURGUNDY AND THE RHÔNE VALLEY
Poitou Charles
Limousin
Ile d'Oleron
Lyon
Rhone Alps
Auvergene
Grenoble
ITALY
Bordeaux
Bay of Biscay
Aquitaine
THE MIDI AND LANGUEDOC
PROVENCE AND THE CÔTE D'AZUR
Provence-Alpes-Côte-D'Azur
Nice
Toulouse
Midi-Pyrénees
Montpellier
Marseille
Languedoc Roussilon
MONACO
Gulf of Lyon
ANDORRA
Liguarian Sea
SPAIN
Mediterranean Sea
N
W
E
S
Majorca
Minorca
0
100 mi
Ibiza
0
100 km

13 Prime Living Locations

The following chapters discuss the characteristics and appeal of the different regions in France. By no means are these the only desirable regions, but they are places where a number of expatriates have decided to live. In fact, they cover about half of France and include the regions where more than two-thirds of the French population lives.

Paris and the Île-de-France

First, of course, is Paris, the cosmopolitan capital and the metropolis surrounding it. In many ways, this is both the head and heart of France—its intellectual, cultural, social, economic and political center. There is no other great city like it and few that equal it: New York, London, Rome, and Tokyo; perhaps Moscow, Cairo, and Beijing. For those seeking the cultural France—the art, the nightlife, the high fashion, the great food—Paris is the place to be. All of its *arrondissements*, the administrative areas into which large French cities are divided, offer potential homes although as in any city, some areas are much more expensive than others.

The region around the city itself, the Île-de-France, more and more shares in cultural and social wealth of Paris as population density increases along with a great transit system. Paris can accommodate only so many people and institutions within its boundaries. Research and academic institutes,

Taking the Measure of Metrics

As you delve into the prime living location chapters, you'll notice the metric measurements used to describe apartments and houses in each region. The metric system is simple to use all by itself, but translating from metric to the American system is complex because of the fractions involved. However, you can make many approximations that, while not exact, make estimating easy.

Note too that housing prices are listed in euros. At the time of publication, one euro equaled about 90 cents.

Distance
1 inch = 2.5 centimeters (2.54 cm)
1 foot = 30 centimeters (30.5 cm)
1 yard = 90 centimeters (91.44 cm)
1 meter = 1 yard, 3 inches, or 3 1/4 feet (39.37 in.)
2 meters = 6 1/2 feet (6 ft. 6 3/4 in.)
10 meters = 11 yards (10 yd., 2 ft., 9 3/4 in.)
1 kilometer = 0.6 mile (0.62 mi.)
1 mile = 1.6 kilometer

Area
1 square inch = 6.45 square centimeters
1 square foot = 929 square centimeters = 0.093 square meters
1 square meter = 10.76 square feet
1 acre = 4,047 square meters = 0.4 hectare
1 hectare = 2.47 acres = 10,000 square meters
1 are = 100 square meters = 120 square yards

---

business, commercial and manufacturing centers have all pushed outward, both following the burgeoning population and attracting more. Many of these suburbs offer small town charm with big city excitement in woodsy settings cut by streams and rivers. It is in Paris and the Île-de-France that one will find the greatest number of Americans, mixed among the 12 million French and scores of other nationalities.

Southern France: The Midi and Languedoc

Between the Atlantic Ocean to the west and the Mediterranean Sea to the east, and between the Massif Central to the north and the Pyrénées to the south, lies Bordeaux and the Midi region, a rich, rebellious land that produces enough wine to fill its famous canal connecting the two seas. The western Pyrénées and into the lowlands are Basque country, where French gives way to a more ancient language, one so different from any other that legend among the devout Catholics of region claims that it took the Devil seven years to learn his first Basque word. The rural northern area drained by the Dordogne river has been much favored by the English and Americans in recent decades, whÎle the great university city of Toulouse, surrounded by rolling plains with fields of grain, sunflowers, and corn reminds one of the American Midwest, has become a high-tech, aerospace center. Sparsely populated Languedoc along the Mediterranean remains largely agricultural, dotted with small farming villages. Besides the hot summers, this area provides easy access to the ski slopes and other winter sport areas of the Pyrénées.

Southeast France: Provence and the Côte d'Azur

In the famed South of France, sandwiched between the Rhône River east to Italy is Provence, a land divided between the chic, densely populated coastline from Marseille to Nice and the dry, mountainous interior. This was not the cradle of Mediterranean civilization but certainly the site of its adolescence. The Côte d'Azur is chic and expensive; the interior less costly but both areas have an international population, having been a vacation favorite with Europeans for nearly two centuries. Aix-en-Provence, not far from either Marseille or Avignon, is a great center for American and other foreign university students, whÎle the Luberon Mountains provide picturesque villages of stone houses. You'll probably find more Americans in Provence than anywhere else in France outside of Paris. *Les Alpes Maritime* (the Maritime Alps), though not as high as their northern cousins, provide winter skiing and summer boating on rivers such as the Durance.

Northwest France: Normandy and Brittany

West of the Île de France and Paris is *Normandie* (Normandy) and the English Channel, both more sheltered from the Atlantic storms that can lash the more westerly coast of *Bretagne* (Brittany). The Seine and numerous other smaller rivers wind through this rolling countryside that is heavily farmed but with pleasant wooded areas as well. Modern transportation—fast and frequent trains and good roads—have brought Paris within reach, the way that Long Island is to New York or Napa is to San Francisco. The Eurostar and the Chunnel have only served to emphasize the proximity of the region to the U.K. It remains a favorite weekend getaway for the English as well as for Parisians, with expensive resorts on the coast and bucolic hideaways further inland. Its central geographic location within the European Union has made Normandy a great distribution hub as well.

East-Central France: Burgundy and the Rhône Valley

The Rhône Valley and *Bourgogne* (Burgundy) constitute, like the Midi, a great wine-producing region. The southern part of this area below Lyon was historically part of Rome's Provence and remains allied in architecture and lifestyle today. Away from the Rhône river as well as along its banks are pleasant villages and market towns; farming—not only grapes, but fruit and olives— is the big industry here outside of the only large city in the region, Lyon. The Alps, to the east, and their summer and winter recreation areas are within easy reach of much of the Rhône valley. In Burgundy, it is much the same— grapes and fruit, although it is too far north for olives. Picturesque little villages are only a few hours from Paris and the regional park of Morvan with its heavily forested hills provides excellent summer recreation and the slopes of the Jura Mountains to the east make a day of skiing or other snow sports quite possible.

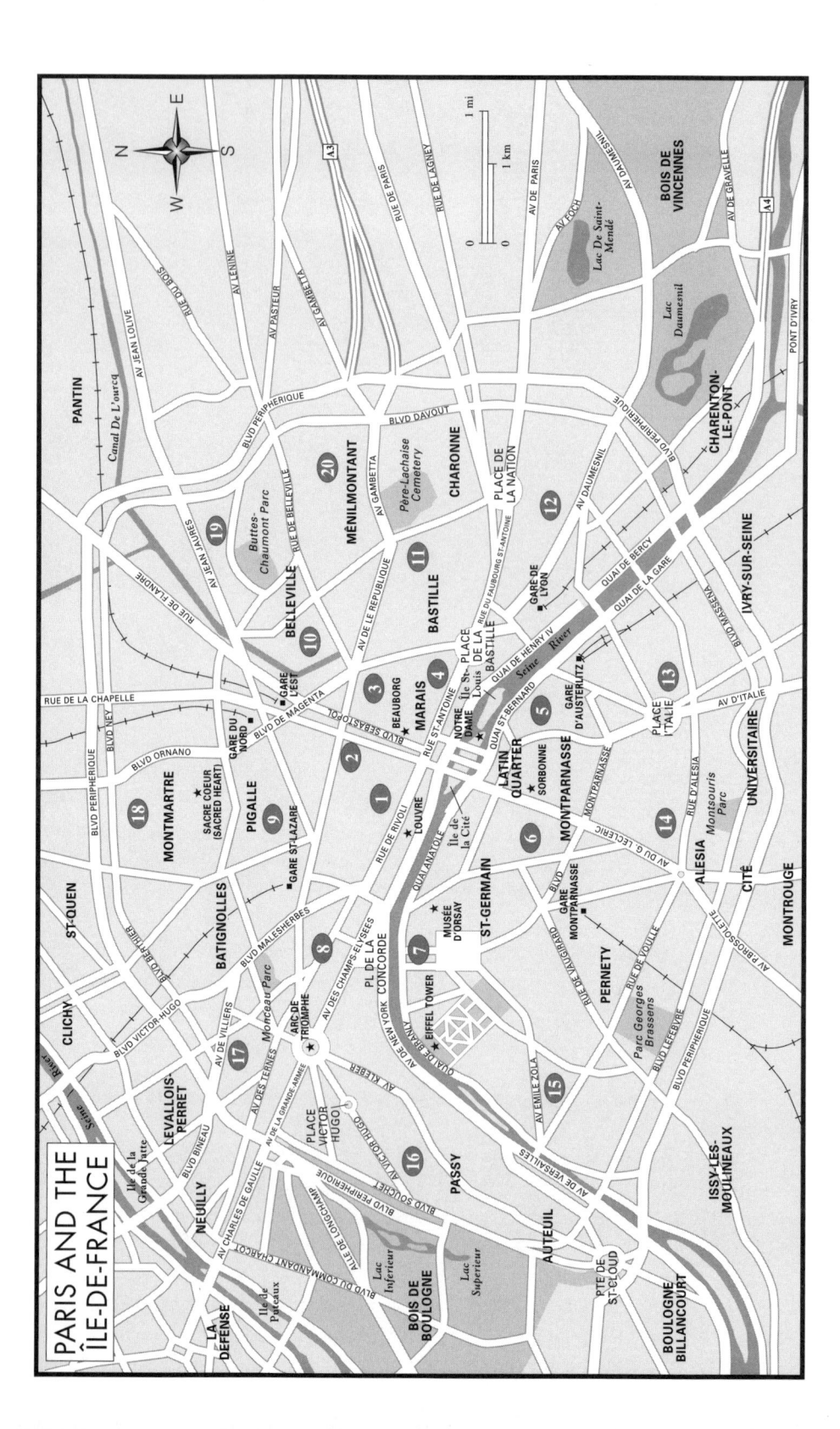

PARIS AND THE ÎLE-DE-FRANCE

14 Paris and the Île-de-France

The French capital and its environs, with more than one-sixth of the nation's population, offer a cosmopolitan ambiance, employment, and cultural opportunities. Your French neighbors in this region are urban and suburban folks, better educated on the average than those in rural areas.

This region is the cradle of the French nation. The Franks who lived here gave their name and language, but it was the city of Paris and the kings who occupied the throne there who gradually came to rule the rest of the country. That remains the case today, despite efforts to decentralize the government and allow more regional decision making. The region also dominates the economy of France; here are located the corporate headquarters and the stock exchange, the greatest employment opportunities, and the greatest concentration of industry and research institutions.

While this dominance was once confined to Paris itself, the past generation has brought such growth that the city could no longer contain it all. The departments that ring Paris now play an increasingly important role.

This is also the region of France where you will find the most Americans living. No one knows exactly how many because many of them have no *carte de séjour*. Some of them are tourists or students who have found ways to remain beyond their original visas; others have independent

Sic transit Paris

Paris and the Île-de-France are well served by public rail transportation. *Le métro*, the subway system, opened its first line a century ago, drawing its name from *La Compagnie du chemin de fer metropolitain de Paris*, the firm that operated it.

Today there are 14 metro lines, and some extend well outside of Paris. Perhaps more importantly, the metro is part of a much larger regional transit network. The metro, the suburban RER (*Réseau Express Régional*), and the national French rail system, SNCF (*Société Nationale Chemins de Fer Français*), combine to provide public transportation for millions of riders daily.

Paris is the densest city in Europe, cramming more than 20,000 people into each square kilometer, 2.5 times as many as in London, for instance. Add 2.5 million cars entering and leaving each day, plus 200,000 tons of merchandise being delivered daily, and efficient public transit becomes a necessity.

The metro system is simple and easily mastered. The various lines are just that—lines with two ends. The trains shuttle from one end of the line to the other with stops in between, usually connecting with one or more other lines. Maps in all the stations show all the stops and connections. It takes approximately 50 minutes to cross the city by metro.

Individual tickets are 1.22 euros ($1.09), but since one is almost never enough, it's cheaper to buy a *carnet* (packet) of 10 for 7.93 euros ($7.13), or one of the various passes available for either tourists or commuters. For less than 1,300 euros ($1,170), one can buy a *carte integrale*, good for a year in all eight zones that form a series of concentric circles around the heart of Paris through which the metro and the suburban RER trains travel.

Paris also has buses. During the day, the metro is much faster because of traffic congestion, but the Noctambuses, marked with a yellow owl in a black circle, run from 1:30 A.M. to 5:30 A.M. These are important because the metro does not run all night. Depending on the line and where you are, you may not be able to catch a train between about 1 A.M. and 5:30 A.M.

---

means and have not bothered with the formalities of a long-stay visa, perhaps not intending to reside permanently in France. Still others may own apartments or homes here and stay for extended periods without actually moving here. In actual numbers, we are talking thousands, not hundreds of thousands.

But the number of Americans living permanently in France has never been great; in the past, the majority have been those with a French mate. Unless you are already acquainted with an American living in France and choose to move nearby, chances are you will have no American neighbors. That does not mean you won't find any Anglophones, however; scattered throughout France in far greater numbers than Americans are British people. Add to these the Dutch, who are almost universally English speakers, the Australians, Irish, Belgians, and Germans, in addition to the French themselves, many of whom speak English, and you have a sizeable English-speaking population.

The RER speeds passengers to the suburbs via lines A, B, C, D, and E, but these are deceptive because each of the lines forks off into branches after getting out of Paris. For instance, Line A to the west has three different terminals: St-Germain-en-Laye, Poissy, and Cergy-le-Haut.

Also, SNCF, the national French rail system, runs lines from Paris. Some of these serve suburban areas, such as the line that goes to Roissy and Charles de Gaulle airport.

The two rail systems, RER and SNCF, complement each other; at many suburban stations you can transfer from one system to the other in order to reach a particular destination.

The advent of so many TGV lines in recent years has given many cities such as Rouen, Chartres, Orléans, and Amiens a boost. Thanks to the trains, each city is now an hour or so from Paris. Consequently, they have become attractive to middle-class families who find better housing available for less than the cost of the commute. To avoid becoming mere bedroom communities, these cities have formed an association, *les Villes du Grand Bassin Parisien*, and have begun their own renewal projects.

The problem facing this transit system, however, is that all of these lines radiate from Paris. They are spokes without a wheel. As the Île-de-France has grown, so have its transit needs. By 2000, two-thirds of the traffic, whether passenger or freight, were within the region—3.5 times the number going into or coming out of Paris and 4.5 times the number within Paris itself. And the percentage is increasing annually.

So, even though public transit to and from Paris is good, public transit around the city is not, forcing many people into their autos to go to work.

To handle the problem, construction has already begun on a series of new tram lines and other projects, such as extensions of metro lines that will eventually form a beltway around the outer edge of the three departments surrounding Paris. This is a multi-billion euro project that will take years to complete. At this point perhaps what is most important is not when it will be completed but that the work has started.

Housing in Paris

Paris is expensive. Think New York and San Francisco and Tokyo. And as in those other cities, even those who can afford the price tags will find the perfect location is not for sale and they will have to make do with something else. The problem is that individual houses seldom come on the market in Paris. In 1999, for instance, about 44,000 pieces of property changed hands, but only about 350 were single-family homes. In the past two years, property prices in many districts have increased 10 to 15 percent or more annually, four or five times the rate of inflation.

Apartments, especially if they include a garage or parking space, are also quite expensive, but at least they can be found. Fortunately, a car is not a necessity in Paris with the metro going nearly everywhere day and night. In fact, many will find a car more trouble than it is worth. A car can always be rented for weekend excursions or vacations, almost certainly for less than the price of maintenance year-round and definitely without the aggravation.

For those who wish to rent a furnished house or apartment for less than the normal French lease of three years but for more than the one-week to one-month vacation stay, Paris and its environs offer far more choices than other regions. For a variety of reasons—perhaps a change in jobs, research abroad, or simply desire for an extended vacation—there are furnished homes available to let or sublet. The owners (or lessors in many cases) have a desirable residence and do not wish to lose it, so they will rent it furnished. Since this region has the greatest density of population and it is expensive and difficult to replace a good lodging, people want to hang on to their homes.

Prices for such a rental are always a matter for negotiation. In a sublet, it is unlikely that you will pay less than the price of the original lease and probably more. Wear and tear or possible damage to the furnishings must also be considered. While you might find a studio or two-room apartment for 450 to 500 euros ($405 to $450) per month, larger accommodations are likely to run in the 1,000 to 3,000 euro ($900 to $2,700) range.

It is the larger apartments, those of four rooms or more, that have shown the greatest increase in price. Studios and two-room apartment prices have risen, but not at the same dizzy rate. The average purchase price of housing in Paris is now about 2,700 euros ($2,430) per square meter. You are more likely to find the price of the more desirable residences closer to 4,500 euros ($4,050) per square meter. In most cases, the price per square meter is greater in smaller apartments than in larger ones. Paris apartments are generally small, many of them studios or two rooms. A two- or three-bedroom apartment of 100 square meters is, by middle-class standards, a big place.

As with real estate anywhere, location and quality are the prime ingredients in any purchase. For the best properties in any given neighborhood, the price may be double or more than the average. At the same time, averages are just that: Some properties will sell for less as well as more. But consider some lower prices carefully. The bargain flat may end up costing more than a newer one by the time the cost of renovations are included. Or a less favored neighborhood may have its delightful streets.

In the 6th, 7th, and 16th *arrondissements* (districts of Paris), the average price per square meter topped 3,050 euros ($2,745) by 2000. Sections of other *arrondissements*, such as the 1st, 5th, and 8th, were just as high or even higher, but these latter ones had some neighborhoods with lower average prices as well. Only in the 10th and the 19th was the average price below 2,000 euros ($1,800) per square meter for the entire *arrondissement*.

One rule of thumb is that you cannot tell what a building will be like just from its exterior. You may be able to judge the neighborhood as desirable or not, but you must get beyond the front door and through the courtyard to learn about a building, no matter how uninspiring it may appear from the outside. In some cases, the façade may be all that is left of the original building. In others, the building may have been a beauty from the beginning and either well maintained or tastefully restored.

The Right Bank, the Left Bank

Paris is divided first of all by the Seine River—*Rive Droite* and *Rive Gauche* (Right Bank and Left Bank). The other primary divisions are the *arrondissements*, the 20 districts of the city. Paris is more or less circular, and the *arrondissements* in the center also form a rough circle. They are smaller, more congested, and generally more prestigious than the higher numbered ones that form the outer circle. Since the metro lines all start at different points around the periphery of the city and weave their way to the opposite side, they tend to cross near the center, giving the inner *arrondissements* the best transportation.

The first four *arrondissements* are all on the Right Bank, although the 4th includes the Île St. Louis and most of the Île de la Cité, islands in the Seine, with the 1st claiming the balance of the Île de la Cité. Given the historic character of these *arrondissements* and the lack of vacant lots, there is no new construction here.

These districts include such landmarks as the Louvre, Nôtre Dame cathedral, and the George Pompidou Center of the Arts, or Beauborg as it is more familiarly known. The Marais, the ancient Jewish quarter, bridges the 3rd and 4th *arrondissements* and includes the luxurious Place des Vosges. Today it has become an area much favored by gay visitors to Paris. These districts also are centrally located with good public transportation and lots of cafes. No less than six metro lines pass through the 1st *arrondissement*, for instance.

The less pricey apartments in any of these districts are likely to be those with a lot of nighttime activity and traffic and a somewhat run-down aspect. Even these will likely be 2,500 euros ($2,250) or

One of the more traditional houses that one might encounter

more per square meter. For a better location and perhaps a view of the Seine or the Tuileries garden, the price nearly doubles.

For the very best properties, which rarely come on the market, the price can exceed 11,500 euros ($10,350) per square meter. In 1999, an apartment of 115 square meters on the Île St. Louis in very bad condition but with an exceptional view, sold for 11,825 euros ($10,642) per square meter, or nearly 1.4 million euros ($1.26 million).

For what are probably the least expensive apartments in these districts, look to the outer edge, near Place de la Republique and along Boulevards St. Denis and Strasbourg.

To the north of this core are a semi-circle of five more *arrondisements*—the 8th, 9th, 10th, 11th, and 12th—in clockwise order from west to east. These vary considerably. The Avenue des Champs Elysées divides the 8th. Property here is expensive on either side of the avenue, as it is around the Place de l'Opera in the 9th, in contrast with some of the seedier neighborhoods in the 10th. These five districts also contain the majority of Paris' train stations. These include the Gare St-Lazare on the border between the 8th and 9th, the Gare du Nord and the Gare de l'Est adjacent to each other in the 10th, and the Gare de Lyon in the 12th.

The average price in these districts is about 2,400 euros ($2,160) per square meter. But near the Place de la Bastille, which sits at the intersection of the 4th, 11th, and 12th *arrondissements*, and not far from the 3rd, or near St. Georges in the 9th, prices are likely to be closer to 4,000 euros ($3,600) per square meter.

In the 9th, Pigalle prices have generally been increasing at an above-average rate. The northern borders of the 8th, 9th, and 10th, marked by the district north of Gare St-Lazare in the 8th, and the metro stops at Clichy between the 8th and 9th and Barbès-Rochechouart between the 9th and 10th are probably the least expensive in these *arrondissements*. There are lots of Turkish and North African restaurants and shops in the 10th and some of the boulevards in these working-class neighborhoods have a shabby appearance. But there are also nicer spots near the St. Martin canal.

Moving further from the center, in the 11th, one finds prices beginning at 1,500 euros ($1,350) per square meter near Belleville, but these are likely to be in older buildings and not in the best condition. More likely the average will be 2,000 euros ($1,800) and up. A neighborhood growing more chic by the month along rue Oberkampf in the 11th is already commanding even higher prices, averaging 3,500 euros ($3,150) per square meter for large apartments in new buildings.

In the 12th, around Place de la Nation, prices average 2,000 euros ($1,800) per square meter for apartments in good condition, with the best going for 5,000 euros ($4,500) per square meter and above. In many cases this reflects the proximity of the Bois de Vincennes, a public park that includes the Paris zoo, the museum of natural history, a horse racetrack, and flower gardens, as well as the convenience of five metro lines nearby. The 12th is home to Bercy, the Ministry of Finance. Nearby is located the Bercy Sports Palace and the American Center and the Bercy business park, a very expensive office and commercial area. New buildings here are some of the least expensive in the *arrondissement*, however, with averages of 3,000 to 3,500 euros ($2,700 to $3,150) per square meter.

The heart of the Left Bank is certainly the 5th and 6th *arrondissements*, home to the Latin Quarter, the Sorbonne, the Jardin-des-Plantes (arboretum), the Luxembourg Garden, Ecole des Beaux Arts, and the Pantheon. Boulevard St-Michel, often abbreviated to Boul' Mich', and Boulevard St-Germain are perhaps the two best-known thoroughfares.

Both of these *arrondissements* are stylish, desirable addresses, often the equal in prestige and price to those on the Right Bank. The 5th may get the nod from the intelligentsia and the 6th from wealthy sophisicates, but there is a good mix in both. Five metro lines serve the 5th *arrondissement*. As in the first four *arrondissements* the historic character and lack of vacant land mean there is no new construction.

For those seeking the cultural France—the art, the nightlife, the high fashion, the great food—Paris is the place to be.

The 5th is on the average the less expensive of the two. Here one can count on paying 3,200 to 4,100 euros ($2,880 to $3,690) per square meter for better apartments. There may be some studio and two-room apartments in bad condition in the 1,500 to 2,750 euro ($1,350 to $2,475) range. For newer ones located strategically near the Sorbonne or Val de Grâce hospital, the price increases and ranges from 4,575 to 7,625 euros ($4,117 to $6,862), with larger units commanding the higher prices.

The 7th *arrondissement*, containing the Eiffel tower, National Assembly and many of the ministries, Musée d'Orsay, and the military academy has seen the greatest increase in prices in recent years—up 15 percent in 1999, for instance. One should expect to pay 6,100 to 9,150 euros ($5,490 to $8,235) per square meter for apartments in newer buildings. The area between Avenue Bousquet and the Champ du Mars is somewhat less expensive, with prices averaging 3,800 to 6,100 euros ($3,420 to $5,490) for older renovated apartments.

As with the Right Bank *arrondissements*, as you move further from the center of the city, prices generally decline. South of the 7th is the 15th, one of three *arrondissements* in the outer ring on the Left Bank. Gare Montparnasse straddles the border between the 15th and 14th, almost where they border on the 6th. The area between Necker hospital and Montparnasse is perhaps the most expensive, averaging 3,350 to 6,100 euros ($3,015 to $5,490) per square meter for apartments in good condition. In other areas, you may find older buildings in fair condition for 2,450 to 4,575 euros ($2,205 to $4117) per square meter.

The 14th to the east has some very nice streets and the beautiful park, Montsouris. Average prices here run 2,450 to 3,650 euros ($2,205 to $3,285) per square meter, with prices going much higher—3,800 to 6,100 euros ($3,420 to $5,490) for newer, larger apartments in favored locations.

The 13th borders the Seine on the east. Here is Paris' Chinatown and Gare d'Austerlitz—it faces Gare de Lyon across the river in the 12th. Place d'Italie, an important metro transfer point, and the new Bibiliothèque Nationale are also here. You can find fair apartments in the 2,150 to 2,750 euros ($1,935 to $2,475) per square meter range, but most of the new or renovated units will run from 3,050 to 4,575 euros ($2,745 to $4,117) per square meter.

The *arrondissements* on the outer periphery of the Right Bank contrast greatly. The 16th on the west side is sandwiched between the Seine and the Bois de Boulogne, a 2,000-acre wooded park that was once the hunting ground of kings and over the years, became a favorite prowl of prostitutes and their clients; today it contains two horseracing tracks. The Arc de Triomphe at its northern border, the 16th contains the Trocadero fountains. It is considered the most bourgeois part of the city, not always a compliment in the French lexicon. But it does have many larger apartments, and prices are accelerating faster than in many other parts of the city—up to 15 percent in 1999.

Here even studios in bad condition will start at 1,500 euros ($1,350) per square meter. Anything in fair condition will range from 2,750 to 4,275 euros ($2,475 to $3,847) per square meter. In newer buildings, one should expect to pay 4,575 to 7,625 euros ($4,117 to $6,862) per square meter.

The southern part of the 17th is very similar to the 16th. However, average prices are lower. Around Place des Ternes and Monceau park, you can find good apartments in the 3,800 to 6,100 euro ($3,420 to $5,490) per square meter range. The northern part, separated by the railroad yards leading to the Gare St-Lazare in the 8th, is less pricey, but few larger apartments come on the market. Average prices here range from 2,300 to 4,575 euros ($2,070 to $4117) per square meter.

The 18th arrondissement surrounds Montmartre, the hill on which *Sacre Coeur* (Sacred Heart) basilica stands. Transportation can be a problem, so it is wise to check for metro lines. Many immigrants live in this district; the neighborhood along Boulevard Barbès, for instance, is heavily African and very colorful. Montmartre itself commands good prices, 3,050 to 6,100 euros ($2,745 to $5,490) per square meter, but many other neighborhoods are much lower. Older buildings in fair condition average from 1,375 to 2,450 euros ($1,237 to $2,205) per square meter and renovated and newer buildings bring 2,450 to 3,800 euros ($2,205 to $3,420) per square meter.

The 19th is probably the most isolated in Paris, so transportation may be a consideration. The area around the Stalingrad metro stop on the border between the 10th and the 19th is also notorious for addicts and drug dealing. Paris' largest park, Buttes-Chaumont, is located in the 19th, as is the National Conservatory. Old buildings in good condition here will bring 1,825 to 2,750 euros ($1,642 to $2,475) per square meter; in new buildings, prices average from 2,450 to 3,650 euros ($2,205 to $3,285) per square meter.

The 20th *arrondissement* contains the famous Père Lachaise cemetery. Most of the neighborhoods are working class and there is a mix of races and ethnic groups. The western neighborhoods along Boulevards Belleville and Ménilmontant are certainly coming up as the 3rd (Marais) and the adjacent 11th have done. The area around Place Gambetta on the eastern side of Père Lachaise has shown big increases in price recently. Apartments in fair condition average from 1,500 to 2,750 euros ($1,350 to $2,475) per square meter, while new buildings go from 2,600 to 4,275 euros ($2,340 to $3,847) per square meter.

Les Banlieues: The Suburbs of Paris

Surrounding Paris, with its more than two million residents, is the rest of Île-de-France, the name of the province comprising Paris and the seven surrounding departments. This region is home to another nine million people. The area of the province is 12,011 square kilometers (4,637 square miles), about the size of three Rhode Islands but smaller than Connecticut. The seven departments form two concentric circles around Paris. The inner ring, or *petite couronne,* consists of three departments. Four more form the *grande couronne.* While in past ages the Paris basin has been rich agricultural land, urban sprawl limits most of the farming to the *grande couronne,* where sugar beets, wheat, and corn are major crops.

The Sarthe département from above

Aid for Academics

Each year hundreds of American researchers arrive in France to pursue their studies at scores of universities and institutes. Most of them are Ph.D. candidates or post-docs—those who have their degree and are pursuing a particular line of research.

Almost all of them need help with housing and many have families. Trying to relocate a household is never simple; to do it in a foreign academic setting can be much more difficult.

Fortunately, there is help available. One source is the Alfred Kastler Foundation, established in 1993 by the Academy of Sciences and based in Strasbourg. Its goals are to guide scientists and scholars through the inevitable red tape and see them comfortably settled as soon as possible in France.

Part of the foundation's efforts include helping the researcher's family establish themselves in the community, entering local schools, finding child care if needed, and so on. However, the foundation's primary goal is to ensure that the scientist's stay in France is productive and that the collaboration between French and foreign researchers continues even when the scientist returns to his or her own country.

Even before arriving in France, the scientist can announce his or her plans and begin to receive advice about necessary documents to prepare as well as practical help obtaining insurance and opening a bank account, both of which can be accomplished via the foundation's website, .

France has dozens of institutions to which are given long names descriptive of their functions. The long names are quickly shortened to initials, resulting in an alphabet soup of acronyms, listed below. Each organization has websites, its address constructed as www.[acronym].fr. The website for CNRS, for example, is www.cnrs.fr.

Public establishments for scientific and technical research:
CEMAGREF *Centre national du machinisme agricole, du génie rural, des eaux et des forêts*
CNRS *Centre national de la recherche scientifique*
INED *Institut national d'études démographiques*

There are no real peaks in this region—Paris sits in a basin. None of the few hills tops 1,000 feet in elevation. However, the numerous rivers feeding into the Seine as it snakes its way to the ocean create a series of valleys and ridges that are covered by many wooded areas.

A regional network of trains called the RER (Réseau Express Régional), whose lines cross Paris and connect with the metro as well as the national rail system, serves as the major public transit system. For either commuting or just occasional forays into the city, the RER plays a major role. In addition, many of the metro lines themselves extend well into the departments of the *petite couronne*.

There is a great deal of difference between the various suburbs, as might be expected. Some are wealthy bastions, others with huge public housing developments have concentrated pockets of poverty and unemployment. One thing to note about the Parisian suburbs, unlike American ones, is that they remain small towns. The largest of them and the only one with a population greater than 100,000 is Boulogne-Billancourt, where Renault was founded.

Most of the suburban growth has taken place since 1950. Beginning in 1954, France began building very large high-rise complexes with more than

INRA *Institut national de la recherche agronomique*
INRETS *Institut national de recherche sur les transports et leur sécurité*
INRIA *Institut national de recherche en informatique et en automatique*
INSERM *Institut national de la santé et de la recherche médicale*
IRD *Institut de recherche pour le développement*
LCPC *Laboratoire central des ponts et chaussées*

Public establishments for industrial and commercial research:
ADEME *Agence de l'environnement et de la maîtrise de l'énergie*
ADIT *Agence pour la diffusion de l'information technologique*
ANDRA *Agence nationale de gestion des déchets radioactifs*
ANVAR *Agence nationale de valorisation de la recherche*
BRGM *Bureau de recherches géologiques et minières*
CEA *Commissariat à l'énergie atomique*
CIRAD *Centre de coopération international en recherche agronomique*

CNDP *Centre national de documentation pédagogique*
CNED *Centre national d'enseignement à distance*
CNES *Centre national d'études spatiales*
CSI *Cité des sciences et de l'industrie*
CSTB *Centre scientifique et technique du bâtiment*
IFREMER *Institut français de recherche pour l'exploitation de la mer*
INERIS *Institut national de l'environnement industriel et des risques*
ONERA *Office national d'études et de recherches aérospatiales*

Public interest agencies:
ANRS *Agence nationale de la recherche contre le SIDA* (SIDA is French for AIDS)
CNG *Centre national de génotypage*
CNS *Génoscope Centre national de séquençage*
OST *Observatoire des sciences et techniques*
RENATER *Réseau national pour la technologie, l'enseignement et la recherche*

500 apartments. (The first of these, Sarcelles, totaled 2,000 units.) A little over a decade later, the emphasis changed. New towns with individual houses, smaller apartment buildings and little shopping streets were created and supplied with transit, libraries, swimming pools, and other civic amenities. These new towns were actually groups of villages and developments with open land between and separate identities.

Another decade later and the emphasis changed again, this time in favor of development centered in older towns. As a result, you can find almost any sort of residence scattered through the departments—the worst of it a hodge-podge of unattractive sprawl, but the best of it superb development in this cradle of the French nation.

THE INNER CIRCLE: HAUTS-DE-SEINE, SEINE-ST-DENIS, AND VAL-DE-MARNE

The most favored towns are those just beyond the most prized outer *arrondissements* of Paris, the 16th and 17th on the west, the 12th through the 15th on the south, and the 20th on the east. These are the *proche banlieues* (nearby suburbs), with excellent transit connections into the city. The suburbs to the west, south, and southwest lie in the departments of Hauts-de Seine (92) and Val-de-Marne (94).

Suburbs to the north and northeast in the department of Seine-St-Denis are the poorest. They have experienced high unemployment and higher crime and delinquency rates than others. But rising costs in the city combined with proximity have begun the process of gentrification.

One town in particular, Montreuil, has been particularly successful in attracting young families. Directly east of the center of Paris, Montreuil (pop. 90,500) is the third largest in the region and culturally active, sponsoring a blues festival and a children's book fair. Prices here were running about 2,000 euros ($1,800) per square meter at the end of 1999 for new buildings with all conveniences and perhaps 16 to 18 percent less for older buildings in top condition.

The prices rise as one follows the curve of the city to the northwest: Les Lilas fetched up to 2,000 euros ($1,800) per square meter for older buildings while the best new ones brought 2,600 euros ($2,340) per square meter. Houses around Place Charles de Gaulle sold for 380,000 euros ($342,000) while others in less favorable areas were half that price.

Just above Les Lilas, in Le Pré St. Gervais some newly constructed luxury apartments of five or more rooms went for 2,750 euros ($3,375) per square meter. But older buildings were under 1,500 euros (41,350) per square meter while houses sold for 200,000 to 250,000 euros ($180,000 to $225,000).

Directly north of the city, proximity and good transit into Paris from the communes of St-Denis and Pantin, Bobigny, and Aubervilliers keep prices in the 1,200 to 2,000 euros ($1,080 to $1,800) per square meter range, depending on condition and other variables.

Further north in the department, they begin to drop. To the northeast in Sevran, four-room houses began at about 140,000 euros ($126,000). In the eastern part of the department, very nice older houses went for 305,000 euros ($274,500).

In the Val-de-Marne, the department on the eastern and southern sides of Paris that takes its name from the Marne River, one favored town is St-Mandé. With Paris on one side and the Bois de Vincennes on another, it has prices ranging up to 4,700 euros ($4,230) per square meter for new large luxury apartments. Further south and further east in Charenton, Joinville, and St-Maurice, prices dropped to the 2,900 to 3,200 euros ($2,610 to $2,880) per square meter range, with older units in good condition dropping to 2,000 to 2,750 euros ($1,800 to $2,475) per square meter.

In Nogent-sur-Marne, which sits near the intersection of autoroutes A3 and A4, new construction in the center of town ranged from 2,450 to 3,800 euros ($2,200–$3,420) per square meter. But older apartments to renovate could be found for less than 1,500 euros ($1,350) per square meter. The few houses that came on the market sold for 230,000 to 305,000 euros. Not far away in Joinville, houses sold between 200,000 and 250,000 euros.

Once away from both the Bois de Vincennes and the Marne, prices drop. At Maisons-Alfort, Vitry- and Ivry-sur-Seine, and Creteil, one could find older renovated buildings in good condition for 1,375 to 1,825 euros ($1,237 to $1,642) per square meter.

Adjacent to the entire western side of Paris is the department of Hauts-de-Seine (92). Those towns close to some of Paris' more expensive real estate in the 15th, 16th, and 17th *arrondissements* and with the Bois de Boulogne also at hand command prices higher than many Parisian neighborhoods. Levallois-Perret, Neuilly-sur-Seine, St. Cloud, and Boulogne all brought between 3,800 and 6,900 euros ($3,420 to $6,210) per square meter on the average for larger apartments in new or newly renovated buildings.

These towns, along with the Bois de Boulogne, are contained within a loop of the Seine, between the river and Paris. The Seine arcs through Paris, exiting the city's southwest corner. Almost immediately, it abruptly turns north and finally northeast, creating this exclusive enclave.

In the northwestern part of the department, the vast business park called La Defense dominates another loop of the Seine. The unpredictable river, after curving around Paris to the north, changes direction again. In a 180-degree turnabout, it meanders southwest toward St-Germain-en-Laye. La Defense lies between these two folds of the Seine. Nearby Nanterre and Courbevoie both have renovated buildings in good condition in the 2,300 to 2,750 euros ($2,070 to $2,475) per square meter range.

THE OUTER CIRCLE: VAL-D'OISE, ESSONNE, YVELINES, AND SEINE-ET-MARNE

Once beyond the *petite couronne*, the possibilities begin to open up. In nearly every direction are historic names and forested land. St-Germain-en-Laye, birthplace of Louis XIV, lies at the south end of the forest of the same name with its golf course and racetrack. (Note: At the north end of this area is one of the world's largest sewer plants. For years, nearby residents have complained of odor.) Southwest is Versailles and further on, Rambouillet. North is Montmorency and Chantilly; southeast is Fontainebleau. Disneyland Paris is to the east.

South of Paris is Orly airport with its nearby TGV line and Rungis, the vast wholesale market that replaced Les Halles in Paris when the Pompidou Centre was built three decades ago. It is also home to a large number of research institutes, think tanks, and schools. An RER line passes through the Chevreuse valley, and the towns along it are very popular. Another TGV line serves the north side of Paris—Charles de Gaulle airport and Disneyland on the east.

Development has generally followed transportation, and locating near a rail line or autoroute may be a convenience for those who anticipate coming and going with some frequency. It can be a mixed blessing, however, when the autoroutes are jammed with commuters and vacationers.

The largest and least expensive department in the province is Seine-et-Marne, covering the eastern 40 percent of province. East of Disneyland is the old city of Meaux (pop. 63,000), famous for its brie cheese. Houses in its historic sections caught between the coils of the Marne River sell for 300,000 and 450,000 euros ($270,000 and $405,000). Apartments are about 1,500 euros ($1,350) per square meter, falling to 1,050 to 1,200 euros ($945 to $1,080) in more modern neighborhoods. Old houses in nearby towns in need of repairs may be found for 75,000 to 120,000 euros ($67,500 to $108,000).

Closer to Paris and near Disneyland is one of the new towns—actually a grouping of separate communes—called Marne-la-Vallée. In the area called Val Maubée, apartments go for between 1,500 and 1,800 euros ($1,350 to $1,620) per square meter. Houses sell for 140,000 to 215,000 euros ($126,000 to $193,500).

> *One thing to note about the Parisian suburbs, unlike American ones, is that they remain small towns.*

South from Meaux along the Grand Morin River are villages such as Crécy-la-Chapelle, known as "Little Venice" for its network of small canals, and Coulommiers, another town famous for brie.

Closer to Fontainebleau is the new town of Melun-Sénart. Here apartments range from 1,300 to 1,450 euros ($1,170 to $1,305) per square meter with houses beginning at 114,575 euros ($103,117). Older houses in these areas go for between 750 and 1,150 euros ($675 to $1,035) per square meter.

At Fontainebleau, houses rarely come on the market. Apartments average 1,500 to 2,300 euros ($1,350 to $2,070) per square meter, but that is only an average. One that was 130 square meters recently sold for nearly 460,000 euros ($414,000).

Directly south of Paris is the department of Essonne (91). Here are numerous university and scientific research institutes. Well served by rail and autoroutes, with Orly not far, it offers areas close to Paris that are wooded and calm. In the valleys of the Bièvre and Yvette Rivers, for example, there is no new construction and you can find apartments costing between 1,450 and 2,500 euros ($1,305 to $2,250) per square meter. Large houses, when they can be found, sell for 230,000 to 400,000 euros ($207,000 to $360,000). Apartments range from 1,500 to 2,000 euros ($1,350 to $1,800) per square meter.

Not all of the departments are so expensive. In Massy, houses sell for 150,000 to 220,000 euros ($135,000 to $198,000). Older apartments may be found for 900 to 1,400 euros ($810 to $1,260) per square meter, with new ones going as high as 1,900 euros ($1,710) per square meter. South of Orly airport in the valley of the Orge River, one must pay 1,500 to 2,000 euros ($1,350 to $1,800) per square meter for new apartments in the towns with good rail service to Paris. Older units—except those overlooking the Orge—range from 850 to 1,150 euros ($765 to $1,035) per square meter.

The department of Yvelines (78) lies east of Paris and the Hauts-de-Seine (92). It contains three historic towns once the homes of French royalty, all with forests and gardens to match: Versailles, St-Germain-en-Laye, and Rambouillet. It is also a department where prices are about the same as Paris. They rose an average of 16 percent in 1999. One reason may be that relatively few properties were for sale.

In Versailles and St-Germain-en-Laye, new apartments ranged from 3,000 to 4,000 euros ($2,700 to $3,600) per square meter, while older units brought 1,850 to 3,000 euros ($1,665 to $2,700). In St-Germain-en-Laye, even units in very bad condition needing a great deal of work brought an average of 750 euros ($675) per square meter.

Rambouillet, much further from Paris, had no new construction but older apartments in better neighborhoods sold for 1,850 to 2,250 euros ($1,665 to $2,025) per square meter. Prices dropped in less desirable areas to 1,100 to 1,350 euros ($990 to $1,215) per square meter.

East of the St. Germain Forest along the banks of the Seine and a good half-hour by train from Paris, you find prices moderating. In Poissy, for example, new apartments sell for average prices between 1,650 and 2,400 euros ($1,485 to $2,160) per square meter, while older ones brought 900 to 1,350 euros ($810 to $1,215) per square meter. New houses were selling for 140,000 to 200,000 euros ($126,000 to $180,000).

Val d'Oise (95) is the northernmost department in the Île-de-France. It stretches east to west across the top of three other departments. Its southeastern corner, bordering Seine-St-Denis and Hauts-de-Seine, is close to Paris and densely populated. At Argenteuil, an industrial city of about 100,000, new apartments average from 1,400 to 1,950 euros ($1,260 to $1,755) per square meter, while older, unrenovated units go for 800 to 1,000 euros ($720 to $900) per square meter.

Further north, the more desirable areas of Montmorency, with its forest, and Enghien-les-Bains, boasting a lake, prices increase. Around the lake, apartments average 2,250 to 3,000 euros ($2,025 to $2,700) per square meter, while away from it and in Montmorency, prices rose from about 1,200 euros ($1,080) per square meter for older apartments up to 2,200 euros ($1,980) for new ones. Houses ranged from 230,000 to 400,000 euros ($207,000 to $360,000).

Moving away from Paris, in towns like Taverny, prices drop, with very small houses selling for 115,000 euros ($103,500) and one in stone going for 200,000 euros ($180,000). In the new town of Cergy-Pontoise and the older town of Pontoise, new apartments sold for 1,400 to 1,650 euros ($1,260 to $1,485) per square meter; older units, from 1,000 to 1,450 euros ($900 to $1,305) per square meter. Stand-alone houses near a golf course begin at 230,000 euros ($207,000).

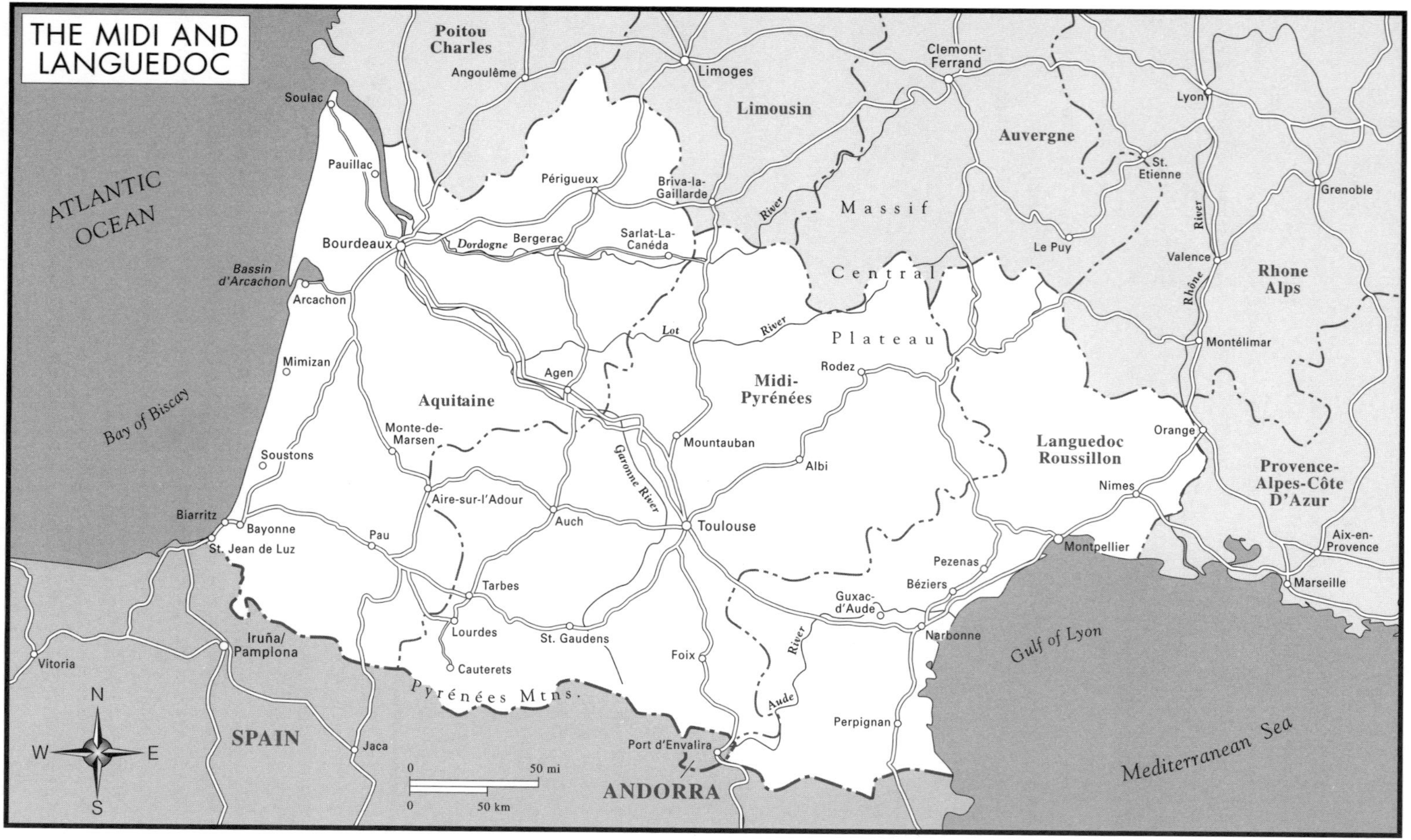
THE MIDI AND LANGUEDOC
ATLANTIC OCEAN
Bay of Biscay
Poitou Charles
Limousin
Auvergne
Rhone Alps
Massif Central
Plateau
Aquitaine
Midi-Pyrénées
Languedoc Roussillon
Provence-Alpes-Côte D'Azur
Gulf of Lyon
Mediterranean Sea
Pyrénées Mtns.
SPAIN
ANDORRA
Angoulême
Limoges
Clemont-Ferrand
Lyon
Soulac
Pauillac
Périgueux
Briva-la-Gaillarde
St. Etienne
Grenoble
Bourdeaux
Dordogne
Bergerac
Sarlat-La-Canéda
Le Puy
Valence
Rhône River
River
Bassin d'Arcachon
Arcachon
Lot River
Montélimar
Mimizan
Rodez
Agen
Monte-de-Marsen
Mountauban
Albi
Orange
Soustons
Garonne River
Aire-sur-l'Adour
Nimes
Biarritz
Bayonne
Auch
Toulouse
Pau
St. Jean de Luz
Montpellier
Aix-en-Provence
Pezenas
Marseille
Tarbes
Béziers
Guxac-d'Aude
Lourdes
St. Gaudens
Narbonne
Iruña/Pamplona
Vitoria
Foix
Cauterets
Aude River
Perpignan
Jaca
Port d'Envalira
0
50 mi
0
50 km
N
W
E
S

15 The Midi and Languedoc

Between the Pyrénées and the Massif Central lies an island of high tech in a sea of wine. Southern France between the Atlantic and the Mediterranean, from the Spanish border along the crest of the Pyrénées as far north as Bordeaux and the desolate southern reaches of the Massif Central, remains one of the least appreciated yet most attractive parts of the country. Whether you prefer the sun and sand of the Atlantic and Mediterranean coasts, hiking and skiing in the steep Pyrénées, or the wooded hills and river valleys of the Massif Central, this region has everything you might want in France except Paris. Exploring this region from west to east to discover the many similarities and significant differences of this area will help you determine where you might locate.

The westernmost of the three regions that comprise this territory is Aquitaine, with three million people in five departments: Gironde, Pyrénées-Atlantique, Dordogne, Landes, and Lot-et-Garonne. Gironde, with Bordeaux as its heart and soul, is the most populous and fastest growing. While the province as a whole grew 3.8 percent from 1990 to 1999, Gironde grew by 5.9 percent. It was rivaled only by Landes, the department immediately south of Gironde, which grew by an even five percent. Bordeaux is Aquitaine's major city.

With its pricey, world-famous wines and historic ties to the U.K., Bordeaux is justly regarded as the most bourgeois area of France outside of

Paris' 16th *arrondissement*. In this city, formality reigns and pedigree is more important than achievement.

Northeast of Bordeaux from Perigeux to Agen, you will find wetter, more rugged terrain and numerous Anglophones, mostly British and Dutch who have retired here or own second homes. The beaches from Bordeaux south to Biarritz and the pine forests behind them provide a great playground most of the year. The southwestern part of Aquitaine is Basque country, where the strikingly different language makes it possible to believe you are no longer in France.

South of Bordeaux, in the middle of the territory (hence, the region's name: the Midi), lies Toulouse, a great city with a fine university and an industrial base. Boeing's only rival, Airbus, is built here, as are the European Ariane rockets. Grapes grow here and there, but are greatly overshadowed in importance by grain.

> *If you love wine, foie gras, armagnac brandy, truffles, cheese, hot summers, mild winters, and stone houses ... this region will appeal to you.*

The eastern third of this vast territory is sparsely populated Languedoc, another great wine-producing area, its southern corner an extension of Catalonia, its inland reaches dry and rugged. Its wide, sandy Mediterranean beaches and similarities to Provence have encouraged an influx of foreigners in the past decade, some of them Americans. They come seeking vacation homes; few have settled here permanently.

The southern part of this territory is dominated by the Pyrénées, standing along the horizon like a wall around Heaven. From them flow rivers such as the Garonne and the Aude, which, along with their tributaries, wind through the plains below. The Pyrénées are as indisputably the southern boundary of France as the Atlantic is its western border.

The northern part of this territory recalls the Pyrénées' rugged terrain without ever competing in magnitude with that range's peaks. The uplift of the Massif Central plateau and bordering hills such as the Montagne Noir contribute greatly to the watershed with rivers such as the Dordogne, Lot, and Tarn flowing into the Garonne and the Herault. The Orb brings their waters to the east.

In the center lies a rich agricultural region producing grain, vegetables, meat, and fruit in abundance. But the region's most widely known crop is wine, from some of the most famous and expensive in the world—the first growths of Bordeaux—to *vin de pays* scarcely known beyond the villages where it is made.

If you love wine, foie gras, armagnac brandy, truffles, cheese, hot summers, mild winters, and stone houses, and prefer to live within easy reach of the big city amenities of Bordeaux, Montpellier, and Toulouse, this region will appeal to you.

Bordeaux

Bourgeois Bordeaux may be known as a haven for the beautiful people, but regular folks live here too. By French standards, it's a relatively big city, with a population of 215,000. Housing choices are varied.

Much of property along the Garonne River in Bordeaux has been undergoing renovation. Old warehouses are being demolished and building façades restored, especially in the neighborhood called Chartrons. On the river itself, prices climbed as much as 15 percent in six months during 1999. Renovated apartments that averaged about 1,375 euros ($1,237) per square meter at the beginning of 1999 were bringing 1,825 euros ($1,642) per square meter by the end of the year.

Little stone one-story houses from the 19th century called *échoppes* that were once the homes of laborers are much prized today and represent an important architectural style in the region. Most of these, away from the center of the city, have already passed 180,000 euros ($162,000). Bigger houses bring even higher prices, on the order of 250,000 euros ($225,000). Those searching for an *échoppe* at a lesser price should cross to the less fashionable side of the river where they are more prevalent and average about 150,000 euros ($135,000). Apartments in that district average 800 to 900 euros ($720 to $810) per square meter.

In the so-called *Triangle d'Or* (Triangle of Gold) in the center of the city, the average price per square meter of new luxury studio and two-room apartments approach 2,300 euros ($2,070) per square meter. Large units bring 1,625 euros ($1,462) per square meter while three- and four-room

The village of Caunes-Minervois, near Carcassonne

units sell for an average of 1,300 euros ($1,170) per square meter. Perhaps the least costly district in Bordeaux is La Victoire. Here one can find old apartments from 800 to 1,000 euros ($720 to $900) per square meter and new ones beginning at 1,150 euros ($1,035) per square meter.

For similar units on the outskirts of the city, prices declined by 10 to 12 percent. For older units, the prices were significantly less, falling to below 1,000 euros ($900) per square meter for all but the best. Houses likewise declined in price away from the center, although in the nicer suburbs among the famous vineyards, prices climb back up. Even small houses here start around 170,000 euros ($153,000).

Wine on Both Coasts

Wine is king in Languedoc, just as surely as it is in Bordeaux. Every wine lover knows the names of the great wines of Bordeaux, such as Châteaux Margaux, Latour, and Yquem. The châteaux were classified in 1855 into first, second, third, fourth, and fifth growths according to quality. It was a ranking based on the track record of the wines over the years. These rankings have gone unchanged, though not unchallenged. Yet they have stood the test of time, if only as a superb marketing tool.

As with most systems of inherited nobility, however, a great deal of snobbery and elitism have grown up around these wines, having little to do with their quality and much to do with the wealth of those who own the estates and those to whom high prices and good taste are synonymous.

Languedoc engages in a different sort of wine trade. In place of the grand châteaux of the 17th and 18th centuries, the bourgeois mansions and the international jet set that the last 150 years have produced on the Atlantic coast, you find small domains and châteaux where the owner may work side by side in the field with the hired hands. Here wine may come from a tin-roofed shed attached to small modern house with a child's tricycle in the yard or from huge cooperatives that serve scores of small farmers with machinery and expertise.

It's a different kind of wine too. This is wine that people drink week in and week out, that you can afford to drink every day. It's wine that you can buy by the liter for less than the price of gasoline, delivered by the same kind of hose and nozzle that delivers gas from the pump.

But don't be led astray by the rural charm of Languedoc wine production. Today the knowledge and skills to make wine of excellent quality are universal. Where once the wines of Languedoc were stored in concrete vats, stainless steel tanks and oak barrels are now commonplace. Carbonic maceration, temperature-controlled fermentation and all the other techniques of modern wine-making are used.

Any country, any region hospitable to *vitis vinifera,* has the potential for making world-class wine. California proved that a generation ago. Now it's being proven in Languedoc, where the plebian reputation of the past works to the wineries' advantage.

In contrast, the Burgundy and Bordeaux regions are extremely limited in the grape varieties they can grow under the French *Appellation d'Origine Contrôlée* (AOC) system, if only because the land is too valuable to do anything else. The AOC restricts the wines so labeled to traditional varieties of grapes for that region; wines that do not conform must be labeled as *vin de pays* or *vin de table* and bring a much lower price.

Languedoc is a patchwork of *vin de pays*

Around Bordeaux

North and east of Bordeaux, vineyards dot both sides of the river. Just above Bordeaux, the Dordogne River joins the Garonne, and the estuary widens and becomes the Gironde. The famous communes of Margaux, Pauillac, St, Julien, and St. Estéphe line the west bank while the lesser-known Cotes du Bourg lies opposite on the eastern side. To the east of Bordeaux lie Libourne and the vineyards of St. Emilion. Southeast of Bordeaux are the vineyards of the sweet wines of Sauternes and Barsac.

Land in these regions is valuable; vines are planted everywhere and the spacious grounds of châteaux elsewhere in France are often absent.

vineyards and AOC regions, some only a few years old with little recognition. Some of these areas produce Rhône-style wines, themselves blends of half a dozen different varieties of grapes, giving all those varieties legitimacy for AOC wines. Still other areas grow chardonnay, cabernet sauvignon, sauvignon blanc, merlot—all of them grapes known around the world.

Thus the wine growers of Limoux who have long used chardonnay and chenin blanc grapes to make a sparkling wine can also bottle these as still wines and compete with chardonnays from all over the world. When wine lovers in London or Amsterdam or San Francisco pits the bottle from Limoux against that from Napa or Burgundy, they consider the taste of the wine in relation to the price, not just the price.

This is part of the Languedoc advantage. A wine grower need not be concerned with the AOC system. Chardonnay grown in Languedoc, for instance, was being sold in Mâcon as Pouilly-Fuissé a few years ago. It was a tip from someone in the region, not from any disgruntled customers, that brought about the fraud investigation.

But Languedoc producers don't have to resort to subterfuge to sell their wines around the world. Often marketed as *"vin de pays d'Oc"* and labeled with name of the grape varietal, they sell well all over Europe and in the States. Robert Mondavi, who collaborated two decades ago with Baron Philippe de Rothschild to produce the $50-a-bottle Opus One in California, now imports cabernet sauvignon, syrah, and five other varietals from Languedoc. In fact, there is wine being produced in Languedoc that cannot be purchased there—it is all being exported.

The most expensive *vin de pays d'Oc* is that of Mas de Daumas Gassac near Montpellier. In 1970, Aimé Guibert set about to produce a world-class wine. Advised by the great French oenologist Emile Péynaud, he did so by planting cabernet sauvignon vines selected from an old Médoc vineyard. The gamble—and a lot of hard work—paid off. Today Daumas Gassac wine sells around the world at top Bordeaux and California prices, when you can find them.

None of this means the traditional AOC wines have been abandoned in Languedoc. Rather, the average has steadily improved as a younger generation of winemakers have taken over, recognizing that mediocre quality is no longer viable economically. Both wine cooperatives and individual growers now routinely produce both AOC wines and *vin de pays* varietals. And their wines are finding a ready market at home as well as abroad, selling out at once-unheard of prices as high as 10 euros ($9) a bottle.

You'll find no bargains these days with the spiraling prices of these wines. Even in St. Emilion, a small vineyard is worth about 60,000 euros ($54,000) per acre. However, house prices in Libourne, about 30 kilometers (18.6 miles) from Bordeaux, and the small villages surrounding it are much less than those in the suburbs surrounding Bordeaux on the other side of the river. Small village houses begin at 50,000 euros ($45,000) and larger homes with gardens, at 80,000 euros ($72,000).

East from St. Emilion is the Dordogne, the department that takes its name from the river. This region is beloved by the English who move to France. Its numerous little villages have proved such a magnet for them that it is widely expected that some of these villages will have British mayors after the 2001 elections now that property owners from other EU countries can vote in French local elections.

Principal towns include Bergerac, Périgueux, and Sarlat. With a population of 30,000, Périgueux is the largest of the three. The entire department contains less than 400,000 people. Water is plentiful as numerous rivers and streams tumble through the rocky escarpment of the Massif Central. Farmhouses and villages line the river valleys and dot the wooded, sometimes rugged landscape. This is the region of Lascaux and other caves with the magnificent prehistoric cave art, perhaps 17,000 years old.

Medieval stone arches, St. Emilion

Much of the land from the Atlantic east, north and west of Bordeaux, is covered with pine forests and lagoons and wetlands until you reach the vineyards along the banks of the Gironde. The Bassin d'Arcachon, a shallow bay and marine preserve, is the most prominent feature on the coast. It stands at the northern end of the great regional park, *Landes de Gascogne*, covering 290,000 hectares (700,000 acres) southwest of Bordeaux.

Close to Bordeaux, Arcachon sits contentedly on its bay with beach and boating and all the recreational opportunities of the regional park not far to the

Abercrombie and Kent

southwest. Across the Gironde from Bordeaux, you will find land in the St. Emilion less expensive than among the vineyards of the great chateaux. Heading along the Dordogne river into the Perigord, the countryside around larger cities such as Libourne, Bergerac, and Sarlat is dotted with small villages. From here to Albi and south to the Garonne you will find little but farms and small villages in wooded, hilly settings. These villages have long been favorites of the British, who have either moved, or own vacation homes, here.

The park is a tremendous recreational area and much of the land between its western edge and the Atlantic beaches is forested and dotted with lagoons. Towns such as Sabres and Pissos in the park itself, and Mimizan, Castets, and Soustons, remain comfortably small yet close to larger cities such as Dax and Mont-de-Marsan.

These towns serve as something of a dividing line between the pine forests of Landes and the uplands leading into the Pyrénées. From Bayonne south, the towns of Biarritz, Hendaye, and St. Jean de Luz line the coast to the Spanish border. From St. Jean de Luz, you can follow highway D918, the Route du Fromage, inland. It leads to St. Jean Pied-de-Port and, from there, deeper and higher into Basque country.

Basque homes always appear neat and freshly painted—usually white with red shutters, except for the large rectangular stones that form the corners of each wall and are left bare, the shape emphasizing the sturdy square structures of two or three stories.

Moving east you remain in Basque country but enter the region of Midi-Pyrénées. In the foothills of the Pyrénées are Pau and Tarbes looking

Pays

The region comprising Bordeaux, the Midi, and Languedoc is a vast one with many *pays*, a word the French use to denote both nations and ill-defined regions without legal boundaries—such as Southern California, or upstate New York, or the American Midwest. In France, *pays* may simply refer to an agricultural region where climate and terrain dictate a certain kind of farming.

I live in a *pays* called Minervois, which today refers to a particular wine region. The farmers here grow the same grapes and produce a similar wine to those of the adjacent Corbières, but a range of hills dominated by Mont Alaric separates the Corbières and the Minervois, just as a spur of the Montagne Noire separates the Minevois from the Cabardes.

An area may also have gone by different names during its long history. What today we call Languedoc, the Visigoths who ruled there in the 5th and 6th centuries called Septimania, a name rarely seen but still remembered today. Languedoc today refers to the political region of Languedoc-Roussillon, rather than the much broader area covering nearly one-half of modern France, where *oc* rather than *oïl* meant yes. Scores of smaller divisions and appellations have been all but forgotten by the wider world during two millennia.

onto the fertile plains to the north. These and other cities further east such as St. Gaudens serve as market towns for the villages in the foothills. Some of these, such as St. Bertrand de Comminges, are quite lovely and have proved attractive for second homes.

Throughout the Pyrénées are slopes and trails for winter skiing, both downhill and cross-country, and for hiking or cycling in the summer. Most of these spots are one to two hours from cities in the warmer plain formed by the Garonne River and its numerous tributaries.

Toulouse

In the center of this territory, in the Midi region, is Toulouse, *la Ville rose*, once a Visigoth capital and now the heart of France's aerospace industry. The Ariane rocket and Airbus jetliners are built here. The super-jumbo Airbus 3XX, capable of carrying 600 passengers and representing an investment of more than 12 billion euros ($10.8 billion) also will be assembled here.

Much of this high-tech industry is built on a population that is well educated. The university of Toulouse continues to attract high-caliber students and professors. Some 110,000 students attend the university on campuses spread throughout the city. Toulouse is second only to Paris as a center of higher learning in France. Some 10,000 researchers work in 340 public and private institutes.

Growth in Toulouse surpassed that in Bordeaux during the last decade. Toulouse itself increased by 8.9 percent to 390,000 people; the surrounding department of Haute-Garonne topped that with a 12.9 percent increase to more than 1 million people. It is the fourth-largest metropolitan area in France after Paris, Lyon, and Marseille.

All this growth resulted in a 15 to 20 percent rise in the number of property sales in 1999 accompanied by a similar increase in prices. The prized small, one-story, four-room *toulousaines* houses near the center of the city now on average exceed 215,000 euros ($193,500). New apartments in the same areas go for around 2,000 euros ($1,800) per square meter.

In the Busca district, a house of 75 square meters sold in 1999 for more than 150,000 euros ($135,000). In the same area, new apartments went as high as 2,400 euros ($2,160) per square meter, while older ones sold for 12 to 15 percent less. In Roseraie, a district on the periphery of the city, tiny houses of 50 square meters with a 300-square-meter garden sell for as little as 66,000 euros ($59,400) while a much larger 170-square-meter house with a bigger garden might bring more than 200,000 euros ($180,000). Apartments in this district can be found for slightly more than 1,000 euros ($900) per square meter.

Toulouse opened a single metro line a few years ago that cuts across the city northeast to southwest. This configuration gave residents who wanted to live near it a wide choice. In the center, around Place du Capitole, the large square in front of city hall, apartments went as high as 1,450 euros ($1,305) per square meter, while at Jolimont, the end of the metro line, they averaged about 1,200 euros ($1,080) per square meter.

Some consider housing built in the 1960s in the southeast section of the city, near the scientific complex of Rangueil, a great bargain. These apartments have modern appointments and are much more spacious than some of the new units elsewhere in the city. They average 600 to 800 euros ($540 to $720) per square meter. This is also a good district to look for houses, since many of those in suburban Ramonville and Castanet not far to the south are priced at the 300,000 euro ($270,000) level.

Around Toulouse

Surrounding Toulouse is a rolling plain with farmhouses dotting the ridgelines and villages tucked away in the folds of the hills. Corn and maize, barley and sunflowers fill the landscape of the Lauragais, as the region is called. Cintagabelle, the home of Prime Minister Lionel Jospin, is not far from Toulouse. The Ariege River flows through here before joining the Garonne near Toulouse. Many of the villages within 10 kilometers (about 6 miles) of Toulouse have become quite suburban as city growth has pushed outward. But beyond them in every direction are villages that retain their agricultural charm. Larger towns such as Auterive to the south or Montauban to the north serve as market centers.

Following the Garonne and the canal that parallels it northwest from Toulouse, the countryside remains much the same until you gradually come upon the Massif Central.

> *Corn and maize, barley and sunflowers fill the landscape of the Lauragais*

This is Quercy, not a department or province, but the name commonly given to the area covered by the departments of the Tarn, the Lot, and the Lot-et-Garonne. Similar and with many of the same features as the Dordogne and Perigord, small farms and villages are typical of the region.

Agen, a city along the Garonne and the canal and the autoroute between Toulouse and Bordeaux, once served as the southern port for the region, loading its produce onto barges. *Prunes de Agen* gained their name not because they were all grown in Agen, but because they were shipped from there. Tobacco is another historically important crop of the region.

Rocamadour, the tiny village built into the side of a cliff where pilgrims came to worship at the altar of the black Virgin, is in the Lot. Truffles and mushrooms, fruit, walnuts, foie gras, and *charcuterie* (cooked meats) are common products. And, of course, wine: Bergerac, Cahors, Gaillac, and Monbazillac are all well-known names to French wine lovers.

South of the Garonne is the department of Gers. Auch (pop. 24,000) is one of the centers and a desirable place to live. Other towns like Condom, Nerac, and Eauze have less than 10,000. Produced here are poultry and foie gras plus *armagnac*, the brandy that many find superior to cognac because it is so often the work of small producers rather than the giant distillers of the rival product.

One little-known crop of the region is *pastel*, a plant of the mustard family, that yields a beautiful blue dye called woad used since prehistoric times. Woad was a source of great wealth in the textile industry centered in Toulouse in the 16th and 17th centuries, before it was replaced by much cheaper indigo from the New World.

Languedoc

The eastern third of this region borders the Mediterranean and presents an entirely different face. Dry, rocky, and sparsely populated, but also warm

In Their Own Words

How do the people in the small villages react to the influx of strangers in their midst? A small country weekly in Languedoc, *La Semaine du Minervois*, asked residents for their reactions in a story about the booming local real estate market.

Here is a translation of what the people, identified only by first name and occupation, said:

Alain, a civil servant: "People say 'the English are buying up everything.' On my part, I think differently, that the arrival of these foreigners brings a new wind; it's beneficial for the activation of a region."

Roselyne, retired: "It gives one a twinge of the heart to see the French heritage become the property of foreign buyers."

Yolande, retired: "The foreign buyers make the price of real estate climb. But they benefit the region by restoring the old houses that are our heritage."

Viviane, retired: "The foreigners who live here are very polite, but we don't have any exchanges with them. First of all, there is the barrier of language and then I have the impression that they remain with their own acquaintances. They don't really try to integrate themselves here. As for knowing if they can bring something to our region, I think so if they come to stay here. But if they buy a second home for vacations, that's different."

Not all the change in rural areas results from foreigners, however. French from the cities are moving to the country and the result is a certain amount of tension between urban and rural ethos. In the 1960s, the average person traveled no more than five kilometers a day. The current average is 30 kilometers (18.6 miles).

This increased mobility, plus the growth of the Paris region, has intensified the pressure on farm country even beyond the Île de France. Between 1965 and 2000, the number of farms dwindled from three million to 700,000.

The experts see an end to the distinction between urban and rural cultures. "After all, everyone watches the same news on television, shops at the same supermarkets, taps the same computer, and uses the same cell phone," said one.

and sunny with excellent beaches and old stone houses, Languedoc is little known even among the French for reasons both historical and geographical.

A thousand years ago, that was not the case. At the first millennium, Languedoc represented the peak of western European culture. The Arab occupation had been repulsed in the 8th century but left behind a residue of learning. The region had suffered little from the Viking invasions that so ravaged the north. Maritime commerce and the cloth trade had enriched it. The poetry of its troubadours, the wealth and refinement of its nobility, and the level of its learning—in literature, architecture and law—all confirmed Languedoc's superiority.

Later centuries were not so kind. The religious and military crusade against the Albigensian heresy—a belief in asceticism held by a people known as the Cathars—brought the region beneath the Catholic heel of the north. Plague, invasion, and religious persecution all swept across in succession. Additionally, the hegemony of Paris overwhelmed the native languages of Languedoc.

Internationally, the Italian Renaissance, the colonization of the New World, and the golden age of the Netherlands all passed beyond its borders. Continental trade routes, well established after a century of crusades to the Holy Land, passed to the north and the great pilgrimages of medieval times fell off. Europe turned to face the Atlantic, no longer the Mediterranean, and Languedoc became in every sense a backwater.

The province is now called Languedoc-Roussillon, the hyphenated latter portion in deference to the Catalan culture that dominates the department of Pyrénées-Orientales on the Spanish border. Historically, the border region has had economic and political ties with Barcelona and the kingdom of Aragon. In fact, the frontier between France and Spain was not set until 1659. Today, the European Union regards the Toulouse-Barcelona axis as an economic region, much as it was centuries before nationalism swept the continent.

Geographically, this eastern-Pyrénées province is less verdant

The town of Sarlat, near the Dordogne River in the Aquitane

Abercrombie and Kent

than its western cousins. Nonetheless, there are prime summer and winter recreational areas—skiing and hiking are the major activities. The lower slopes are dotted with vineyards. Collioure on the coast and Céret in the mountains are villages once frequented by artists such as Picasso. Towns such as Limoux, south of Carcassonne, and St. Paul de Fenouillet, northwest of Perpignan, are gateways to the Pyrénées without being high in the mountains. Ceret, a French Catalan town beloved by artists for more than a century, is another one.

The major city in Languedoc is Perpignan (pop. 105,000). Like most of the French cities on the east side of the Mediterranean, it is situated away from the sea itself, less subject to flooding and beyond the inlets and shallow *étangs* (lagoons) that cut the wide, sandy beaches north of where the Pyrénées meet the sea. Campgrounds abound near the water. Some of these beach towns are only summer resorts with little or no independent life. Businesses close between October and Easter and the streets are empty.

Going north from Perpignan, the larger towns are Narbonne, Béziers, Montpellier, capital of the province, and Nîmes. Between Béziers and Montpellier is the Bassin de Thau, a large bay filled with oyster and mussel beds.

Montpellier

Montpellier, with its quarter of a million inhabitants, is the largest and youngest of the Languedoc cities, dating back only to the 10th century. Once part of Aragon, Montpellier was sold by Jacques III of Mallorca to the king of France in 1349.

Montpellier's university, particularly the medical school, is one of the oldest in France, dating to the beginning of the 13th century. Like Toulouse, Montpellier grew rapidly in the last decade. The city itself gained 8.1 percent in population and the department, the Hérault, increased 12.8 percent. (Languedoc-Roussillon registered the highest percentage growth of any province in France during the 1990s: 8.4 percent.)

Despite its growth, Montpellier is less expensive than Toulouse or Bordeaux. Prices increased 5 to 10 percent in 1999, while the number of sales went up 20 percent. The difference is partly due to the fact that prices of older buildings remained stable. In the center of the city, much sought after despite the traffic and lack of parking, you'll pay 1,200 to 1,500 euros ($1,080 to $1,350) per square meter. There is little new construction here.

In the Beaux-Arts district, which is close to the center but has parking and wider streets, a 70-square-meter three-room apartment of quality with a swimming pool sold for 92,000 euros ($82,800). Finding larger units in the district is difficult. In new buildings, you'll pay 1,700 to 2,000 euros ($1,530 to $1,800) per square meter.

A small house and garden runs close to 200,000 euros ($180,000) in the

Boutonnet district. In the less classy Figuerolles, you can find apartments between 600 and 800 euros ($540 and $720) per square meter while small houses sell between 65,000 and 150,000 euros ($58,500 to $135,000) depending on size, condition, and location.

On the outskirts of the city, you can expect prices to drop 10 to 15 percent and slightly more in the suburbs.

Around Montpellier

Along the western side of the Mediterranean beaches is another sea, a sea of grapevines dotted with villages, cut by canyons and streams and divided at times by brush-covered hills. From Perpignan to Nîmes, from the Mediterranean to the Montagne Noir are vineyards with small orchards of apples, apricots, olives, and fields of melons or asparagus interspersed.

The Corbières is a particularly rugged region, with grapes in the valleys and steep rocky ridges above. Its western end, southeast of Carcassonne is mountainous and forested, stopping the grapevines only temporarily as they commence again in the Aude river valley leading north to Carcassonne. In the north, the Corbières gives way to the rolling plain of another wine region, the Minervois, cut by the Canal du Midi as it winds toward Béziers and the sea.

Not many kilometers west of Carcassonne, the land becomes more fertile, and the vineyards yield to fields of grain and sunflowers that continue to Toulouse and beyond. To the north the Montagne Noir, rugged hills and canyons much colder in winter than the plains, are often covered with snow during winter. These form the southeastern edge of the Massif Central.

One picturesque view after another

Beyond them is the regional park of Haut Languedoc, sparsely populated even in the summer months.

North of the park and northeast of Montpellier, you climb up to a flat plain about 4,000 feet in elevation. This is the area known as the Larzac plateau, wind-swept and desolate, perhaps, but the thousands of sheep that pasture here provide the milk for Roquefort cheese, all aged in the caves beneath the tiny village of Roquefort-sur-Soulzon.

North and northwest of Montpellier is the department of Gard, containing the province's second-largest city, Nîmes, and the beautiful Roman aqueduct, Pont du Gard. An especially picturesque town in the Gard is Uzès, once a wealthy duchy and now filled with well-preserved and restored stone buildings.

The northernmost department in Languedoc is Lozère. It is the least populated department in France, with 73,500 people.

Houses in many of the little villages scattered through Languedoc appear relatively cheap. One could buy a shell of a village house for 10,000 euros ($9,000) and spend 7,000 ($6,300) more just to remove debris and strengthen the walls so that they would support floors above the ground level. After that, you could put in floors, windows, wiring and plumbing, and finish the walls. Before completion, additional costs would top 30,000 euros ($27,000), with you, the owner, doing much of the work yourself.

Renting

If you plan to rent while looking for property to buy, you should be able to find a four- or five-room unit of 100 to 125 square meters (1,000 to 1,250 square feet) for 600 to 1,000 euros ($540 to $900) per month in the cities throughout the region. The difficulty may be in leasing a rental for less than three years, the length of the normal lease in France. In small villages, shorter leases may be more likely, although you may have to take a house rather than an apartment.

Also, the typical rental unit is unfurnished. During off-season, you might find the owner of a furnished vacation property rented in the summer by the week willing to take a longer-term tenant at an advantageous price since otherwise the unit would remain empty. In such an arrangement, however, heating will be a point of negotiation between you and your landlord.

One strategy to finding a rental is to enlist the aid of your real estate agency. Tell them you are looking for property to buy but want to live in the area for a few months before deciding; can they help you find a rental? Even if you do not buy anything from them immediately, they still stand to profit from the rental finder's fee—and they gain more time to find the right property for you.

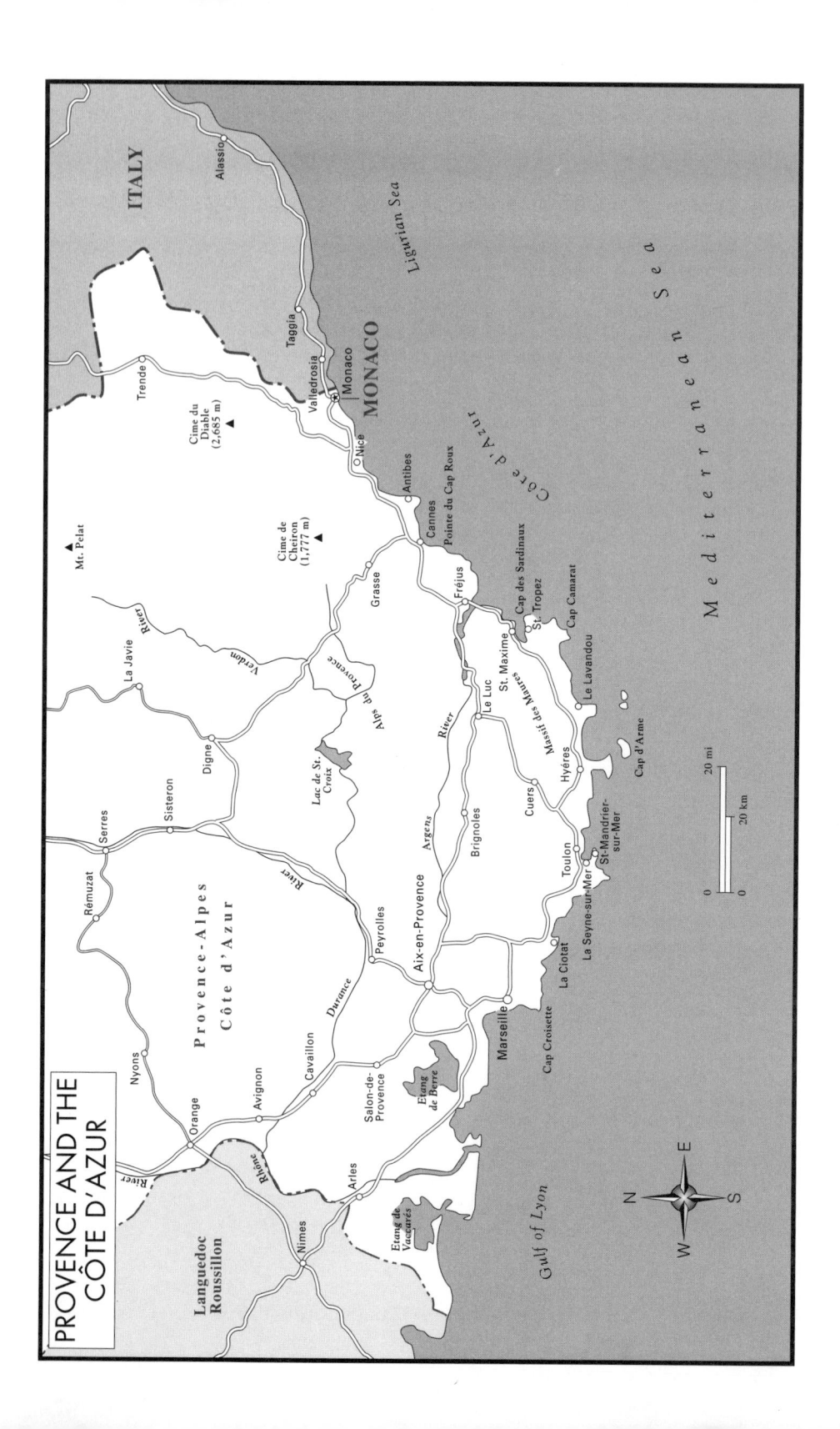

PROVENCE AND THE CÔTE D'AZUR

16 Provence and the Côte d'Azur

Anyone charmed by Peter Mayle's tales of life in Provence will automatically be a candidate for residence in this region. The towns that surround the *Parc régional du Lubéron*, such as Cavaillon to the west and Peyrolles-en-Provence to the south, are beautiful places to live.

But the modern French région of Provence-Alpes-Côte d'Azur (PACA) contains much more than the Lubéron. The coast from Marseille to Nice includes the wealthy sophistication of Cannes and St. Tropez. Inland, the rich agricultural and recreational areas contain villages such as Moustiers-Ste-Marie. The lower Rhone valley south of Avignon has such Roman towns as St-Remy-en-Provence, a place rich in history and pleasant to visit.

From Marseille to Nice stretches France's "gold coast." It's not called that, of course. Part of it is the Riviera, and a much larger portion, the Côte d'Azur, the Sky Blue Coast. As you would expect in this ritzy region, glamour and the good life don't come cheap.

Nice stands at the eastern edge of the region. About 30 kilometers (18.6 miles) east of this Riveria resort lie Menton, the warmest place in France, and the Italian border, with Monaco nestled in between. West of Nice are the playgrounds of the rich and famous—Antibes, Cannes, St. Tropez. Further west is the great naval base of Toulon and the wines of Bandol, marking the end of the Côte d'Azur. A short distance east of Bandol rise the limestone cliffs called Les Calanques, a plateau separating the great industrial port of Marseille from the rest of this coastline.

Provence in Prose

For hundreds of thousands of years, humans have occupied the land today we call Provence. For all of recorded history, Provence has attracted the peoples of one civilization after another—Greek, Roman, Visigoth, Saracen, Frank, Viking, French, English, German, Russian, American. Much has been written to explain its charms. Here is a sampling:

"Inland Provence is everywhere composed of the same unvarying elements: limestone spurs and plateaux *(a very hard and massive limestone); platforms of ancient rock, only partially eroded; plains and valleys generally rather narrow; and depressions like the one surrounding the ancient twin* massifs *of the Maures and the Esterel. But these elements are shuffled by the caprice of the relief which combines them to form new landscapes at every turn."*
—Fernand Braudel, The Identity of France, translated by Sian Reynolds

"These are the villages of beautiful view, scenic walks, and tranquility, where nearly every home boasts a cypress tree to the north, a Provençal welcome sign that also serves as a natural windbreak, and where every town big enough to support a café also has an alley-like stretch of ground for boules, *the bowling-like game that is still played for hours on end by old men in worn navy bérets."*
—Patricia Wells, The Food Lover's Guide to France

"We looked through the window at the old stone tub, bright with flowers. It would take at least four men to move it away from the garage and into the garden, and organizing four men in Provence was, as we knew, not something that could be arranged overnight. There would be visits of inspection, drinks, heated arguments. Dates would be fixed and then forgotten. Shoulders would be shrugged and time would pass by. Perhaps by next spring we would see the tub in its proper place. We were learning to think in terms of seasons instead of days or weeks. Provence wasn't going to change its tempo for us."
—Peter Mayle, A Year in Provence

"Thus in Provence you will find the jovial and the libidinous. But in the cathedrals of Provence, you will see almost no leering gargoyles and almost no vomiting peasants, copulating apes and be-pitchforked fiends. . . . It is indeed one of the chief joys of that sweet land that the Gothic there has practically no existence. And the grotesque as a characteristic is as absent from the lives of the Provençaux as from their arts. They had instead traditions of beauty, discipline, frugality and artistic patience."
—Ford Madox Ford, Provence

The region, called PACA for Provence-Alpes-Côte d'Azur, consists of six departments. It is France's third most populous, with 4.5 million people. Despite the attraction of the weather, it grew only slightly during the 1990s.

PACA is a politically conservative region with a population of wealthy retired people and military personnel. It is also the stronghold of the xenophobic National Front, whose demagogic leader, Jean-Marie Le Pen, has made a career of anti-Semitism and anti-immigration. A split in party ranks and financial scandals seem to have cost the National Front some of its political clout, but it remains influential. When a similar party came to power in Austria in 2000, the National Front was quick to express approval and give support despite widespread European concern.

But the region is far more diverse than the reputation the National Front has given it. Cities such as Avignon, Aix-en-Provence, Marseille, and Nice are too sophisticated to be limited in such a fashion. For a month every summer, Avignon, not Paris, becomes the theatrical capital of France and perhaps of Europe as hundreds of stage productions unfold in a great festival of drama and dance.

North of the coast live thousands of small farmers and artisans—potters, ceramicists, furniture makers, painters, and sculptors. Industrial Marseille has a large blue-collar base. The influence of Italy next door and the hundreds of thousands of tourists from virtually every nation in the world who throng here every year all mix into an unforgettable melange.

Nice

Nice is surely the capital of the Côte d'Azur, as well as the prefecture of the department, with nearly half a million people in the metropolitan area. It is an old city—as old as any in France—with a modern face. It is also an expensive city, where property prices rival those in Paris, yet it is as far away from Paris as you can get and still be in France. Paris is more than 900 kilometers (558 miles) distant. Lyon marks the halfway point between the two cities.

Human habitation in Nice dates back 400,000 years, yet for centuries it was not part of France—from 1388 until Napoleon III won Savoy back for France in 1860. In fact, Genoa and Turin are as close as Marseille to Nice.

Much of the city is new. In 1860, Nice had a population of 40,000 and the growth since then has been both industrial and cultural.

Two non-Mediterranean nations have strongly influenced the modern development of Nice. The first is Great Britain. The English had been habitués of the city since the 18th century, when Great Britain was allied with Savoy. The House of Savoy ruled from medieval times until the 19th century. It was an area that ebbed and flowed with the fortunes of war, and at times included what is now Switzerland, southeastern France, Italy's Piedmont, Sicily, and Sardinia. With a strong local colony that has remained constant, the English established what is probably the city's best-known feature, the Promenade des Anglais, the broad avenue fronting the beach of the *Baie des Anges* (Bay of Angels).

The other is Russia. Beginning in the mid-19th century, wealthy Russian nobles began settling in Nice. They competed to create grand estates. The largest Orthodox cathedral outside of Russia is St. Nicolas in Nice, built

> *As you would expect in this ritzy region, glamour and the good life don't come cheap.*

by a Russian architect with German brick and Italian tile. Other Orthodox churches include St. Michel-Archange in Cannes and a chapel in Menton.

Housing prices in Nice rose 10 to 15 percent in 1999 and continued increases seem certain. Whether they will continue at the same rate is difficult to say. At the moment there is a wide range of prices, often determined by views of the sea, or neighborhood more than quality of construction.

New buildings around favored areas such as Place Massena sell for up 3,350 euros ($3,015) per square meter. Not far away, along the Quai des Etats-Unis, prices are 4,500 euros ($4,050) and up per square meter. Prices along the Promenade des Anglais are less because of traffic and the noise it generates. Nonetheless, the average price there is about 3,250 euros ($2,925) per square meter.

In other areas away from coast, prices drop to around 2,450 euros ($2,205) per square meter. Older buildings are less, down to 2,000 euros ($1,800) per square meter, with prices dropping as you move north away from the coast. But it is difficult to find anything, even ill-favored and in need of renovation, below 900 euros ($810) per square meter until you reach the outskirts of the city.

Houses start at 300,000 euros ($270,000) and many exceed 700,000 euros ($630,000). At the edge of the city, you might find homes beginning at 230,000 euros ($207,000).

If you wish to rent an apartment in Nice, you will be able to do it—for a price. Rather than the 600 to 1,000 euros ($540 to $900) per month you might pay for four or five rooms in other French cities, expect to pay 1,000 to 1,500 euros ($900 to $1,350) in Nice for comparable quarters, more if you

A view of Avignon, at night

require greater luxury. The world-famous coastal resort towns such as Cannes and Antibes are even pricier.

Inland, the department of Alpes-Maritime is far less densely populated, with half of its one million residents in Nice and the surrounding metropolitan area. The autoroute parallels the coast, as does highway N7 from the Italian border to Cannes.

Cannes-Antibes

Cannes was a small fishing village until the middle of the 19th century. In 1834, England's Lord Brougham was stopped from wintering in Nice by a cholera epidemic. He stayed instead in Cannes, enjoying it so much that he built a home and returned there every winter until his death 34 years later. Other wealthy English followed, along with Russians. In 1939, capitalizing on its reputation as a watering hole for the wealthy, Cannes opened its first film festival September 1, only to close it two days later for the war. The year after the war another festival was scheduled, assuring Cannes' place in the world of celebrities and wannabe celebrities.

No surprise, then, that housing is expensive here. In the Cannes-Antibes area, both sales and prices rose significantly in 1999—sales increased by 20 percent and prices by 10 percent. But there is considerable variation in price depending on the usual factors of view and location.

In Antibes, for instance, prices range from about 1,100 to 5,000 euros ($990 to $4,500) per square meter. For three rooms with a view of the sea, you'll pay a bare minimum of 150,000 euros ($135,000). On Cap d'Antibes, a house with a garden begins at 800,000 euros ($720,000).

Cannes is more expensive than Antibes. Here prices begin at 1,200 euros ($1,080) per square meter and climb to 12,000 euros ($10,800) for properties along the Boulevard de la Croisette, fronting the water. More reasonable prices are found inland near boulevards Carnot and République. For a house with a swimming pool in the posh neighborhood called La Californie, prices begin at 1.5 million euros ($1.35 million).

Around Cannes

Leaving Cannes on N85 and driving northwest about 17 kilometers (10.5 miles), you climb into the foothills to Grasse (pop. 42,000), a center of the perfume industry. This picturesque city of steep narrow streets served as a winter vacation spot for Queen Victoria.

In the center of town, villas of 130 square meters with some land sell for 150,000 to 230,000 euros ($135,000 to $207,000). In the old city, some apartments sell for less than 100 euros ($90) per square meter, but these need total renovation. Those that have had even a little bit of work done fetch 750 euros ($675) per square meter.

In the outlying districts of Saint-Antoine and Saint-Jacques, houses with gardens sold for between 250,000 and 400,000 euros ($225,000 and $360,000) in 1999. Apartments in the same areas ranged from 1,000 to 1,800 euros ($900 to $1,620) per square meter.

West of Cannes, both N7 and the autoroute A8 curve inland while the coastline bows out. N98 is the highway that hugs the coast down to St. Tropez. There, N98 cuts inland, and it is D559 that heads back to the water for 40 kilometers (25 miles) before rejoining N98 about 17 kilometers (10.5 miles) before that route arrives in Hyères, a town of about 50,000 people that is part of the Toulon metropolitan area.

Toulon and its great harbor, two-thirds of the way from Nice to Marseille, was the site of one of Napoleon's early victories when, in 1793 as an artillery captain, he seized it from the royalists who were backed by an English and Spanish fleet.

Toulon itself is much smaller than Nice, with about 180,000 people in the city compared to Nice's 320,000. The two metropolitan areas are nearly the same size, however; Toulon's metro population is about 450,000. Without the cultural wealth of Nice, it nonetheless has a great deal to offer, especially in views of the sea.

Along the coast east of the harbor, what were once small fishing villages such as Le Mourillon and Cap Brun have now been engulfed by the city and have become prized residential areas. Here new apartments run between 1,500 and 2,150 euros ($1,350 and $1,935) per square meter, the view often accounting for the difference in price.

Older houses here range between 1,200 and 2,000 euros ($1,080 and $1,800) per square meter. A villa with surrounding garden approaches 500,000 euros ($450,000). Away from the coast, prices drop and newer apartments sell for 950 to 1,500 euros ($855 to $1,350) per square meter.

North of the city is Mont Faron, with superb views of the harbor. Here a villa of 120 square meters but with steeply sloped yard costs about 230,000 euros ($207,000). New apartments of good quality sell for 1,900 to 2,200 euros ($1,710 to $1,980) per square meter.

On the west side of the city, which is not so highly regarded but nonetheless offers good views, villas begin at 1,100 euros ($990) per square meter.

Between Toulon and Marseille on D559 are two coastal towns worth noting. The first is La Ciotat (pop. 31,000), noted for shipbuilding over the centuries and hard hit by the recession of the 1990s. Along with its modern port, it also has an old fishing port and very nice beaches. Nine kilometers (5.5 miles) down the road is the smaller of the two, Cassis (pop. 8,000) Noted for its excellent white wine, the town's beaches are small but the harbor is filled with pleasure craft. Marseille is 30 kilometers (18.6 miles) away.

Marseille

"A considerable town," the writer M.F.K. Fisher said of Marseille. She was right.

Marseille does have its unlovely side. To the northeast, oil refineries and other industry on the Etang de Berre (a large lagoon adjoining the city) make undesirable neighbors. A great port city, Marseille has all the warts of any large city. As a sprawling, brawling gateway to France and northern Europe for 2,600 years, it has a large immigrant population from North Africa and the Near East.

Marseille has been pillaged and conquered and threatened and bombed. Early in its history, the residents made the mistake of siding with Pompey against Caesar, and it cost them dearly. Marseille suffered plagues. No king has ever made it his home, and no religion considers it a shrine. But Marseille has endured and grown, celebrated for its vitality and *joie de vivre*.

The southern part of the city, which rises up from the port like an amphitheater, is the most desirable. This takes in the 7th, 8th, 9th, 11th, and 12th *arrondissements*. In the Longchamp district, for instance, older apartments with *tomettes* (hexagonal terra-cotta floor tiles) and fireplaces usually sell for less than 1,000 euros ($900) per square meter. Around the train station in the 1st *arrondissement*, prices are half that, but the area is being rehabilitated and prices are rising.

Northeast of Marseille is the Camargue Parc Naturel, a wild region rich in natural beauty.

Rents for small apartments of 20 square meters near the university run 220 to 250 euros ($198 to $225) per month, marketed to the student population. In other areas, a studio of 25 square meters goes for 300 euros ($270) per month, a two-room for 300 to 400 euros ($270 to $360) per month.

The neighborhood of Roucas-Blanc in the 7th *arrondissement* has something of the character of a village. Villas there begin at 305,000 euros ($274,500). Apartments in the same neighborhood run 1,500 to 2,000 euros ($1,350 to $1,800) per square meter. Elsewhere, villas start at 230,000 euros ($207,000).

From near the lighthouse to the entrance of the old port, the Corniche du President J. F. Kennedy runs south more than five kilometers (3.1 miles) overlooking the harbor of Endoume. Apartments along the Corniche cost 1,600 to 2,200 euros ($1,440 to $1,980) per square meter. Villas are in the 500,000 to 700,000 euro ($450,000 to $630,000) range.

Aix-en-Provence

Thirty kilometers (18.6 miles) north of Marseille is Aix-en-Provence. These two cities and the suburbs between them account for about 1.4 million of the Bouches du Rhone department's 1.8 million people.

Aix-en-Provence is a lively city, full of students, grand mansions, and markets. This was the home of painter Paul Cézanne, who returned here when Paris failed to appreciate his work. In many ways this is the "capital" of Provence, as it was when it was the home of the Provençal counts.

Whereas Marseille is a worldly city poised at the edge of the sea, Aix-en-Provence, despite its students and sophistication, remains landlocked, part of a great inland empire.

In the center of old Aix, where parking places are rare, apartments sell for 1,500 to 2,150 euros ($1,350 to $1,935) per square meter. Moving south, in the area of the hospital and university, prices decline to 1,400 to 1,700 euros ($1,260 to $1,530) per square meter. In the desirable Torse neighborhood, new building begin at 2,300 euros ($2,070) per square meter, while older units go for under 2,000 euros ($1,800) per square meter. Houses are in the 230,000 to 280,000 euro ($207,000 to $252,000) range.

Aix-en-Provence is the gateway to the region. Many of the towns and villages mentioned below, such as St. Maximin la Ste., Baumes, Brignoles, and Le Luc, are potential places to live. Leaving Aix and going east on the autoroute A8 or the smaller N7 that runs alongside it, you are on the overland route to Cannes and Nice. St. Maximin la Ste. Baumes, a town of 10,000 situated in an old lake bed, is 45 kilometers (28 miles). Its magnificent basilica was saved from destruction in the revolution by Napoleon's brother Lucien, who turned it into a warehouse and used the organ to play the *"La Marseillaises."*

Heading east another 16 kilometers (10 miles) further is Brignoles (pop. 12,000), once famous for its plums and the bauxite mined in nearby hills. Another 25 kilometers (15.5 miles) east is Le Luc, an agricultural town of about 7,000. Grapes and olives are grown throughout the plain of the Var, and Le Luc sits at the intersection of A8 and A57, the autoroute that runs down to Toulon and then Marseille. From Le Luc, A8 continues east to Fréjus, Cannes, and Nice.

Southwest of Le Luc is the Massif des Maures, rugged country indeed, with few villages or inhabitants. This oval plateau rises up from the coast and extends from Fréjus to Toulon. The two autoroutes border it on the north and west, and the Mediterranean contains it on the south and east. Numerous towns and villages crowd the coast, but there are few far inland in this hilly, difficult terrain.

East of Aix-en-Provence is the Camargue, the flat, watery delta of the Rhône. Much of the Camargue is now a regional park, but the western side is not. In either case, birds and fish abound in the shallow, reedy lagoons. Products includes salt, rice, and reeds, which are harvested for making thatched roofs. The Camargue is a worthy place to visit, rich in natural beauty, but would not be considered a prime living location.

The dryland parts of the Camargue are France's Wild West, home to cowboys and horses and cattle. The horses are typically white, a particular breed, and the cattle black with curved horns. In times past, they ran wild.

The gateway to the Camargue is Arles. Just above Arles, the Rhône divides into two branches, the Petit Rhône and the Grand Rhône. Arles sits

The town of Arles, near Avignon

Archie Satterfield

astride the Grand Rhône, the older city on the east side, with its 2,000-year-old arena and the countryside that so delighted Vincent van Gogh. The two forks spread apart and by the time they reach the open sea some 30 kilometers (18.6 miles) away, they are 60 kilometers (37 miles) apart, creating an immense triangle that is the regional park.

Aix, Arles, and Avignon form another triangle that encloses a charming section of Provence, mostly rolling plains but with the range of rocky hills called the Apilles more or less in the middle. The Apilles are not high, just peaks of 250 to 400 meters (800 to 1,300 feet), but inspiring in their naked crags.

Arles is the smallest of the three cities, with a population of 55,000. Arles itself is split by the Rhône; the older city on the eastern side is more interesting and intimate than its western sister. Today Arles is no longer the sleepy Provençal town that Vincent van Gogh knew in 1888, but it remains a city of charm. About 20 kilometers (12.4 miles) north of Arles, facing each other across the Rhône are two smaller but no less interesting towns, Tarascon and Beaucaire.

Les Baux, reached from either Arles or Salon-en-Provence via D17 and D5, is absolutely spectacular. The village sits on a massive outcropping of rock nearly a kilometer long and 200 meters wide. All fields below the rock are planted with olives, vineyards, and fruit trees. Jutting more than 100 meters (325 feet) above the surrounding terrain, its sheer bulk dominates the countryside. The beauty is so breathtaking that, in this village of 500 people, there are two Michelin one-star restaurants and one two-star.

Ten kilometers (6.2 miles) north on D5 is St. Rémy de Provence, a town of 10,000 about 20 kilometers (12.4 miles) south of Avignon. The modern city stands not far from the ruins of a pre-Roman settlement called Glanum the Romans added to. Their ruins still remain, including an 18-meter-high (TK-feet) mausoleum, baths, and temple. St. Rémy's tree-lined boulevards and cafés show contemporary life is also alive and well here.

Avignon

Avignon, with nearly 200,000 people in the metropolitan area, is another great Provençal city and comparable in housing prices to to Aix. The prefecture of the department of the Vaucluse, Avignon is 36 kilometers (22.3 miles) from Arles via N570 and 78 kilometers (48.3 miles) from Aix-en-Provence via N7. Avignon stands beside the Rhône, where the Durance River joins it.

In the past, as today, an important factor in building a great, beautiful city was the wealth of the inhabitants. Magnificent buildings, whether mansions or churches, were expensive, and impoverished people could not afford grand constructions.

Luberon: Provence at Its Rustic Best

Created in 1977, *Parc régional du Lubéron* (Luberon Regional Park) covers 165,000 hectares (400,000 acres) enclosing 67 communes. Park headquarters are in Apt, a town of 12,000 in the north-central part.

Manosque, near the Durance on the park's eastern side, is about 40 kilometers (25 miles) from Apt. Cavaillon, near the western edge and famous for its melons, is about 32 kilometers (19.8 miles) away. From north to south the park's dimension varies greatly, narrowing to 13 kilometers (8 miles) at the western end, bulging to 33 kilometers (20.4 miles) in the middle, and slimming back to 20 kilometers (12.4 miles) on the east.

Within these boundaries lie towns and villages of rustic beauty, such as Gordes and Rousillon, where the colorful ochres—usually warm tones of yellow, rust, and beige—used in Provençal buildings are still quarried. (Ochres are minerals crushed into a powder and used to color the stucco of buildings.) Hiking trails and little roads barely wide enough for one car, let alone two, crisscross the park. The streams that run down its hills empty into the Durance River, which forms the park's southern boundary.

Much of the vegetation in the southern part of the park is *garrigue*, the brush composed of live oak, pine, Scotch broom, and thyme that thrives so well in the rocky, arid soil common to Mediterranean France. In the north, where water is more plentiful, the green forests are oak. The Luberon Mountains, contained within the park, are not high. Le Mourre Nègre, the tallest peak, stands just 1,125 meters (3,750 feet).

Among the prominent features of Luberon park are the medieval stone villages that cling to the sides and upon the tops of the hills. As agricultural practices changed in the last century, people moved away. Today, that trend has reversed and many of the stone houses have been restored as second homes. The tourist industry has provided jobs for others and the villages are alive again.

Other, newer towns contained within Luberon are also noteworthy. From Avignon, highway N100 runs to the east through the park. But before entering the park, the highway passes through l'Isle sur la Sorgue (pop. 15,000), a town justly famous for its antiques. With more than 150 antique dealers, this city has become a prime stop for anyone interested in old furnishings. Thanks to abundant water, in times past l'Isle sur la Sorgue was an important site for tanning, as well as cloth and paper making. Today many of the old water wheels remain in place, lending to the town's charm.

Apt (pop. 12,000) is by far the largest of the Luberon towns, 34 kilometers (19.8 miles) from l'Isle sur la Sorgue. It is also the liveliest, due to its bustling Saturday market, its site as park headquarters, and its central location. This area is *Le Petit Luberon*, the western part of the park where the peaks of the Luberon Mountains stand less than 2,000 feet.

Southwest of Apt 11 kilometers (6.8 miles) lies Bonnieux (pop. 1,500). It rests between *Le Petit* and *Le Grand Luberon*. Rousillon is about the same distance to the northwest and Gordes a few kilometers further. Saignon, another hill village, is just three kilometers (1.8 miles) southeast of Apt. These are all small villages. With a population of 2,000, Gordes is nearly twice the size of Roussillon.

For a different view of the Luberon, come into the park from Aix, crossing the Durance River on highway D556 into Pertuis. From Pertuis, take D956 six kilometers (3.7 miles) to La Tour d'Aigues, a town of 3,300 that sits amid vines and cherry trees. The waters of the Durance keep things green here. Its 16th-century Italian château now houses a museum of ceramics.

Looking at the Palace of the Popes in Avignon, you can see the wealth that the church fathers had accrued. It covers 15,000 square meters, or nearly four acres. Actually, it is two palaces. Pope Benoit XII razed the old Episcopal palace in 1334 and had a virtual fortress built that is now called Palais Vieux.

A mere eight years later, Pope Clément VI found it not to his taste and ordered construction of the Palais Neuf. Clement knew how to throw a party. His banquet hall covered a quarter of the area of a football field; the feast marking his election to the papacy required the slaughter of 118 cattle, 1,023 sheep, 101 calves, and 914 young goats. The 50,000 tarts baked for the party took 39,980 eggs.

All that medieval wealth has turned into modern splendor. Avignon becomes an immense theater every summer with the best-known festival in France. About 500 plays, dances, concerts, and spectacles of all sorts take place throughout the city during the month of July. Space is at a premium whether for sleeping, dining, or presentations. But the festival has made Avignon the most theatrically-oriented city in France.

Northeast of Avignon about 40 kilometers (24.8 miles) lie the slopes of Mont Ventoux, the "giant of Provence," a peak of 1,909 meters (6,200 feet). It appears so dramatic because it rises as a solitary pyramid, capped with snow in the winter.

Several cities around its western side are worth noting. From Avignon on D942 28 kilometers (17.3 miles), you come to Carpentras (pop. 25,000). This town came into its glory when Pope Clement V decided to settle here before going to Avignon. (The papacy governed Avignon and the surrounding region from 1229 until the revolution.) As church territory, the region became a refuge for Jews when Philip IV expelled them from France.

North of Carpentras 27 kilometers (16.7 miles) on D938 is Vaison-la-Romaine, a pleasant town of almost 6,000 on the northwest side of Mont

The Vaucluse rock formation, near Gordes in the Vaucluse region

Ventoux. An old medieval village occupies the heights, while a modern town stands below, the Ouvèze River dividing the two.

The wisdom of the ancients was demonstrated in 1992 when the river flooded and 37 people were killed and 150 homes destroyed. The ancient bridge to the upper village survived, however. Extensive ruins of the Roman city Vasio that once occupied were unscathed.

Nyons lies 16 kilometers (9.9 miles) north of Vaison-la-Romaine with Mont Ventoux to the south. Olives are the big crop here and groves of trees line the surrounding fields. With a population of 6,300, Nyons is also a center for distillation of lavender and other aromatic plants, as well as a truffle market.

This whole region between Avignon and Nyons, on both sides of the Rhône and east to Mont Ventoux, is really an excellent area. Roman ruins abound, superb wine comes from towns like Gigondas and Beaumes-de-Venise, and cities like Orange (pop. 26,000) and Valreas (pop. 9,000) provide plenty of commercial activity. Across the Rhône to the west, more wine is produced in areas such as Tavel. The rugged, sparsely populated Ardèche, with its lengthy river canyons, provide excellent summer recreation.

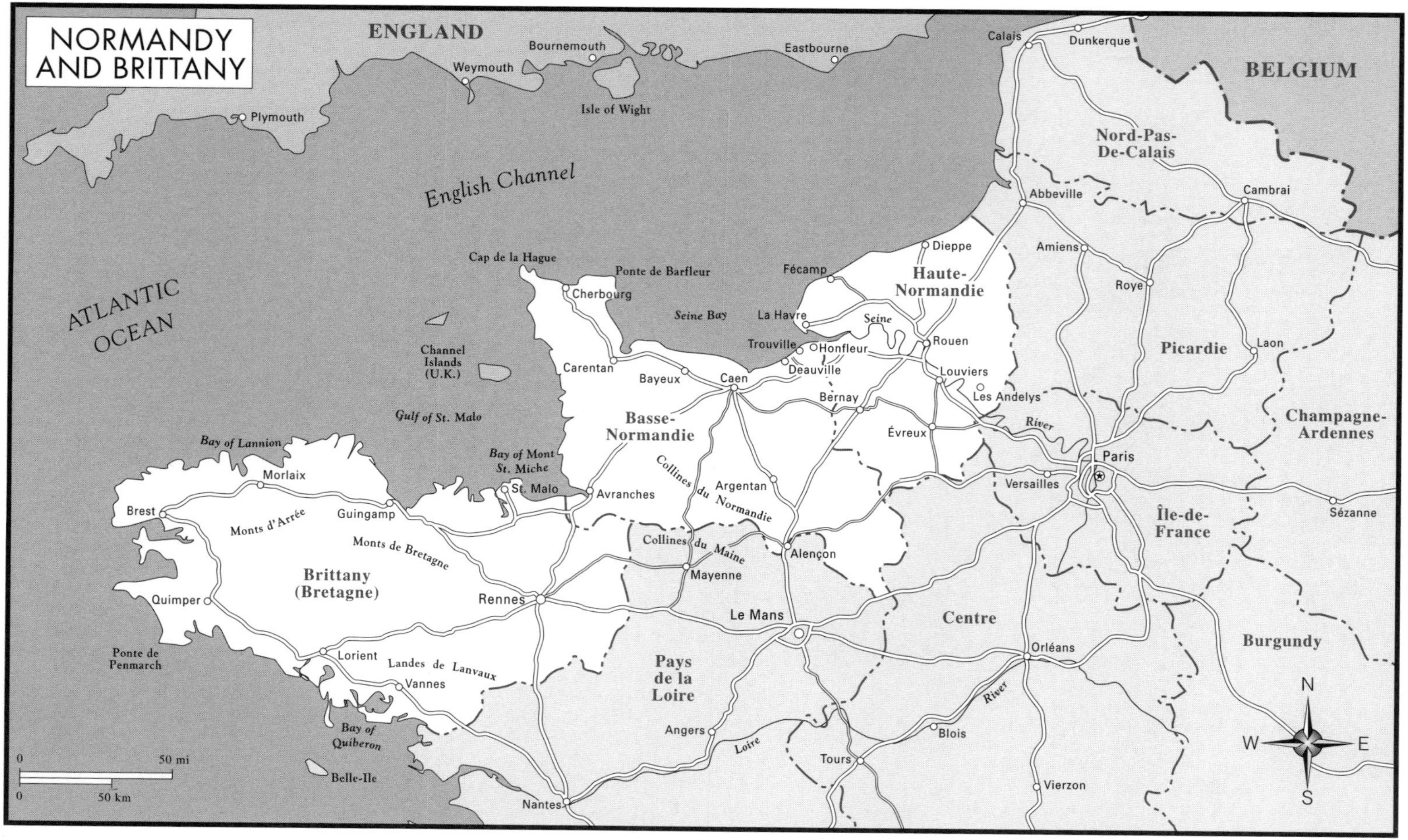
NORMANDY AND BRITTANY
ENGLAND
BELGIUM
Plymouth
Weymouth
Bournemouth
Isle of Wight
Eastbourne
Calais
Dunkerque
Nord-Pas-De-Calais
Abbeville
Cambrai
English Channel
ATLANTIC OCEAN
Cap de la Hague
Ponte de Barfleur
Cherbourg
Seine Bay
Fécamp
Dieppe
Haute-Normandie
Amiens
Roye
La Havre
Seine
Rouen
Picardie
Laon
Channel Islands (U.K.)
Trouville
Honfleur
Deauville
Louviers
Les Andelys
Carentan
Bayeux
Caen
Bernay
Évreux
River
Champagne-Ardennes
Gulf of St. Malo
Basse-Normandie
Bay of Lannion
Bay of Mont St. Miche
St. Malo
Avranches
Collines du Normandie
Argentan
Paris
Versailles
Sézanne
Morlaix
Brest
Monts d'Arrée
Guingamp
Monts de Bretagne
Collines du Maine
Alençon
Île-de-France
Mayenne
Brittany (Bretagne)
Quimper
Rennes
Le Mans
Centre
Pays de la Loire
Burgundy
Ponte de Penmarch
Lorient
Landes de Lanvaux
Vannes
Orléans
Bay of Quiberon
Angers
Blois
Loire
Tours
Vierzon
Belle-Ile
Nantes
0
50 mi
50 km
N
W
E
S

17 Normandy and Brittany

Adjacent regions, both close to the U.K., Normandy and Brittany are quite different in character. Normandy still attracts day-tripping Parisians and British emigrants alike with its rural charm, fresh seafood, and storied past. Brittany is wilder and woollier, at least politically. Its historical push for independence, its conflicts with the central government, whether royal or revolutionary, are echoed today in resurgent Breton nationalism.

Normandy

Normandy's greatest attraction may be its proximity to both Paris and London, combined with its good beaches, good food, and opportunities for an upper-middle class lifestyle. Pleasure boats, both sail and motor, abound, as do gold courses and horse farms. Orchards and grazing cattle make every country lane a pastoral scene.

The coastal towns north of Le Havre such as Fécamp and those to the southwest from Honfleur to Houlgate offer boating, bathing, and easy access to the U.K. The villages and towns along the Seine river are nearly within commuting distances of Paris and Rouen. The inland river valleys between Mont-St-Michel on the Atlantic and the Eure on the eastern side are dotted with villages not far from market towns like Alençon, Argentan,

Le Trou Normand and Other Delights

Normandy gained its reputation as a gourmand's paradise long before *la nouvelle cuisine*. *Leger* (light) is not the word that comes to mind when you look at typical menu.

The reliance on the local farms emphasized butter, cream, beef, and eggs. Aside from today's health concerns, the greatest challenge these meals present is finishing them.

To help overcome the problem, Normans call upon another local product and add a special course in the middle of meal. The pause that refreshes the Norman appetite calls for a neat shot of Calvados, the brandy distilled from apple cider. When looking for good Calvados, age is important—12 to 15 years minimum and 20 to 40 preferably.

The common belief is that the alcohol cuts grease; a more scientific answer is that it dilates the wall of the stomach, easing the overstuffed feeling. Whatever, the result is renewed vigor when the cheese course is brought out.

Cheeses are one of the glories of Normandy. *Livarot, pont l'evêque, neufchâtel*, Brillat-Savarin, and, probably the best known of all, camembert. Camembert is actually a modern cheese, unlike many others in France, such as roquefort and *cantal*. Its creator was Marie Harel, a Norman cheesemaker who hid a priest from Brie fleeing the revolutionary Terror in 1790. In gratitude, he showed her how to make brie and she turned around and invented camembert. When a rail line from Alençon to Paris opened in 1863, one of her descendants introduced Napoleon III to the cheese. He liked it and it immediately gained a reputation.

But packaging proved a problem, as the ripe cheese tended to run on its straw pallet. When someone hit upon the round box of thin wood, the famous cheese could go anywhere. During World War I, it became a symbol of France because it was part of every French soldier's rations.

Ironically, the popularity of camembert worked against Normandy because for decades the cheese could be made anywhere and still be called camembert. However, in 1993 the best of camembert was granted an AOC (*Appelation d'Origine Contrôlée*). Today, camembert so labeled must come from Normandy.

Dreux, and Vimoutiers. These villages offer a pastoral lifestyle and the recreational possibilities of the *Parc naturel régional de Normandie*.

For generations, when Parisians went to the beach, they invariably headed northwest following the Seine River to the English Channel and the coast of Normandy. The beach resorts and fishing villages and ports all along the coast with their tall, half-timbered houses offered a welcome change from city life. With modern transportation, the journey is scarcely longer than the average American commute and many people whose work is on the fringes of the Paris area are taking advantage of the fact, positioning themselves at some midway point between the metropolis and the beach.

The Seine Valley effectively divides Normandy into an upper and lower region. Haute-Normandie includes the departments of Seine-Maritime and Eure, separated by the Île de France. Basse-Normandie encompasses the departments of Calvados, Manche, and Orne.

With the exceptions of Rouen, Le Havre, and Caen, there are no large cities in Normandy and agriculture remains its primary industry. The lush fields of the Seine Valley and the smaller farms of Basse-Normandie continue to produce grain and produce and cheese just as they have for centuries. Further south and west, the land becomes hillier and and more forested, cut by numerous rivers flowing into the sea. The small towns of these valleys often contain both delightful, unpretentious places and more luxurious manors. Basse-Normandie has made a valiant effort in recent years to attract new industry and create jobs by offering subsidies and other enticements to investors.

The beaches remain prime tourist attractions, with hundreds of thousands trekking annually to Mont St-Michel. But the wooded parklands offer equally pleasant recreation. Both because of historical ties and proximity to the U.K., Normandy has long been a favorite destination on the continent for the British. The opening of the tunnel under the English Channel has only increased this interest. While there are relatively few Americans, there are lots of English speakers among the population.

Driving northeast from Paris on A-13, the Autoroute de Normandie, you parallel the Seine. The terrain changes slowly, flattening out as you move toward the English Channel. This is the land the Norsemen saw as they came up the rivers in the 8th and 9th centuries: well forested along the Seine, green, fertile fields, and villages and monasteries rich and ripe for the taking.

> *Orchards and grazing cattle make every country lane a pastoral scene.*

And take they did, laying waste to the land and returning to the sea with their treasure. But not all of them left for good. Many Norsemen returned as conquerors rather than raiders and settled. They came to dominate the region, giving it their own name. Within two centuries they were firmly in control of the countryside and recognized by France, with whom they were allied. In 1066, the ruler of Normandy, William the Bastard, crossed the Channel to become William the Conqueror.

HAUTE-NORMANDIE

Just across the line from Île de France on the right bank of the Seine is Giverny, where Claude Monet lived and worked from 1883 until his death in 1926. Today the Fondation-Monet maintains his house and gardens, a very popular day trip from Paris. The beauty of the spot makes it easy to see where the founder of the Impressionist movement drew his inspiration. In fact, many of his paintings were scenes from this garden.

Across the road from Monet's house and garden is the Museum of American Art, showing the paintings of the many Americans who flocked to Giverny beginning in 1880 to work in the same milieu as Monet himself. The larger town two kilometers northeast is Vernon on the crossroads of N15 and D181.

Although both departments cover approximately the same area, the Eure has a little less than half the population of Seine-Maritime—less than one person per square kilometer. The northern part of the department—along the Seine leading from Paris, approaching Rouen and continuing west to the coast—contains more than half of the population of 540,000.

But the proximity of Eure to Paris has helped it to grow by five percent in the last decade. Not only have city folk come seeking second homes, but many of them are arriving intending to become full-time residents. As the metropolitan area of Paris has expanded, so have employment opportunities outside the city, allowing people to live further away because they are not commuting all the way into the city.

On the right bank of the Seine, the town of Les Andelys, population 8,500, offers a panoramic view of the valley. Paris is 100 kilometers (62 miles) away and Rouen 40 kilometers (25 miles). The town is called Les Andelys because there are actually two of them—Petit and Grand. Commanding the river is Château Gaillard, built in 1196 by Richard the Lionhearted, king of England and duke of Normandy, to bar the French from Rouen. It was in the old market of Rouen where the English, after a five-month trial, burned 19-year-old Joan of Arc at the stake.

On the right bank, about 25 kilometers (15 miles) west of Les Andelys and 100 kilometers (62 miles) from Paris is Louviers, a town heavily damaged in 1940 but very well restored. Some 35 kilometers (21 miles) south of Rouen, Louviers stands at the head of the Eure valley and highway D836 parallels the river, leading to Pacy-sur-Eure and then changing its number to D16 when it crosses the border into the Eure-et-Loir department continuing to Dreux.

The garden in front of Monet's house at Giverny, in Haute-Normandie

Archie Satterfield

Due south of Louviers is Evreux, prefecture of the Eure and, with 60,000 people, its largest city. South to Dreux and west to Bernay is thinly populated country with small villages. Much of this area is the Pays d'Ouche, a wooded plateau difficult to farm. The town Conches-en-Ouches lies about 20 kilometers (12 miles) southwest of Evreux on D830.

The two principal cities of Haute-Normandie, Rouen and Le Havre, both lie in the department of Seine-Maritime. Le Havre, France's greatest port on the Atlantic, was heavily bombed during World War II. It was rebuilt according the plans of Auguste Perret, known as "the magician of reinforced concrete." The population is 250,000. Heavily industrialized, most of the city lacks the charm of yesteryear.

Rouen, the capital of the region and a university city, is the smaller of the two but sits in the center of a much larger metropolitan area. The population of Rouen itself is 106,000, but when the 33 communes surrounding it are included, the count reaches nearly 400,000 people. However, the area as a whole has shown little growth in the past decade.

As a result, prices remain stable. The most desirable neighborhoods are on the right bank or near the cathedral just across the river, where new, quality apartments did not pass 2,000 euros ($1,800) per square meter. In the other parts of the center of the city, prices for new buildings remained below 1,500 euros ($1,350) per square meter and older units below 1,200 ($1,080). For instance, a large apartment of 140 square meters near the train station meters sold for 158,500 euros ($142,650). Many of the older, renovated units away from the center sold for less than 1,000 euros ($900) per square meter.

Moving out north from the center, a few large houses of 300 square meters in Bois-Guillaume and Mont St.-Aignan, both close to the beltway and the new metro line, were selling for 450,000 euros ($405,000). However, closer in to the center most houses were 1,000 to 1,250 euros ($900 to $1,125) per square meter.

In some areas such as St. Andre and on the right bank near the Jardin des Plantes and between Grand-Quevilly and Sotteville, houses approached 1,400 euros ($1,260) per square meter. However, a rarely available house in the traditional half-timbered style called *colombage* in old Rouen will exceed that price.

In general, houses in the immediate suburbs remain equal in price to those in Rouen, but face a lesser tax burden and are therefore cheaper to own—115,000 to 200,000 euros ($103,500 to $180,000) depending on size and appointments.

The coast and two great fishing ports lie about 65 kilometers northwest and north of Rouen. Fécamp, once the capital of the French cod fishing industry, is the smaller of the two, with a population of 21,000. Cod fishing as practiced in the past has all but died here, and pleasure craft have replaced many fishing boats in the harbor. Such industry as has survived deals now with drying fileted cod into flat, stiff pieces to be reconstituted by French housewives and made into *brandade*.

Dieppe, where 7,000 Allied troops staged a reconnaissance raid in 1942 testing German defenses, is the beach closest to Paris. At two hours from that city, it remains an active commercial fishing port as well as a harbor for pleasure boats and a transfer point for fruit such as bananas and pineapples from Africa. It is also the port where the Newhaven car ferry docks. Old houses of four and five stories, their ground floors devoted to commerce, line the waterside.

All of this maritime activity merely continues a long tradition in Dieppe, population 36,000. Some claim that a Dieppois, Jean Cousin, sailed along the coast of Brazil and set foot in the New World four years before Christopher Columbus.

The estuary that forms Dieppe's harbor is created by the Béthune and Varenne Rivers. Near their confluence, about 8 kilometers (5 miles) southeast of Dieppe on highway D1, lies the village of Arques, population 2,500. It was from here that William sailed to conquer England. Southeast beyond the village the land rises, covered by the Forêt d'Eawy.

BASSE-NORMANDIE

Along the western border of the Eure lie the three departments of Basse-Normandie: Calvados, Manche, and Orne. This is the area that most Americans think of as Normandy. Here are the beaches of D-Day—Omaha and Utah. In France, June 6, 1944, is called *Jour J* and the invasion itself, *Le Débarquement*.

The Seine, as it winds through Rouen on its way to La Manche

Mickey Mouse

William the Conqueror's military success marked the beginning of centuries of warfare and rivalry between France and England. The warfare ended after six centuries but the rivalry continues today. Oddly, it was the conquest of England that eventually gave the world Mickey Mouse. This is how it came about.

Two knights who sailed with William were Hugues d'Isigny and his son Robert, both from the Norman village of Isigny near the mouth of the Vire, the river that separates Omaha and Utah beaches. The two knights stayed in England; gradually the family name was Anglicized, first to Disgny and then to Disney. In the 17th century, some of the family emigrated to Ireland and in 1834, to North America. In 1901, a fourth son was born to Elias Disney in Chicago. His parents named him Walter.

Here also are the resorts of Deauville and Trouville, so often seen in films, and one of the most-photographed sites in France, Mont St-Michel.

Today, except for the monuments and memories, much of the land has reverted to its centuries-old pursuits—beef, cream, cheese, butter, apples, cider, and calvados, the brandy distilled from apple cider.

This region's overall population of 1.4 million—less than it was in 1826—grew very little in the past decade, but some consider that a victory because numbers had been declining significantly. A large percentage of the population is rural—60 percent in the Orne and Manche and 30 percent in Calvados—and its decline marked the movement from farms to cities outside the region.

Some credit for this decline goes to the strenuous efforts that have been made to bring light industry to the region. There is some foreign investment—Japanese, American, and other European corporations have opened parts distribution warehouses and research facilities. Besides location, the lure includes subsidies and tax breaks for the investors, and a lower average wage than Paris.

Most of the businesses in the region are French, however. Besides producing food products, the area is home to a number of small factories and shops fabricating metal and plastic parts for machinery and consumer appliances.

Caen, the largest city of the region, has a metropolitan population of about 200,000, with slightly more than half that number in the city itself. Located on the Orne River about 12 kilometers (7.5 miles) south of the coast, Caen was heavily damaged during the war, living up to the origin of its name: "field of combat."

Less than two hours from Paris, Caen is served by 15 trains daily. A canal built alongside the river in the 19th century has given the city easy access to the sea, and there are docks for pleasure boats in the city.

Caen home prices have risen only slightly since 1999, although the better properties have not gone begging. New apartments in the center of the city run up to 2,000 euros ($1,800) per square meter, but most are closer to

1,700 euros ($1,530) per square meter. Older units run from 800 to 1,250 euros ($720 to $1,125) per square meter, the difference often arising from the amount of renovation required. One unit of 180 square meters on the very desirable rue du Vingtième-Siècle sold for 244,000 euros ($219,600) and needed major work.

The market for houses is on the outskirts and the suburbs, where a home on a golf course will cost up to 200,000 euros ($180,000). On the right bank of the river, small houses of about 100 square meters built in the 1920s and little changed since the war sell for between 100,000 and 150,000 euros ($90,000 and $135,000). In the better neighborhoods of St. Paul and Haie-Vigné, the price for the same size property rises to between 140,000 and 200,000 euros ($126,000 and $180,000).

Those who wish to rent for a few months while looking for property to buy should be able to find four- or five-room units in the 600 to 1,000 euro ($540 to $900) range. The difficulty may be in obtaining it furnished for less than the traditional three-year lease. One possible solution is to find a house that is ordinarily rented to summer vacationers by the week and persuade the owner to let you have it for a longer period at a lesser rate during a time when it might otherwise stand vacant.

At the mouth of the Seine is the charming town of Honfleur, population 8,500. A few kilometers across the estuary from Le Havre, it could not be more different from that industrial center. Honfleur's tiny harbor is surrounded by narrow, colorful buildings five to seven stories high; shops and restaurants line the quai. The elegant new suspension bridge, Pont de Normandie, unites these two faces of France.

Le Havre, where river meets sea

Samuel de Champlain sailed from Honfleur to found Quebec in 1608. Today, just as in 1608, fishing boats dock there to unload the fish and fresh shellfish that is part of the Norman diet. Alongside the port is the church of Ste. Catherine and its belltower, constructed all of wood. The church was built at the end of the Hundred Years' War. The shipyard workers, all skilled axmen and carpenters, wanted to thank God for the departure of the English. Deciding not to wait for architects and masons, the raised the church themselves with the material they knew best.

In Honfleur, houses of about 90 square meters, with a small garden, range from about 1,000 to 1,200 euros per square meter. Larger homes with bigger gardens cost about 1,200 to 1,500 euros per square meter, and well-renovated old homes in *colombage* (half-timbered) with gardens cost up to 1,900 euros per square meter. These prices also apply to the resort towns of Trouville and Deauville, discussed below.

Following D513 along the coast from Honfleur 18 kilometers (16 miles), you come to at Trouville and Deauville, both popular resort towns. At Cabourg, D513 turns inland to Caen, about 25 kilometers (22.5 miles) away. The coast from the mouth of the Orne west are the beaches of D-Day: Sword, Juno, Gold, Omaha, and Utah. D514 hugs the shoreline until the shore itself turns north to form the Cotentin peninsula.

> *It was in the old market of Rouen where the English, after a five-month trial, burned 19-year-old Joan of Arc at the stake.*

This area is called Presqu'île du Cotentin because of the low, marshy region that makes it nearly an island and separates it from the rest of Normandy. Cherbourg and its magnificent port lies at its tip. Cherbourg is the second largest metropolitan area in Basse-Normandie, with a population of about 95,000.

To the east of Cherbourg about 27 kilometers (24 miles) on D901 is one of France's prettiest villages, the little fishing port of Barfleur, population 600. Barfleur faces back toward France, somewhat protected from the Atlantic by the width of the peninsula. Its houses are made from granite. The massive church of St. Nicolas dominates the town.

In the opposite direction, about 20 kilometers (12 miles) west of Cherbourg, is La Hague, site of a nuclear waste dump and nuclear fuel reprocessing center. Environmentalists have repeatedly complained that the site is unsafe, a charge vigorously denied by authorities. La Hague was closed a few years ago after its capacity was reached.

The department of Manche, population 481,000, covers the Cotentin peninsula. At its southwest corner, where the north-south shoreline makes a right angle turn to the west, is Mont St-Michel. This magnificent structure and site draws hundreds of thousands of visitors every year. A mass of granite swept by the tides, the abbey and church that surmount it, the old

William the Bastard

Argentan is 60 kilometers from Caen via N158. Almost midway between the two cities is Falaise, population 8,000, the birthplace of William the Conqueror. The story of his birth explains why, until 1066, he was called William the Bastard.

William's father was Robert the Magnificent, duke of Normandy, who as a 17-year-old youth became enamored of Arlette, the beautiful daughter of a rich tanner. Robert first spied Arlette as he returned from hunting one day; she was at the *lavoir*, her skirts pulled up around her thighs doing the family wash.

From then on, Robert watched from the castle every day as Arlette went to the fountain for water. Robert, who is suspected of having poisoned his brother Richard III in order to succeed him as duke of Normandy, asked Arlette's father if he could take her as a concubine. Her father was enraged, but finally said Arlette could decide for herself. She agreed, but refused to go secretly to the castle. Instead, she waited for the drawbridge to be lowered and entered proudly on horseback. The chronicles of the era reported that "when the time that Nature required had passed, Arlette had a son named William."

15th- and 16th-century houses at its base, truly deserve the title of *"Patrimoine Mondial"* bestowed by UNESCO in 1979.

East of Mont-St-Michel bay, you'll pass through both the department and town of Mayenne on N12. Although Mayenne, population 13,500, belongs in the Pays de la Loire region, this northern part is much closer in spirit to Normandy than to the Loire Valley. The 110 kilometers (68 miles) almost due north from Mayenne to Caen on D23 and D962 passes through the regional park of Normandy and towns and villages such as Domfront, population 4,400, where pears rather than apples are grown and made into cider.

Another village is Clécy, population 1,200, center of what is called *Suisse Normandie*, a somewhat fanciful appellation given to the area because the massive rock formations reaching heights of 120 meters (390 feet) recall the Swiss landscape. Clécy is the center of a great recreational area for hiking in the Orne River valley.

Some 60 kilometers (54 miles) east of Mayenne is Alençon, prefecture of the Orne, third department of Basse-Normandie. Alençon (pop. 30,000), considered the "capital" of the Basse-Normandie région (Caen being the actual capital), is famous for its lace. When lace and lace-making became very popular in France in the mid-17th century, the government feared that too much money was going out of the country to purchase it. Colbert, King Louis XIV's right-hand man, decided to build a lace-making factory in Alençon and to forbid imports of foreign lace. The effort was successful, and the beauty and quality of Alençon lace remain legendary.

Alençon also boasts a Nôtre Dame cathedral of its own, built during the English occupation of the Hundred Years' War, that is well worth visiting. An ornate sculpture by Jean Lemoine adorns the façade while the windows were created by master craftsmen in the 1500s.

About 45 kilometers (28 miles) north of Alençon via N138 and N158 is Argentan (pop. 16,500), the subprefecture of the Orne. Like Alençon, it is a forested area and was noted for its lace. A particular style, quite different from that of Alençon, was developed by Benedictine nuns in the abbey here.

Housing prices in both Aleçon and Argentan are comparable to those closer to the coast—around 900 to 1,500 euros per square meter of living space. However, houses in this area are usually in better condition, and often include more land (often up to a hectare, or 2.4 acres, rather than 1,000 square meters or less) and perhaps an outbuilding or two that could be converted to living space.

For reference, Rouen lies 150 kilometers (93 miles) north of Alençon via N138; Paris, 200 kilometers (124 miles) via N12; and Chartes, 120 kilometers.

Brittany

The town on the east side of the bay of Mont St-Michel is Avranches, population 8,700. From here south on A84 it is 80 kilometers (50 miles) to Rennes, capital and largest city of *Bretagne* (Brittany). The region grew by 3.8 percent in the 1990s to a population of 2.9 million. Rennes, with a population of 250,000 in the metropolitan area, and the surrounding department, Ille-et-Vilaine, was where much of the growth occurred.

This growth has boosted property prices in the area. The choicest properties in the center of the city approach 2,300 euros ($2,070) per square meter. New apartments in the neighborhoods of Oberthur, Mail, Mabilais, and St. Martin—not far from the center—are less expensive: 1,700 to 2,000 euros ($1,530 to $1,800) per square meter. Older units drop below 1,500 euros ($1,350) per square meter.

Buildable land within a 20-kilometer (12-mile) radius of the city sells for 60 to 90 euros ($54 to $81) per square meter, bringing the cost of a suburban house of 100 square meters to 140,000 to 185,000 euros ($126,000 to $166,500). Older houses are available at the bottom of this range.

As mentioned above, given the resurgence of Breton nationalism in Brittany, and the subsequent fatal bombing of a McDonald's in the spring of 2000, you should be aware that the independence movement, however misguided, must be taken seriously. Check with the U.S. State Department's travel advisory website at www.travel.state.gov before you go.

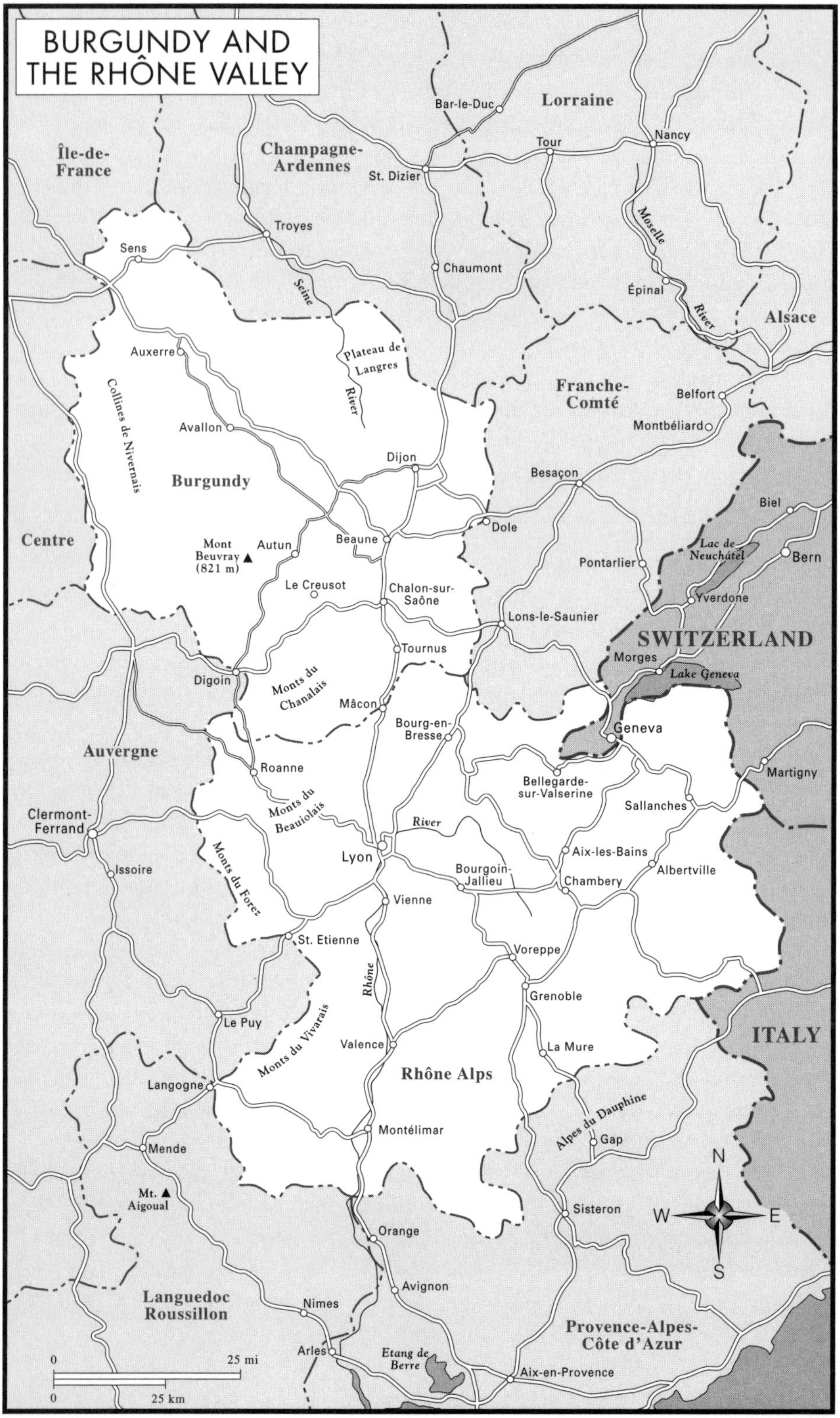
BURGUNDY AND THE RHÔNE VALLEY
Lorraine
Bar-le-Duc
Nancy
Tour
Île-de-France
Champagne-Ardennes
St. Dizier
Moselle
Troyes
Sens
Chaumont
Épinal
Seine
River
Alsace
Plateau de Langres
River
Auxerre
Franche-Comté
Belfort
Collines de Nivernais
Avallon
Montbéliard
Dijon
Burgundy
Besaçon
Biel
Dole
Centre
Mont Beuvray ▲ (821 m)
Autun
Beaune
Lac de Neuchâtel
Bern
Pontarlier
Le Creusot
Chalon-sur-Saône
Yverdone
Lons-le-Saunier
SWITZERLAND
Tournus
Morges
Lake Geneva
Digoin
Monts du Chanalais
Mâcon
Bourg-en-Bresse
Geneva
Auvergne
Roanne
Bellegarde-sur-Valserine
Martigny
Monts du Beauiolais
Sallanches
Clermont-Ferrand
River
Lyon
Aix-les-Bains
Issoire
Monts du Forez
Bourgoin-Jallieu
Chambery
Albertville
Vienne
St. Etienne
Voreppe
Rhône
Grenoble
Le Puy
Monts du Vivarais
Valence
La Mure
ITALY
Rhône Alps
Langogne
Alpes du Dauphine
Montélimar
Gap
Mende
N
Mt. ▲ Aigoual
W
E
Sisteron
Orange
S
Avignon
Languedoc Roussillon
Nimes
Provence-Alpes-Côte d'Azur
0
25 mi
Arles
Etang de Berre
Aix-en-Provence
0
25 km

18 Burgundy and the Rhône Valley

Dominating the eastern-central part of the country, these two regions offer many advantages to those who would move to France. Burgundy and the Rhône Valley are two very different areas bound by the common thread of wine.

The Rhône Valley is really an extension of modern-day Provence. Its architecture, agriculture, terrain, and climate are similar to those in that southern region. And although home to a lively tourist industry, the Rhône region lacks the seacoast that attracts so many people to the South of France. All the better if you prefer to avoid the crowds! The "capital" of the Rhône region is Lyon, an urban French jewel rivaled only by Paris.

Burgundy lacks a great city like Lyon, but takes no back seat in the charm department. The wealth of the past is easily visible in its well-maintained villages replete with stone houses capped by slate roofs. The region's proximity to Paris has made it, like Normandy, a favorite weekend retreat for city dwellers. And of course, it is famous for its wines. Although those produced in the area south from Dijon to Beaujolais are the best known, grapes grow throughout the region, as do cherries and other fruits. The thickly forested hills of Morvan regional park provide both winter and summer recreation.

Outdoor enthusiasts will delight to discover both Burgundy and the Rhône Valley afford easy access to eastern ski slopes all winter long.

Burgundy

Living in Burgundy places you about halfway between Paris and Lyon; you can easily keep a luncheon date in either city. But it also places you near the unmatched ski slopes of the Alps. For the ski addict, who has a partner who prefers to live in the lowlands, this may be an ideal compromise.

If the slopes attract you, a good place to live might be a village near one of the eastern towns closer to Lyon, such as Louhans or Macon.

If Paris is the draw, finding a place near Semur-en-Auxois would be ideal. You would be close to the Autoroute A-6, the TGV stop at Montbard and also be close to both Dijon and Beaune. Semur-en-Auxios, like both Autun to the south and Avallon to the west, lies close to the Parc naturel régional du Morvan, with great recreational possibilities.

The vineyards of Chablis, even closer to Paris, are famous in their own right, with cherry orchards, cattle farms and picturesque villages set in small river valleys.

Transportation is the key to Burgundy and the upper Rhône valley. Both the TGV trains and the autoroutes have brought Paris and Lyon close together. But both are contained within a narrow corridor. For those who need or want the access they provide, there is a premium to pay. For those who are willing to keep their distance, the countryside has much to offer.

The Rhône Valley

In centuries past, Burgundy was a powerhouse that could threaten the French throne. It was Burgundy that aided the English and bargained away Joan of Arc. "Happy as a duke in Burgundy" is a common saying. Even today, the modern region covers 31,000 square kilometers (19,220 square miles), more than all of Belgium, a land that the Burgundians once ruled.

Today it exists in a precarious state, the southwestern parts of the region hemmoraging population. Cities like Mâcon, Chalon/Saône, and Le Creusot lost eight to 10 percent of their population during the 1990s. Some see the region as little more than a corridor between Paris and Lyon; wealthy Parisians see it as a perfect weekend getaway—an hour or two from home. Its famous

Archie Satterfield

vineyards still produce their liquid gold but face stiff competition worldwide and lack the possibility to expand production of their best wines.

Burgundy's problem—some say its saving grace—is that it largely remains a pastoral land in an industrial world. Its rich agricultural tradition continues to provide some of the finest meat (Charolais beef, Bresse chickens), cheese (*langres, epoisses, charouce*), and wine (chablis, chambertin) in the world.

But as the monks who have inhabited its many beautiful monasteries would say, "Man does not live by bread alone." He (or she) also needs the employment that the region cannot provide at this time.

Burgundy's two poles are Paris and Lyon, the region stretched on an axis between the two. The northwest corner of one of its four departments, Yonne, borders the Île de France. Sens, one of that department's major cities, lies about 115 kilometers (71 miles) from Paris via A5 and 55 kilometers (34 miles) from Fontainebleu on N6. Once a powerful Roman city, Sens today is a pleasant subprefecture of 27,000 people. Its walls have come down; in their stead are boulevards and promenades.

At the other end, in the southernmost department of Saône-et-Loire, is Mâcon. The prefecture of the department, Mâcon (pop. 37,000) sits on the banks of the Saône River and gives its name to the southern part of Burgundy's wine region. Here begins the transition to the Midi. The climate moderates from northern Burgundy, and the rounded Roman roof tiles appear. Lyon is 75 kilometers (46 miles) further south via A6.

> *Burgundy and the Rhône Valley are two very different areas bound by the common thread of wine.*

Between these two extremes rolls some very pleasant countryside. Leave Paris on A5 but cross over to N6 at Sens. Following N6 along the Yonne River brings you to Auxerre (pop. 40,000), the prefecture of the department of Yonne. Twenty kilometers (12 miles) east is Chablis, the village of 2,500 that bestowed its name on some of the greatest white wine in the world. Besides grapes, cherry orchards abound along the banks of the Yonne.

Continuing on N6 for a little more than 50 kilometers (31 miles), you arrive in Avallon (pop. 8,600). from a granite promontory Avallon overlooks the valley of the Cousin River. Once a fortified city, its stone houses with their turrets and chimneys remain an impressive sight. Avallon is the northern gateway to the *Parc Régional du Morvan* (regional park of Morvan). This mountainous region of granite cliffs, abundant rainfall, and thick forests reaches heights of 900 meters (2,925 feet).

Outside Avallon, pick up A6 (*Autoroute du Soleil*) to Pouilly-en-Auxois, a village of 1,300 situated at the mouth of the 3,333-meter (10,832 feet) tunnel through which the Burgundy canal passes in transferring from the

Rhône basin to that of the Seine. Here you take highway A38 to go 43 kilometers (27 miles) to Dijon.

DIJON AND ENVIRONS

Unlike most cities in the region, Dijon, Burgundy's largest with more than a quarter of a million people in the metropolitan area, gained population in the 1990s. Its growth was based not only on employment opportunities, but also on the beauty of the city itself. Dijon is known as France's greenest city because of the number of parks and open spaces.

Moreover, Dijon has done much to conserve its rich heritage from the dukes of Burgundy and French kings. It remains a city of substantial buildings and numerous churches. Some 30,000 students study at its university. Boats and barges dock here serving Burgundy's excellent network of canals. And, of course, it remains the prime place to begin a tour of the region's vineyards.

All of this means that housing prices are going up, perhaps not so quickly as in some cities but rising nonetheless.

Luxury apartments in new buildings in the center of the city sell for about 1,600 euros ($1,440) per square meter while older units of good quality go for about 1,200 euros ($1,080) per square meter. For the few large apartments of 100 square meters, the price reached 200,000 euros ($180,000).

> *For the ski addict, who has a partner who prefers to live in the lowlands, this may be an ideal compromise.*

In the southern part of Dijon, near Colombière park, a calm neighborhood with lots of greenery, prices ranged from 1,000 to 1,500 euros ($900 to $1,350) per square meter for older units and up to 2,300 euros ($2,070) per square meter for quality units overlooking the park itself. Individual houses sold for about 1,500 euros ($1,350) per square meter.

Less expensive was the neighborhood of Bourroches near the periphery of the city's southwest sector. Here apartments built in the 1960s ranged from about 600 to 1,000 euros ($540 to $900) per square meter, and houses built in the 1930s began at 130,000 euros ($117,000).

In the suburban hills of Talant and Fontaine, houses ranged between 230,000 and 460,000 euros ($207,000 to $414,000). On the east side of the city, houses sold for 150,000 to 190,000 euros ($135,000 to $171,000). However, it should be noted that some of the suburbs around Dijon lost population during the 1990s.

From Dijon south to Lyon and beyond, the road N74 leads past one famous vineyard and commune after another. Fixin, Gevrey-Chambertin, Morey-St. Denis, Chambolle Musigny, Vougeot, Vosne-Romanée, Nuits-St. Georges—and that's only the first 16 kilometers (10 miles)!

Beaune, another 22 kilometers (13.5 miles) south, is a city devoted to wine—wine grapes, wine-making, wine-selling, wine-tasting, with a little food and a lot of tourism thrown in for good measure. The 22,000 Beaunois have much to celebrate. Their medieval walled city, once the home of the dukes of Burgundy, is impeccably maintained.

In historic Beaune, houses for sale are rare indeed. However, you will find four- and five-room apartments, with about 100 to 110 square meters of space, available. These cost about 1,200 to 1,500 euros per square meter. Outside the historic walls of Beaune, in the more modern sections of the city, housing prices are comparable to those of Dijon. Properties drop in price as you move out into the rural areas to the northwest, southwest, and southeast of the city, well beyond the fabulous vineyards of the Cote d'Or that run south from Beaune. Here you will pay 600 to 800 euros per square meter for a house of 100 square meters with 2,500 to 5,000 square meters of land.

Although the autoroute A6 leads south toward Lyon, many roads cross it or branch off to the east and west. Fifty kilometers (34 miles) west of Beaune on D973 is Autun (pop. 18,000), another Gallo-Roman city. The wooded, rolling landscape serves as a gateway to the southern part of the Morvan park, and the TGV stops about 25 kilometers (15.5 miles) away in Le Creusot.

The land west of A6, south from Beaune, is *La Bresse Bourguignonne*, a *pays* ignored by the nobility in the past and therefore virtually unknown today, standing in the shadow of *La Bresse Savoyarde* to the south. The more southerly region benefits from its connection to Marguerite of Austria and its capital, Bourg-en-Bresse.

The streets of Kaysersberg, in the Alsace region, north of Burgundy

But it is in *La Bresse Bourguignonne*, in Louhans, 37 kilometers (23 miles) southeast of Chalon-sur-Saône on highway N78, where the poultry-producing brotherhood of *"poulardiers de Bresse"* has its headquarters. Louhans (pop. 6,140) has more to offer than chicken farms. It is a market town with a street bordered by arcades—the upper floors of the buildings

Strasbourg: The Jewel of Alsace

Napoleon believed the Rhine River was a fitting northern border for France, an article of faith he was unable to persuade the Duke of Wellington to accept. Nonetheless, the Rhine does now serve (for some 125 miles) as France's border with Germany, in Alsace.

While Alsace as a whole may not be as remarkable as other parts of France, the city of Strasbourg is a jewel well worth considering for residence. A cosmopolitan city for centuries, Strasbourg has gained new status as the site of the European Parliament. The region is sure to gain importance as the European Union evolves.

Now a city of a quarter million, with 400,000 in the metropolitan area, Strasbourg grew more than five percent during the 1990s. Traffic problems associated with this growth have not been ignored. Nearly 200 kilometers (125 miles) of bicycle paths complement a new tramway that eases congestion in the city.

Meanwhile, the distinctive Alsatian wines and cuisine have gained followers worldwide. Some of the best are produced in villages around Colmar, 75 kilometers (46.5 miles) south of Strasbourg. Those who prefer small villages will find Ribeauville (pop. 4,800), Kaysersberg (pop. 2,750), and Riquewihr (pop. 1,100) attractive.

All three villages are among the vineyards and within 15 kilometers (9.3 miles) of Colmar, a lively city of 84,000. Strasbourg itself is less than an hour away. Kaysersberg, on N415, was the birthplace of Albert Schweitzer, the French medical missionary and musician who won the Nobel Peace Prize in 1952 for his work in Africa. Riquewihr has survived numerous wars virtually unscathed, and its residents have preserved its old 16th-century houses, walls, and streets.

Strasbourg itself has preserved much of its historic past. Now in vogue, the city is pricey. The scarcity of buildable land has boosted prices of new construction, and older buildings have followed the market upward. Some of the most expensive property, when it can be found, is near l'Orangerie, the park designed by Le Nôtre in 1692 adjacent to the Palais d'Europe and the European Parliament. Here the houses go for 600,000 euros ($540,000) or more. Rare apartments cost 2,800 euros ($2,520) per square meter and up.

On the other side of the Canal de la Marne in the Roberstau district, however, prices drop to 2,150 euros ($1,935) per square meter for the best places and to 2,000 euros ($1,800) per square meter or lower for the rest. The same prices may be found in the very charming but very noisy Petite France, with its medieval façades along the river Ill.

Elsewhere in the city, in the areas of Neudorf and Illkirch, you can find new units from about 1,750 to 2,000 euros ($1,575 to $1,800) per square meter. Older ones run 1,350 to 1,500 euros ($1,215 to $1,440) per square meter. By going to the periphery of the city, you might find new units below 1,500 euros ($1,440) per square meter and older ones for about 1,000 euros ($900) per square meter.

On the city's periphery, homes of 120 square meters with 500-square-meter gardens range from 200,000 to 280,000 euros ($180,000 to $252,000).

jutting out over the sidewalk and supported by pillars—that may be the longest such in France.

Chalon-sur-Saône, 70 kilometers (43 miles) south of Dijon, marks the point where the autoroute A6 begins to follow the course of the river that will join the Rhône at Lyon. A metropolitan area of 77,000, the city lost eight percent of its population in the 1990s, although the department of Saône-et-Loire lost just 0.3 percent.

Despite its problems, the city offers streets of beautifully restored old houses with half-timbered façades. Its semi-annual market for fur and leather dates back to the Middle Ages, as does the city's *carnaval*. Nearby villages such as Givry and Mercurey produce excellent wines.

Twenty kilometers (12 miles) south on A6 is Tournus, the town that stands at the north end of Le Mâconnais, the southernmost wine region of Burgundy. With 6,500 people, Tournus was once an important abbey and today retains some narrow streets and old-stone charm.

Dijon is known as France's greenest city because of the number of parks and open spaces.

From Tournus to Mâcon 35 kilometers (22 miles) lies Mâcon. With just a few more than 34,000 people, it is another Burgundian city that lost population in the 1990s. Nonetheless, it remains a lively, pleasant place, with its wines to keep the economy stable if not growing. Northwest of Mâcon about 20 kilometers (12 miles) via N79 is Cluny, one of the largest and most famous of the medieval Benedictine monasteries.

Just south of Mâcon are the communes of Pouilly and Fuissé, which give their names jointly to another well-known white Burgundy wine, Pouilly-Fuissé. It is here that the region ends. Beaujolais becomes the wine across the line in the region of Rhône-Alpes and the department of Rhône.

The Rhône Valley

Historically the Rhône Valley was an extension of Rome's Provence—*La Provincia*. Roman legions followed the Rhône north from Marseille, and Caesar followed the same river down from the Alps when he came to conquer Gaul. With that conquest, attention shifted northward. The confluence of the Rhône and Saône, not far from the Roman garrison already established at Vienne, proved a natural site; a Roman colony was founded there in 43 B.C. By 27 B.C., it became their capital. In 2000 years, Gaul has never lost its status as a commercial and intellectual center.

The Rhône River geographically dominates the valley. Most of the region's towns line its banks. But you need only venture a few kilometers east or west of the Rhône to find smaller, quieter villages, populated by

French people as they have been for centuries. You won't find a lot of Americans living here year-round, although many own second homes in the region.

Today the Rhône-Alpes is France's second-most-populous region, with 5.6 million people. Of that total, 1.2 million live in the Lyon metropolitan area.

LYON

Few would dispute Lyon's title as France's second city. Like Paris, it is so huge and diverse, it seems unfair to single out particular aspects for praise or note. Commerce and trade, the reasons for which Rome founded the city, continue today as the city's lifeblood. It was wine and silk in the past, today it is wine and pharmaceuticals; art and architecture and music and sculpture yesterday, the same today; transportation and banking—Lyon has it all.

> As for the wine, the French like to say that Lyon is watered by three rivers: the Rhône, the Saône, and the Beaujolais.

Including cuisine. Lyon is the home of famous chef Paul Bocuse, whose family have been restaurateurs here since 1765. It's not just Bocuse, however, that makes Lyon a capital of gastronomy. It's the whole region—in fact, Bocuse's restaurant is located in a suburb of Lyon. There are the Troisgros brothers in Roanne, 88 kilometers (55 miles) to the west, and La Pyramide in Vienne, 30 kilometers (18.5 miles) to the south, a restaurant where Bocuse himself once plied his trade. A number of excellent Lyon restaurants are named "Mère so-and-so," recognizing Mother as the original chef or at least the inspiration for so much of the cuisine.

As for the wine, the French like to say that Lyon is watered by three rivers: the Rhône, the Saône, and the Beaujolais. While the Saône follows a wiggly course due south, paralleled by A6, the Beaujolais river of wine comes from the vine-covered hills west of that autoroute. The area's vineyards go under the general name of Côtes du Rhône, but the better ones have developed numerous individual appellations, such as Condrieu, Hermitage, and Cornas.

While Lyon stands as a gateway to Provence and the Midi, it also lies at the intersection of routes to Italy, Switzerland, Germany, and Spain, as well as Paris, Brussels, and London. Thus, the population, produce, commerce, and ideas of Western Europe have passed through Lyon over the centuries in one direction or another. These influences, coupled with the city's contemporary verve, account for Lyon's cosmopolitan flavor.

There is a range of housing in Lyon, at a range of prices. The most sought-after areas include neighborhoods such as Brotteaux, the old depot near La Tête d'Or park, where prices recently increased 15 percent. Just across the Rhône in La Croix-Rousse, and in La Presqu'île, the narrow strip

A Question of Taste

Italy gave us the fork and France taught us what to put on it. On that point, many of us would agree. But how the French nation came to dominate cuisine and cooking in the West remains one of the great unsolved puzzles of the world. It's not as if no one else had a chance. Everyone must eat and most of the basic ingredients—meat and poultry and common vegetables and fruits—have been widely available for centuries, at least in temperate zones. Yet the French, as a society, have accepted that the transformation of these raw materials into palatable meals is an art form, and they honor it as such.

The French, as a society and a culture, care about taste in a way the United States and many other nations simply do not. As individuals, Americans are just as capable farmers and chefs as the French. But as a nation we produce tomatoes that have shelf life, not taste—our supermarkets install special lighting to make them appear red. Our daily bread is balloon bread, produced by a few large corporations and sold all over the country. Instead of trying to improve the taste of our food, we cheapen it.

In contrast, the French revel in the taste of things and the subtle differences that individual cooks, or a few kilometers, can make. Is the wine of Paulliac superior to the wine of Margaux? Is the wine of Gevrey-Chambertin better than that of Nuits-St. Georges? These are serious questions to the French, not in the sense of "mine's better than yours" but in the sense of "can you taste the difference?" Nuance delights the French.

Contrary to the American notion of "French food," the cuisine of France is very diverse, both in its ingredients and in tastes favored in particular regions. One area uses butter, for example, another olive oil, still another goose fat. In the Alps cheeses are made from cows' milk, in the Pyrénées sheep's milk, in Provence goats' milk. Oysters from the Mediterranean are prepared differently from oysters from the Atlantic; cider from Normandy tastes different from cider from Brittany; sausage from Lyon is not the same as sausage from Toulouse.

Further increasing the culinary possibilities, each *pays* has its own version of the regional specialty. Toulouse, Castelnaudary, and Carcassonne—cities only about 30 miles apart—each lay claim to the truly authentic *cassoulet*. Should a cook use lamb or duck or both? I'll have another helping of each one before I answer that, thank you.

The French take *le bon gout* so seriously, they educate their children in it. French parents send their children to tasting classes the way Americans send theirs to tennis camps. And what's a sophisticated palate for but to savor a meal? A two-hour break at noon is still common, and people go home for lunch on workdays, or dine out if they live too far away. The big family meal at noon on Sunday remains a tradition.

Food, its taste and quality, remains of great concern to the French as a society; they not only honor the best producers and the best chefs, they seek them out. Michelin's *Guide Rouge,* the celebrated listing of the best in French restaurant cuisine, marked its 100th year in 2000. Every year, a great agricultural show is held in Paris. And every year, both the president and the prime minister attend.

As in any art form, decadence and indulgence occasionally overtake refinement. But always, taste—the taste of the fresh ingredients, the true flavors of the food—reasserts itself and a new wave crashes onto the old shore. So long as good taste is paramount, the quality of the cuisine will not flag.

---

of land in the heart of the city between the two rivers just before they join, some new buildings are going for 3,000 euros ($2,700) per square meter.

This price is indicative of the disparity between costs in the fashionable heart of a great city and the more residential neighborhoods. The average, even in excellent areas, is well below the 2,000 to 2,300 euros ($1,800 to $2,070) per square meter range.

Not far south of Brotteaux, where Paul Bocuse runs a *brasserie* (restaurant with bar), around the Part Dieu train station, apartments 20 to 40 years old sold for 1,000 to 1,200 euros ($900 to $1,080) per square meter.

Neighborhoods further to the east, the 3rd and 8th *arrondissements* that have gained in popularity, include Monplaisir and Montchat. In Monplaisir, some houses of 110 square meters with a 300-square-meter garden sell for between 250,000 and 275,000 euros ($225,000 and $247,500), while new apartments sold for 1,600 to 2,000 euros ($1,440 to $1,800) per square meter. A metro line offers good transportation into the heart of the city.

In Montchat, which has something of a village atmosphere, there are small houses built in the early 1900s that sold for 230,000 to 260,000 euros ($207,000 to $234,000). Here older apartments sold for 1,100 to 1,300 euros ($990 to $1,170) per square meter, while new ones sold between 1,500 and 2,300 euros ($1,350 to $2,070) per square meter.

Toward the periphery of Lyon, the suburbs on the east side are favored because of easier access to the city. In Genas, for example, a house can be purchased for about 225,000 euros ($202,500). The north and east-side suburbs from Caluire to Ecully are less favored because of the heavy traffic. Suburban prices for a house of 120 square meters with a 500-square-meter garden ranged from 200,000 to 280,000 euros ($180,000 to $252,000).

An olive tree

St. Etienne and Environs

Some 60 kilometers (37 miles) southwest of Lyon via A47 is St. Etienne. It might have become the dominant city in the region had it not been overshadowed by Lyon. With more than 300,000 people in the metropolitan area, St. Etienne has been a city of heavy industry for centuries. It was once known as Armeville because it exploited nearby coal deposits to become the arms manufacturing center of France, even before firearms.

In 1746, the royal arms manufacturing was established here; less than a century later the first French railroad was built here. Manufacturing continues, but times and technology change. In the last decade, the city of St. Etienne lost 10 percent of its population; the department of Loire, of which St. Etienne serves as prefecture, lost 2.4 percent.

Much of St. Etienne's loss has been from the center of the city, where traffic and parking are very difficult. One result has been a stable market and low home prices here. In the Marandinière district, a house of 130 square meters with a 500-square meter garden sells for 80,000 to 110,000 euros (72,000 to 99,000). Large apartments in the same area were priced around 500 euros ($450) per square meter.

In the neighborhoods of Montplaisir and St. François there are small houses and apartments on the side of the hill that sell for about 600 euros ($540) per square meter, while new ones are priced about 1,500 euros ($1,350) per square meter. A house of 100 square meters with a garden of 700 to 800 square meters sells for about 110,000 euros ($99,000).

Very popular and much sought-after in St. Etienne are houses near golf courses. These sell for 105,000 to 160,000 euros ($116,000 to $144,000), while new apartments nearby approach 2,000 euros ($1,800) per square meter. However, older units brought 800 to 1,000 euros ($720 to $900) per square meter.

Between St. Etienne and the Rhône lies *Parc régional du Pilat* (Pilat regional park), a varied landscape. Along the river are vines; just below Vienne lie the famous Côte Rôtie, the "roasted slopes," the oldest vineyards in the valley of the Rhône, and Condrieu, a village of 3,200 famous for the *viognier* grape. Inland, the hills are pastureland and in the uplands, forests of beech and pine.

As the Rhône continues south from Lyon, the highway number alongside the river changes from A6 to A7. The autoroute stays on the east side of the river after Vienne, sometimes moving kilometers away to avoid the congestion and the valuable vineyards close to the river.

On the west side of the river is the department of Ardèche, lightly populated with 286,000 people. Near Tournon-sur-Rhône, a town of 9,500 on the east side of the river and Tain-l'Hermitage with 5,000 people on the opposite shore, the vineyards widen considerably on both sides of the river.

On the east side of the river is the department of Drôme, taking its name from the river that flows out of the Alps and into the Rhône about 25 kilometers (15.5 miles) south of Valence. Valence, a metropolitan area of about 110,000, is 18 kilometers (11 miles) south of Tournus-Tain and prefecture of the department. The vineyards stop at the Drôme for about 20 kilometers (12 miles), appearing again near Montelimar, where they become Côtes du Rhône, Coteaux du Tricastin, Côtes du Ventoux, and other regions of Provence.

On the west side of the Rhône are the gorges of the Ardèche River, a wonderful recreational area. The river enters the Rhône between Montelimar and Orange. The east side of the river is the plain of Tricastin, filled with vineyards and olive and fruit trees. Along the river are nuclear installations.

Part V
Earning a Living

---
19. Working in France
---

19 Working in France

Just as in the United States, there are many options for earning your daily bread in France. Whether you want to start your own business in France or be a salaried employee, chances are good you can find a niche once you navigate the sometimes tricky terrain of French regulations.

Owning Your Own Business

Starting or buying a business is a far more complex process in France than in America. Those who intend to come to France and start a business should understand from the start that the process is quite different than in the United States. Business in France is regulated; one does not simply decide to put up a sign, open the door, and wait for customers to beat a path to it. In many instances, it is necessary to show proof of education or experience to conduct such a business. You cannot simply declare yourself to be a manufacturer of widgets and set about producing them.

The first step is the departmental *Chambre de Commerce et d'Industrie, Chambre d'Agriculture,* or *Chambre de Métiers.* Unlike in the States, where such organizations are private, voluntary associations, in France they are governmental agencies that regulate and control most of the business in the country. For example, France Telecom will not put your name or business in the Yellow Pages unless you are registered with one of the chambers. Nor will you be considered professional or commercial by other firms and individuals unless you are so registered. For instance, the merchants' association in our village was considering hiring a particular band to play at the annual two-day festival that attracts several thousand people. When someone noticed that the band had no *siret* number (the registration number signifying a legal business), it was immediately dropped from consideration. If you wish to open a business that will attract the general public, you must follow certain steps.

Suppose you want to open a cybercafé. Even if you plan to sell drinks only to be carried off the premises, you'll need a license. Perhaps your idea is to guide American tourists around France, booking their rooms or escorting them to historic sites; such a business must abide by regulations, such as hours of operation and pricing. Even a business as simple as renting rooms in your home—a *chambres d'hotes* or bed and breakfast—requires registration with the local *Chambre de Commerce et d'Industrie* or *Chambre d'Agriculture*. It is the *Chambre d'Agriculture* that operates the *Gites de France* organization, whose members around the country in rural areas rent furnished apartments or houses by the week or furnished rooms by

The French Enterprise

In deciding to open a business in France, you should consider the various possible structures, each of which has ramifications for liability and tax consequences. In general, these structures correspond to common forms in the United States.

The simplest form of business is the sole proprietorship, *l'Entreprise Individuelle*. As the name implies, there is a single owner who is responsible. A spouse who also works in the business is a *conjoint collaborateur*. For a small business unlikely to generate sales in the millions of francs or hire dozens of employees, this structure may be fine. This small business may also qualify for a special tax plan called a *forfait* or *micro-regime* that avoids direct collection and payment of the TVA.

It does have disadvantages, however. The owner is personally liable for the business debts and must pay all of his or her own Social Security costs (retirement and health care). What's more, the owner has no worker's compensation coverage if he or she is injured or falls ill on the job. The business ends with the death of the owner and may involve tax levies.

A single owner who seeks limited responsibility and the advantages of a small corporate structure might form a EURL, *l'Entreprise Unipersonnelle à Responsabilité Limitée*. This is basically a small corporation formed by a single investor who also usually runs the business. An investment of 50,000 francs ($6,896) is required to form a EURL. Two or more investors form a SARL, *la Société à Responsabilité Limitée*. It also requires a minimum investment of 50,000 francs.

La Société en Nom Collectif, SNC, is a partnership. The law fixes no minimum investment for its formation, and the partners are responsible for the debts of the business. This operates much like *l'Enterprise Individuelle* as far as Social Security and health insurance are concerned, but the SNC may not use the simplified tax regimes.

La Société Anonyme, SA, is the formal corporate structure for big business. It requires a minimum investment of 250,000 francs ($34,482) and must employ an auditor.

the night to vacationers. However, in some departments, Agriculture officials may discourage foreigners from participating in this program and you will find the *Chambre de Commerce* more welcoming.

Many foreigners think that a B&B would be an ideal business to run in France. It is certainly a possibility to support yourself from such a venture, but do the arithmetic first. You're legally entitled to a maximum of five rooms to rent. When you start out, you're doing well if you can rent each room 60 nights a year at 50 euros ($45) per night, giving you a gross annual income of 15,000 euros ($13,500) per year. Double either your occupancy rate or your room rate and you are up to 30,000 euros ($27,000) gross. (You cannot expect any business to operate at 100 percent capacity or production in the beginning. After 10 years in the business, our rooms are now fully occupied about 100 nights a year.) Considering the investment and the labor involved, that is not going to make you rich. Someone earning the minimum wage but working 35 hours per week earns more than 11,500 euros ($10,350) per year—and their benefits are paid and they get five weeks vacation.

Part of the regulation of business in France also involves qualifications—who can do what. Some occupations have educational and experience requirements. Others may be regarded as incompatible; for instance, an accountant or architect may not also be a merchant.

Moreover, in French law a distinction is made between a merchant (*commerçant*) and a craftsman (*artisan*). Both are self-employed but they fall into separate categories. Fishermen and farmers are also separated. And certain occupations are reserved in principal for French citizens. These occupations include undertakers, insurance brokers, and gambling casino staff. However, international treaties have modified this and American citizens may qualify for entry into these professions.

OBTAINING THE CARTE DE COMMERÇANT

If you wish to legally engage in business in France, you first step is to obtain a *carte de séjour*, the residency permit that permits you to stay in France longer than three months. Your second step is to get a *carte de commerçant étranger* (foreign merchant's visa). Application for this may be made at a consulate in the United States.

A wiser course may be to first visit the *Chambre de Commerce et de l'Industrie* (CCI) in the department where you intend to locate. The local CCI may have studies of needs in the region and will be able to tell you the requirements for an application. The CCI is also a good place to test the water: How are you as a foreigner received? How many others in the area operate a similar business, for example, what's the competition?

Here they can guide you through the application process. They'll explain the various documents you need and tell you of possible subsidies and tax breaks. These last two items are subject to change depending on the condition of the economy and the policies of the government in power. For instance, in late 1999, the value-added tax (TVA) on labor for home renovation was lowered from 20.6 percent to 5.5 percent to encourage employment of craftsmen. In the spring of 2000, the TVA itself was cut one percent to 19.6 percent.

The CCI may be bureaucratic, but those who want to do business in France must come to terms with it. It is the prefecture that will eventually grant the *carte de commerçant étranger,* but you must satisfy the CCI also. With both agencies, patience is a necessary virtue.

Farmers and fishermen must work through the *Chambre d'Agriculture* and craftsmen through the *Chambre des Métiers*. It is much the same process. Those who would establish a subsidiary of a foreign company are also placed in a separate but similar category.

The advantage of working through the prefecture and CCI, rather than through the consulate in the States, is that you're a step closer to the results. With the consulate, there is a greater time lag as papers are transmitted back and forth; on the scene, you can discuss matters directly with the officials involved. There may be some problems with your initial plan that would not be immediately apparent to a consular official, and being on the scene you can modify your plan much more effectively.

The CCI is also the source of information concerning subsidies, tax reductions, and other government programs to encourage employment and development. France, particularly in recent years, has made a great effort to locate new businesses within depressed areas and to bring young people into the work force. Employers may benefit through direct subsidy, reduced taxes, relaxed work rules, or some combination of these, depending on the industry and locality involved.

Besides your passport, among the required documents for a *carte de commerçant* application will be your marriage license if you are married, confirmation of a divorce, death certificate for widows, and a police record. Like any other document you are required to submit, these will have to be translated into French by a specially qualified translator. Either the local prefecture or the consulate to which you apply will have a list of translators whom they will accept.

While legal translating is a specialty, it underscores the need to gain fluency in French. Imagine trying to operate any sort of a business if you cannot understand your customers or your suppliers! There are degrees of fluency and areas of specialized vocabulary, of course; but finance, insurance, and legal matters in the United States are difficult enough for the lay person fluent in English to comprehend. You may well be able to hire someone to translate for you but for professional help, the price is often high: one translator quoted a price of 600 francs per hour. Nonprofessional translators may not be knowledgeable enough about business affairs to provide the level of help you need.

Social Security and Business Taxes

Once you have gained *commerçant* status and permission to open your business, you can start paying taxes—not income taxes, they come later—but Social Security and health insurance, which are mandatory and part of the same system. These are based on the income of the business, but since the business will have no track record, they will be fixed provisionally for a small business at 3,100 euros ($2,790) the first year and 3,700 euros ($3,300) the second year. After that, the actual revenues will determine these charges.

The French Social Security system is not as unified as the American one, although it is evolving in that direction. Different economic sectors have separate plans managed by different agencies. For instance, salaried employees fall under one set of rules, farmers under another, merchants under still another. Benefits vary somewhat according to the nature of your business. Businesses are required to enroll in a particular plan; it is not a free choice.

The French tax rate on companies—a EURL or a SARL (see sidebar), for instance, grossing less than 50 million francs per year—is 33.33 percent on operating profits. For larger grosses, this increases to 41.6 percent.

Fortunately, there are numerous ways to reduce the tax. The first two years of such taxes are exempted for companies opening in certain locations, followed by a diminishing percentage in the next three years. Firms creating new jobs or hiring the unemployed will find benefits that will largely offset the new salaries. Profits that are reinvested are also taxed at a lower rate, as are long-term capital gains on specific fixed assets. However, France differs from all other EU nations in that it does not tax corporate profits earned outside of France. Corporate tax situations—whether involving branches of U.S. corporations or the establishment of a subsidiary—are a matter for accountants and other tax experts.

Working for Someone Else

The French economy has gradually pulled out of the recession of the '90s. Europe was years behind the United States in doing so and by the end of the century had yet to match America's unprecedented growth. Nonetheless, unemployment has dropped steadily from 1998, and rising real estate prices and increased new construction attest to very real recovery. That, plus booming growth of e-business with its seemingly insatiable demand for technically qualified personnel and increasing multinational operations, now make employment a possibility.

The massive package of tax cuts proposed by the government late in the summer of 2000 will largely affect salaried employees, stockholders, and corporations. Estimated to be worth nearly 20 billion euros ($18 billion) over three years, the cuts are substantial and roughly comparable to the ones Germany made several months earlier. However, given the likely inflation resulting from the rapid rise in oil prices and the continued weakness of the euro, the overall impact remained to be seen.

It remains extremely difficult for foreigners to qualify for the professions, such as medicine, law, architecture, and accounting in France because of educational requirements. You need only imagine the difficulty a French physician or attorney might have practicing in the United States to understand the hurdles involved. While such transatlantic transplants do exist, they are exceedingly rare.

While doctorate degrees from American universities are recognized as the equivalent of the same degree from a French university, they are the only such degrees. Below a Ph.D., there are few parallels for transfer of credit. Each dossier is handled on a case-by-case basis, depending on the schools involved. Anyone who wishes to join that elite group of professionals who were educated in the United States but practice in France should begin by applying to the Ministry of Education.

There are other ways to earn money in France. If you buy a property and later resell it at a gain; write a novel and sell it to an American publisher; own a house and rent it to someone; trade stocks on the Internet through a U.S. brokerage—these are all things you can do legally, as long as you pay the proper taxes and obey any other regulations.

Income Tax: No Escape

Foreigners who live and work in France will inevitably fall under the French income tax regime. While a tax convention with the United States prevents double taxation, rest assured you will be taxed by one of them. If you are a long-term salaried employee, whether for a French or American firm, you have no choice under the law: You will be taxed in France and must seek credit when filing taxes in the United States.

For the American who does business in France, there is the question of domicile, or residency. If you are domiciled in France—not necessarily the same thing as owning a house in France and having a *carte de séjour* or *carte de commerçant*—you are obliged to pay taxes in France on your income worldwide. Moreover, France, like other European nations, assesses a wealth tax; that is, it taxes an individual on their net worth above a limit of approximately $700,000. This tax is one reason that many of France's wealthiest people have moved out of the country.

For tax purposes, several criteria determine whether you are considered to be domiciled in France. The first criterion is if your main residence in France; second, if you earn income in France, whether salaried or self-employed, unless the activity and earnings are incidental; third, if your center of economic interest is in France. The tax is assessed on the basis of the household—that is, the total income of spouses (or unmarried partners) and children.

Persons who are not domiciled in France are taxed only on income from French sources, including:

- Income from real property located in France or from rights connected with such property.
- Income from French movable property and any other stocks and shares invested in France.
- Income from *exploitations* (business concerns) located in France.
- Income from professional activities, whether employment or not, carried on in France or from for-profit transactions carried out in France.
- Capital gains on the transfer, for financial consideration, of property or rights of any kind and profits derived from transactions, in particular those carried out by real estate brokers when such profits are connected with *fonds de commerce* (businesses) operated in France as well as real property located in France, real property rights connected therewith, or shares in unlisted companies whose assets mainly consist of such property and rights.
- Capital gains on the transfer of corporate rights resulting from the transfer of rights pertaining to companies having their head offices in France.
- Compensations, including salaries, in consideration of artistic or athletic performances provided in France.

Taxpayers domiciled outside of France who receive income from French sources or have one or more homes at their disposal in France, must normally file a tax return. However, the convention against double taxation may well negate any taxes due in France. There is also a minimum income provision that exempts anyone whose income after deductions is less than approximately 7,000 euros ($6,300)— the figure is adjusted annually—and 7,700 euros ($6,930) for those 65 or older.

"Working Black"

Say you're not a salaried employee, you have no plans to open a business in France, and your income from U.S. sources is not sufficient to live on. Your thoughts might turn to working odd jobs—teaching English as a private tutor, being a handyman, gardening, creating websites, doing computer programming, that sort of thing. The French call this *"travail au noir"* ("working black"), and it is technically illegal. It can get you in difficulties, perhaps even deported.

What's more, you are unlikely to make much of a living at it, at least not until after you have established some contacts with potential clients. Some French people work in this fashion, of course; they have friends and families and many receive some sort of public assistance such as unemployment insurance or RMI, the general welfare aid extended to citizens with no other means of support. In some instances, the French who "work black" also have a regular job in the same field. They already have health insurance and other benefits and work on the side as means of increasing their income without increasing their taxes. Or their partner or spouse may have regular employment and therefore they have benefits as family members. Yes, it is illegal for them to do this, just as it would be for you. And it is not advisable.

Consider the bigger picture. Unlike in the United States, in France health care and Social Security are the same system. In France, whoever pays into Social Security through employment or self-employment is also enrolled into the national health plan, as are those who are born in the country or have gained legal residency in a fashion that entitles them to it, such as by marriage, or as dependent children.

Americans who receive long-stay visas have had to show both sustainable income and proof of health insurance, so there is neither a need nor a provision for them to become part of the French Social Security system. But the foreigner who arrives in France as a tourist and decides to stay illegally encounters the "Catch-22" of the French system. He can't be hired without being eligible for Social Security and he can't be eligible for Social Security as an illegal alien. And unlike their American counterparts, French employers have too much to lose and too little to gain in hiring illegal foreigners.

To hire someone and not pay the Social Security tax on their wages is considered a serious matter in France. It's a simple law and easily enforceable. By linking employment, health care, and welfare in a single national system, France has limited its illegal immigration problems.

All this is not to say that the French have strict control of their borders. *Au contraire*, almost anyone with a valid U.S. passport will pass through police checks with no difficulty no matter how long they have been in the country unless they have already come to the attention of the police. The automatic three-month tourist visa remains valid in practice if not in theory far beyond three months. International airports are now the primary checkpoints. But the French do control employment and welfare—costs to the state that affect the standard of living of its citizens. If someone remains in France illegally, but pays their own way and does not injure anyone, they are usually left alone.

The point is not whether or not you may slip past the authorities. The point is that to build a life for yourself within a French community, you must do so within the confines of the French legal system. It is certainly possible to live in France on income from the United States; that is what the *carte de séjour* permits you to do. But to try to live and work in France without the proper credentials is a gamble that cannot pay off in the long run.

Part VI
Appendix

20. Useful Resources

… Appendix

French Consulates in the United States

There are 10 French consulates in the United States, including the one adjoining the embassy in Washington, D.C. Each consulate serves the surrounding geographical area. Apply for your visa application at the consulate nearest your residence. If applying in person, check hours of operation before you go; visa applications may be accepted only during certain hours. You can find links to consulates' websites at www.france-consulat.org.

ATLANTA
3475 Piedmont Road, NE
Suite 1840
Atlanta, GA 30305
Tel: 404/495-1660
Fax: 404/495-1661

BOSTON
31 St. James Ave.
Park Square Building
Suite 750
Boston, MA 02116
Tel: 617/542-7374
Fax: 617/542-8054

CHICAGO
737 N. Michigan Ave.
Suite 2020
Chicago, IL 60611
Tel: 312/787-5359
Fax: 312/664-4196

HOUSTON
777 Post Oak Blvd.
Suite 600
Houston, TX
Tel: 713/572-2799
Fax: 713/572-2911

LOS ANGELES
10990 Wilshire Blvd.
Suite 300
Los Angeles, CA 90024
Tel: 310/235-3200
Fax: 310/312-0704

MIAMI
One Biscayne Tower
Suite 1710
2 South Biscayne Blvd.
Miami, FL 33131
Tel: 305/372-9799
Fax: 305/372-9549

NEW ORLEANS
1340 Poydras St.
Suite 1710
New Orleans, LA 70112
Tel: 504/523-5772
Fax: 504/523-5725

NEW YORK
10 East 74th St.
New York, NY 10021
Tel: 212/606-3680

SAN FRANCISCO
540 Bush St.
San Francisco, CA 94108
Tel: 415/616-4910
Fax: 415/397-7843

WASHINGTON, D.C.
4101 Reservoir Road, NW
Washington, D.C. 20007
Tel: 202/944-6000
Fax: 202/944 6212

U.S. Embassy and Consulates in France

Following are the addresses and phone numbers of the various U.S. consulates in France. However, not all of these offer all the services that an American citizen might require. Check with the consulate in Paris for full details. These offices are closed on all French and U.S. holidays.

PARIS
U.S. Consulate
2, rue St. Florentin
75001 Paris
Tel: 01.43.12.47.08
Fax: 01.49.27.92.65

U.S. Embassy
2, avenue Gabriel
75008 Paris
Tel: 01.43.12.22.22
Fax: 01.42.66.97.83

MARSEILLE
U.S. Consulate
12, boulevard Paul Peytral
13086 Marseille
Tel: 04.91.54.92.00
Fax: 04.91.55.09.47

STRASBOURG
U.S. Consulate
15, avenue d'Alsace
67082 Strasbourg
Tel: 03.88.35.31.04
Fax: 03.88.24.06.95

LYON
U.S. Consulate
16, rue de la République
69289 Lyon Cedex 2
Tel: 04.78.38.36.88
Fax: 04.72.41.71.81

RENNES
U.S. Consulate
30, quai Duguay Trouin
35000 Rennes
Tel: 02.23.44.09.60

TOULOUSE
U.S. Consulate
25, allée Jean Jaurés
31000 Toulouse
Tel: 05.34.31.36.50
Fax: 05.34.41.16.19

NICE
U.S. Consulate
31, rue du Marechal Joffre
06000 Nice
Tel: 04.93.88.89.55
Fax: 04.93.87.07.38

Institutions in France Teaching French as a Foreign Language

AIX-EN-PROVENCE
Ecole Populaire Supérieure Suédoise d'Aix-en-Provence
I.S. Aix-en-Provence
Université de droit, d'économie et des sciences d'Aix-Marseille. Institut d'Etudes Françaises pour Etudiants Etrangers.
Université de Provence – Service Commun d'Enseignement du Français aux Etudiants Etrangers. SCEFEE

AMBOISE
Eurocentres Amboise

ANGERS
Centre International d'Etudes Françaises

ANNECY
Institut Français d'Annecy

ANTIBES
Centre International d'Antibes – Institut Prévert
Institut d'Enseignement de Français Langue Etrangère de Nice

AVIGNON
Centre d'Etudes Linguistiques d'Avignon
Université d'Avignon et des pays de Vaucluse – Centre de Cours Internationaux d'Avignon

BESANÇON
Centre de Linguistique Appliquée

BÉZIERS
Centre Hobson

BORDEAUX
Bordeaux Language Studies
Université Michel de Montaigne Bordeaux III. Département d'Etudes de Français Langue Etrangère

BOULOGNE-SUR-MER
Université d'été de Boulogne/Mer des Universités de la Région Nord/Pas-de-Calais

BREST
Centre International d'Etudes des Langues

CAEN
Université de Caen – Centre d'Enseignement Universitaire International pour Etrangers

CANNES
Collège International de Cannes

CAP D'AIL
Centre Méditerranéen d'Etudes Françaises

CHAMBÉRY
Institut Français de Chambéry
La Cité des Langues
Université de Savoie – Institut Savoisien d'Etudes Françaises pour Etrangers

CLERMONT-FERRAND
Université Blaise-Pascal – Service Universitaire des Etudiants Etrangers

DIJON
Alliance Française de Bourgogne
Centre International d'Etudes Françaises de l'Université de Bourgogne

FOUSSAIS-PAYRÉ
Centre International des Langues et Cultures

FRONTENAUD
La Cardere – Institut culturel de langue française

GRENOBLE
Université Stendhal Grenoble III – Centre Universitaire d'Etudes Françaises

HYÈRES
Institut d'Enseignement de la Langue Française sur la Côte d'Azur

LA ROCHELLE
Eurocentres La Rochelle
Institut d'Etudes Françaises de La Rochelle

LILLE
Centre de Langues, Relations Internationales et Formation d'Etudiants Etrangers
Université Charles de Gaulle/Lille III Département des Etudiants Etrangers

LISIEUX
Centre d'Etudes de Lisieux – CEFA Normandie

LYON
Alliance Française – Lyon
Institut de Langue et de Culture Françaises
Institut Lyonnais pour la Diffusion de la Langue et de la Culture Françaises
Institut National des Sciences Appliquées – Service de Français Langue Etrangère
Université Lumière/Lyon 2
Centre International d'Etudes Françaises

MANOSQUE
Centre International des Langues

MENTON
Université d'Eté de Menton

MONTPELLIER
ABM
Alliance Française
Association européenne d'éducation et de culture
Association pour la promotion des rencontres entre étudiants étrangers et français – Institut Culturel Français
Centre de Français du Centre International de Hautes Etudes Agronomiques Méditerranéennes
C.E.R.CL.E
Ecole Klesse
Ecole Méditerranéenne
Institut Linguistique du Peyrou
Institut Méditerranéen d'Etudes Françaises
Montpellier Espace Langues
Novalangue
Université Paul Valéry Montpellier III – Institut d'études françaises pour étudiants et professeurs étrangers

NANCY
Centre d'Accueil et de Formation Linguistiques
Cours d'Eté pour Etudiants Etrangers – Université Nancy 2
Université Nancy 2 – Service universitaire des étudiants étrangers

Nantes
Espace Langues Etudiants. CIFOE
Université de Nantes – Centre d'Enseignement du Français Langue Etrangère

Nice
Actilangue – Ecole privée de Langue Française
Alliance Française
Alpha-B Institut Linguistique
Azurlingua
France Langue
IDIOM
International House
Centre de Langues Riviera
Pluriel Langues
Université de Nice Sophia-Antipolis -Cours audiovisuels de langue française pour étudiants étrangers
Université de Nice Sophia-Antipolis Etudes Françaises pour l'Etranger

Orléans
Université d'Orléans Programmes Internationaux

Paris
Accord – Ecole de Langues
Alliance Française
Cours de Langue et Civilisation Françaises de la Sorbonne
Direction des Relations Internationales/Enseignement – Chambre de commerce et d'industrie de Paris
Ecole de Langue Française pour Etrangers
Ecole Internationale de l'Accueil Franco-Nordique
Ecole Internationale de Français et de Formation En Langues
Ecole Suisse Internationale de Français Appliqué
L'Étoile
Eurocentres Paris
Formation Postuniversitaire Internationale
France Langue
Institut Britannique de Paris - Département d'Etudes Françaises
Institut Catholique de Paris ILCF/Cours Universitaires d'été
Institut Parisien de Langue et de Civilisation Françaises
Language Studies International
Paris Ecole des Roches Langues
Paris Langues
Université Paris III – Institut de Linguistique et Phonétique Générales et Appliquées

Pau
Université de Pau – Institut d'Etudes Françaises pour Etudiants Etrangers

Perpignan
Université de Perpignan – Centre d'Etudes Françaises pour Etudiants Etrangers
S.U.R.I.
Université de Perpignan – Université d'été

Poitiers
Université de Poitiers – Centre de Français Langue Etrangère

Rambouillet
Institut International de Rambouillet

Reims
Université de Reims – Centre International d'Etudes Françaises

Rennes
Langue et Communication
Maison des Langues
Université Rennes 2 – Centre International Rennais d'Etudes de Français pour Etrangers

Rouen
Alliance Française

Royan
Centre Audiovisuel de Royan pour l'Etude des Langues

Saint-Etienne
Université Jean-Monnet/Centre International de Langue et Civilisation

Saint-Germain-en-Laye
Yvelines Langues New

Saint-Malo
Centre d'Etudes des Langues de Saint-Malo

Saint-Pierre et Miquelon
Francoforum. Institut de langue française de Saint-Pierre-et-Miquelon

Sèvres
Centre International d'Etudes Pédagogiques

Strasbourg
CIEL de Strasbourg
Université des sciences humaines de Strasbourg – Institut International d'Etudes Françaises

Toulon
Campus International

Toulouse
Alliance Française – Toulouse Midi-Pyrénées
Institut Universitaire de langue et de Culture Française
Université Toulouse-Le Mirail – Centre d'Enseignement du Français Langue Etrangère

Tours
Centre Linguistique pour Etrangers
Institut de Touraine
Université de Tours – Centre d'Enseignement du Français aux Etudiants Etrangers

Vendôme
Alliance Française du Val de Loire
Verneuil-sur-Avre
Ecole des Roches

Vichy
Cavilam
Villefranche-sur-Mer
Institut de Français

Taking the Measure of Metrics

The metric system is simple to use all by itself, but translating from metric to the American system is complex because of the fractions involved. However, you can make many approximations that, while not exact, make estimating easy. Here are some of them, followed by more precise figures.

DISTANCE
1 inch = 2.5 centimeters (2.54 cm)
1 foot = 30 centimeters (30.5 cm)
1 yard = 90 centimeters (91.44 cm)
10 centimeters = 4 inches
1 meter = 1 yard, 3 inches, or 3 1/4 feet (39.37 in.)
2 meters = 6 1/2 feet (6 ft. 6 3/4 in.)
10 meters = 11 yards (10 yd., 2 ft., 9 3/4 in.)
1 kilometer = 0.6 mile (0.62 mi.)
1 mile = 1.6 kilometer

AREA
1 square inch = 6.45 square centimeters
1 square foot = 929 square centimeters = 0.093 square meters
1 square meter = 10.76 square feet
1 acre = 4,047 square meters = 0.4 hectare
1 hectare = 2.47 acres = 10,000 square meters
1 are = 100 square meters = 120 square yards

VOLUME
1 quart = 0.95 liter
1 liter = 1 quart, 2 ounces
1 gallon = 3.8 liters
10 liters = 2.65 gallons

WEIGHT
1 ounce = 28.35 grams
100 grams = 3.5 ounces
1 pound = 454 grams or 0.45 kilogram
500 grams = 1.1 pounds
100 lbs. = 45 kilograms
1 kilogram = 2.2 pounds
100 kilograms = 220 pounds

SPEED (approximate)
50 kph = 30 mph
90 kph = 55 mph
110 kph = 70 mph
130 kph = 80 mph

TEMPERATURE
-4° Fahrenheit = -20° Celsius
14° F. = -10° C.
32° F. = 0° C.
50° F. = 10° C.
68° F. = 20° C.
86° F. = 30° C.
104° F. = 40° C.
212° F. = 100° C.
To change Centigrade to Fahrenheit, multiply degrees by 1.8 and add 32; after 32° F., each 10° C. = 18° F.

Shoes and Clothing Sizes

French shoe and clothing sizes are quite different from American ones since they are derived from the metric system rather than from U.S. feet and inches. Thus, men think of women with hourglass figures as 91-57-91, rather than 36-23-36.

In general, French men seem to have smaller feet than Americans; finding the equivalent of a 12 or 13 shoe size may be difficult. In women's shoes, equivalents are not exact.

Since so many articles of clothing are made outside of the countries where they will be sold, many of them now carry labels denoting size equivalents. Also, many stores in France display a chart showing corresponding sizes. In any case, it is always wise to try on any article of clothing prior to purchase since there is often variation in size between manufacturers, regardless of the size marked on the label.

WOMEN'S CLOTHING SIZES

American	8	10	12	14	16	18	20
French	36	38	40	42	44	46	48

MEN'S CLOTHING SIZES

American	34	36	38	40	42	44	46
French	44	46	48	50	52	54	56

SHIRT COLLAR SIZES

American	14	14 1/2	15	15 1/2	16	16 1/2	17
French	36	37	38	39	40	41	42

WOMEN'S SHOE SIZES

American	6	6 1/2	7	7 1/2	8	8 1/2	9
French	36	37	37	38	39	41	42

MEN'S SHOE SIZES

American	7	8	9	10	11	12	13
French	40	41	42	43/44	44/45	46	47

Radio Frequencies

French radio networks are all over the dial. The national networks each broadcast their program throughout the country but on different frequencies in different areas. Following are the dial numbers on which you'll find these networks in the various departments. (Remember, the comma functions as a period in French notation.)

AIX-EN-PROVENCE (13100)
France Inter: 91,3
France Culture: 99
France Musiques: 94,2
France Info: 105,3
RF Provence: 103,6

AMIENS (80000)
France Inter: 92
France Culture: 97
France Musiques: 89,3
France Info: 105,5
RF Picardie: 100,2

AVIGNON (84000)
France Inter: 97,4
France Culture: 90,7
France Musiques: 93,2
France Info: 105,2
RF Vaucluse: 100,4

BEAUNE (21200)
France Inter: 95,9
France Culture: 93,7
France Musiques: 99,2
France Info: 104,8
RF Bourgogne: 103,7

BESANÇON (25000)
France Inter: 98,7 or 90,6
France Culture: 89,3 or 93,5
France Musiques: 95 or 96,2
France Info: 104,4
RF Besançon: 102,8

BIARRITZ (64200)
France Inter: 89
France Culture: 96,1
France Musiques: 92,7
France Info: 105,5
RF Pays Basque: 101,3

BORDEAUX (33000)
France Inter: 89,7
France Culture: 97,7
France Musiques: 93,5
France Info: 105,5
FIP Bordeaux: 96,7
RF Bordeaux Gironde: 100,1

BOURGES (18000)
France Inter: 94,9
France Culture: 88,5
France Musiques: 91,8
France Info: 105,5
RF Berry Sud: 103,2

CAEN (14000)
France Inter: 99,6
France Culture: 91,5
France Musiques: 95,6
France Info: 105,5
RF Normandie Caen: 102,6

CLERMONT-FERRAND (63000)
France Inter: 90,4 or 90,8
France Culture: 98,4 or 98,8
France Musiques: 95,5 or 95
France Info: 105,5
RF Puy de Dôme: 102,5

DIJON (21000)
France Inter: 95,9
France Culture: 93,7

France Musiques: 99,2
France Info: 105,1
RF Bourgogne: 103,7

GRASSE (6130)
France Inter: 96,3 or 100,2
France Culture: 88,7 or 101,9
France Musiques: 99,6 or 92,2
France Info: 105,3
Radio Bleue: 100,7
FIP Côte d'Azur: 101,1

GRENOBLE (38000)
France Inter: 99,4 or 89,9
France Culture: 88,2 or 92,8
France Musiques: 91,8 or 95,5
France Info: 105,1
RF Isère: 102,8

LILLE (59000)
France Inter: 103,7
France Culture: 98
France Musiques: 88,7
France Info: 105,2
FIP Lille: 91
RF Fréquence Nord: 94,7

LIMOGES (87000)
France Inter: 93
France Culture: 89,5
France Musiques: 97,5
France Info: 105,5
RF Limoges: 103,5

LYON (69000)
France Inter: 99,8 or 101,1
France Culture: 88,8 or 94,1
France Musiques: 92,4 or 98
France Info: 105,4
FIP Lyon: 87,8

MONTPELLIER (34000)
France Inter: 89,4
France Culture: 97,8
France Musiques: 92,9 or 102,7
France Info: 105,1
RF Hérault: 101,1

MULHOUSE (68100)
France Inter: 95,7
France Culture: 88,6
France Musiques: 91,6
France Info: 105,5
RF Alsace: 102,6

NANCY (54000)
France Inter: 96,9
France Culture: 88,7
France Musiques: 91,7
France Info: 105,9
RF Nancy Lorraine: 100,5

NANTES (44000)
France Inter: 90,6
France Culture: 94,2
France Musiques: 98,9
France Info: 105,5
FIP Nantes: 95,7
RF Loire Océan: 101,8

NICE (6000)
France Inter: 100,2
France Culture: 101,9
France Musiques: 92,2
France Info: 105,7
FIP Côte d'Azur: 103,8

ORLÉANS (45000)
France Inter: 99,2
France Culture: 95,8
France Musiques: 90,7
France Info: 105,5
RF Orléans: 100,9

PARIS (75000)
France Inter: 87,8
France Culture: 93,5 or 93,9
France Musiques: 91,7 or 92,1
France Info: 105,5
Radio Bleue: 107,1
FIP PARIS: 105,1

PAU (64000)
France Inter: 87,9
France Culture: 95,7

France Musiques: 91,5
France Info: 105,5
RF Pau Béarn: 102,5

PERPIGNAN (66000)
France Inter: 92,1
France Culture: 99,8
France Musiques: 97,2
France Info: 105,1
RF Roussillon: 101,6

POITIERS (86000)
France Inter: 97,7
France Culture: 92,3
France Musiques: 95,5
France Info: 105,5
Le Mouv': 87,6

REIMS (51100)
France Inter: 96,8
France Culture: 98,8
France Musiques: 89,2
France Info: 105,5
RF Champagne: 95,1

RENNES (35000)
France Inter: 93,5
France Culture: 98,3
France Musiques: 89,9
France Info: 105,5
RF Armorique: 103,1

ROUBAIX (59100)
France Inter: 103,7
France Culture: 98
France Musiques: 88,7
France Info: 105,2
FIP Lille: 91
RF Fréquence Nord: 87,8

ROUEN (76000)
France Inter: 96,5
France Culture: 94
France Musiques: 92
France Info: 105,7
RF Normandie Rouen: 100,1

STRASBOURG (67000)
France Inter: 97,3
France Culture: 87,7
France Musiques: 95
France Info: 104,4
FIP Strasbourg: 92,3
RF Alsace: 101,4

TOULON (83000)
France Inter: 92
France Culture: 97,1
France Musiques: 94,9
France Info: 105,8
RF Provence: 102,9

TOULOUSE (31000)
France Inter: 87,9 or 103,5
France Culture: 95,7 or 90,5
France Musiques: 91,5 or 93,1
France Info: 105,5
Le Mouv': 95,2

TOURS (37000)
France Inter: 95 or 99,9
France Culture: 88,7 or 97,8
France Musiques: 96,7 or 92,2
France Info: 105,5
RF Tours: 98,7

TROYES (10000)
France Inter: 95,3
France Culture: 97,9
France Musiques: 91,4
France Info: 105,5

VALENCE (26000)
France Inter: 99,8
France Culture: 88,8
France Musiques: 92,4
France Info: 105,4
RF Drôme: 87,9

Chronology of French Kings, Emperors, and Presidents

KINGS

MEROVINGIAN DYNASTY

	REIGN
Merovich	447–458
Childeric I	458–482
Clovis I	482–511
Childebert I	511–558
Clothaire I	558–562
Caribert	562–566
Chilperic	566–584
Clothaire II	584–628
Dagobert I	628–637
Clovis II	637–655
Clothaire III	655–668
Childeric II	668–674
Thierry III	674–691
Clovis III	691–695
Childebert II	695–711
Dagobert III	711–716
Chilperic II	716–721
Thierry IV	721–737
(interregnum)	
Childeric III	743–751
(died 754)	

CAROLINGIAN DYNSASTY

Pepin the Short	751–768
Charlemagne	768–814
Louis I, the Debonair	814–840
Charles I, the Bald	840–877
LouisII, the Stammerer	877–879
Louis III	879–882
Carloman	882–884
Charles II, the Fat	884–888
Odo, count of Paris	888–898
Charles III, the Simple	898–929
(interregnum)	
Louis IV, the Foreigner	936–954
Lothaire	954–986
Louis V	986–987

CAPETIAN DYNASTY

Hugh Capet	987–996
Robert II, the Pious	996–1031
Henry I	1036–1060
Philip I	1060–1108
Louis VI, the Fat	1108–1137
Louis VII	1137–1180
Philip II, Augustus	1180–1223
Louis VIII, the Lion	1223–1226
Louis IX (St. Louis)	1226–1270
Philip III, the Bold	1270–1285
Philip IV, the Fair	1285–1314
Louis X	1314–1316
Philip V, the Tall	1316–1322
Charles IV, the Fair	1322–1328

VALOIS DYNASTY

Philip VI	1328–1350
John II, the Good	1350–1364
Charles V, the Wise	1364–1380
Charles VI, the Fool	1380–1422
Charles VII, the Victorious	1422–1461
Louis XI, the Spider	1461–1483
Charles VIII	1483–1498
Louis XII, Father of his People	1498–1515
Francis I	1515–1547
Henry II	1547–1559
Francis II	1559–1560
Charles IX	1560–1574
Henry III	1574–1589

BOURBON DYNASTY

Henry IV	1589–1610
Louis XIII	1610–1643
Louis XIV, the Sun King	1643–1715
Louis XV	1715–1774
Louis XVI	1774–1793
(interregnum)	
Louis XVIII	1814–1824
Charles X	1824–1830

ORLEANS DYNASTY
Louis Philippe   1830–1848

EMPERORS

BONAPARTE
Napoleon I   1804–1815
Napoleon III   1852–1870

PRESIDENTS

THIRD REPUBLIC
Adolphe Thiers   1871–1873
Patrice de MacMahon   1873–1879
Jules Grévy   1879–1887
Sadi Carnot   1887–1894
Jean Casimir-Périer   1894–1895
Félix Faure   1895–1899
Émile Loubet   1899–1906
Armond Fallières   1906–1913
Raymond Poincaré   1913–1920
Paul Deschanel   Feb.–Sept. 1920
Alexandre Millerand   1920–1924
Gaston Doumergue   1924–1931
Paul Doumer   1931–1932
Albert Lebrun   1932–1940

FOURTH REPUBLIC
Vincent Auriol   1947–1954
René Coty   1954–1958

FIFTH REPUBLIC
Charles de Gaulle   1959–1969
Georges Pompidou   1969–1974
Valéry Giscard d'Estaing   1974–1981
François Mitterand   1981–1995
Jacques Chirac   1995–

Index

A
accommodations: See housing
air travel, 26, 121
Aix-en-Provence, 20, 198-200
appliances, 131-132
arrondissements, 152-154, 162-167: See also Paris
attitudes, 60-61
Avignon, 200-203

B
banking, 98-99
bed-and-breakfasts: buying, 232
Bordeaux, 177-182
Brittany, 15, 215
Burgundy, 19, 155-156, 217-228
buses, 115-116
business: buying, 231-234; permits, 233-234; running a, 231-234; taxes, 235

C
Cannes-Antibes, 195-197
cars, 116-120: buying, 119-120; insuring, 120; renting, 120; repairing, 120; rules of the road, 117-118; tax, 120
carte de commercant étranger (foreign merchant's visa), 233-234, 236
Carte de séjour (residency permit), 125-127, 236, 239: See also visas.
children, moving with, 133-134
citizenship: See visas
class, 51-52
clothing sizes, European, 249
communications, 81-89
computers, 83-85, 87, 131-132
constitution, 4-5
consulates, 242-243
cost of living, 24-26, 34, 94-98: eating out, 26; entertainment, 26; food, 25; household goods, 26, 96; housing, 25, 95
Côte d'Azur, 19, 155, 191-203
cuisine, 57
culture, French, 7, 51-62, 73-74
culture shock, 60-61

currency: See euro and money
customs and excise, 129-130

D
daily life, 79-121
de Gaulle, Charles, 4, 76
dental treatment, 104-105
départements, 16-18, 109
Dijon, 220-222
doctors: See health
drinking water, 110-111
driving, 26, 116-120

E
economy, 23
education, 6, 40, 52
electricity, 142
email, 83-85
embassies, 243
employment, 134-135, 231-239; permits, 34, 235-236; self-employment, 231-234: See also working
environmental issues, 108-111
euro, 23, 91-94: See also money
Europe, currency, 91-94
European Union (EU), 24-25, 77-78, 93-94

F
food, 95
francs: See money
French: See language
French Revolution, 71

G
gasoline, 118
geography, 13-22: See also Prime Living Locations
Giverny, 208-209
government, 4-5, 75

H
health, 103-111: costs, 104; care, 104-105; for expatriates, 104-105; environment, 108-111; hospitals, 107-108
health insurance, 105-107
history, 63-78, 253
home, building a, 146-150

Index

home ownership, 138-139, 142-146
hospitals, 107-108: See also Health
household goods, 129-131
housing, 11, 95-96, 137-150: classifieds, 138; home building, 146-150; home ownership, 138-139, 142-146; renting, 138-146. See also prime living locations and individual cities

I

Île-de-France, 153-154, 167-173
income tax, 236-237
immigration, 125-128: See also visas.
importing, 129-131
insurance: See cars, health insurance, and housing.
Internet service, 83-85, 131-132, 135

L

language, 22, 32, 34, 39-49; accents, 46; instruction in the United States, 41-42; instruction in France, 42-46, 244-247
Languedoc, 19, 154-155, 175-188
literature, 46-49
Louis XIV, the Sun King, 68-70
Lyon, 224-226

M

magazines, 87, 89
mail (La Poste), 85
maps, 2, 112, 152, 158, 174, 190, 204, 216
Marseille, 197-198
Massif Central, 20, 183
medicines, 107
metric conversion, 154, 248
Midi, the, 20, 154-155, 175-188
Mitterand, 77-78
money, 91-102: banking, 98-99; euro, 23, 93; social security, 101-102; taxes, 99-101
Montpellier, 186-188
mortgages, 142-146
moving to France, 128-150: appliances, 131-132; housing, 137-150; household goods, 129-131; pets, 132-133

N

Napoleon, 71-72

National Assembly (Assemblée Nationale), 4-5
newspapers, 87-88
Nice, 19, 193-195
Normandy, 15, 74, 204-215
nuclear power, 109

P

Paris, 11, 14, 153-154, 159-173: arrondissements, 153-154, 162-167; housing, 162-167; Les Banlieues (suburbs), 14, 167-173; transportation system, 160
people, French, 51-62
pets, 132-133
pharmacies, 107
politics, 21
Poste, La (mail), 85
prime living locations, 153-228: Paris and the Île-de-France, 159-173; the Midi and Languedoc, 175-188; Provence and the Côte d'Azur, 191-203; Normandy and Brittany, 205-215; Burgundy and the Rhône Valley, 217-228
property, buying, 138-139, 142-146
Provence, 19, 155, 191-203

R

radio, 87
radio frequencies, 250
rail system, 11, 15, 26, 113-115, 218
real estate agents, 35
regions, of France, 14-15, 21, 181
religion, 22-23
renting, 138-146, 188: See also housing and prime living locations
residency permit (carte de séjour), 125-126, 236, 239
Rhône Valley, 155-156, 217-228

S

shoe sizes, European, 249
smoking, 108: See also health
social security, 101-102, 235
St. Etienne, 227-228
Strasbourg, 19, 222
symbols, of France, 14-15, 21

T

taxes, 99-101

telephone service, 81-83
television, 85-87
time difference, 34
Toulouse, 182-184
touring France, 33
train travel, 11, 15, 26, 113-115, 218
transportation, 26-27, 113-221: air travel, 121; buses, 115-116; cars, 116-120; trains, 11, 15, 26, 113-115, 218

V
Versailles, 69

visas, 21-22, 30, 125-128, 133: carte de séjour, 125-126; carte de commerçant étranger, 233-234; student visas, 127-128; work permits, 134-135

W
work permits, 134-135 See also carte de séjour and visas.
wills, 130
wine, 178-179, 180
working, 134-135, 213-239

About the Author

On the day he was 50 years old, Terry Link and his wife bought a vacant bakery in a little village in the South of France. After signing the papers, they flew back to San Francisco and packed up their belongings, quit their jobs, and started a new life. That was a decade ago.

The change was immediate: Instead of the daily deadlines that he had faced in more than 25 years of newspapering, there was plumbing and wiring and 3-foot-thick rock walls to confront to turn their new home into the bed and breakfast he and his wife now operate.

Link was born in Madison, Wis., but grew up on a small farm in the Imperial Valley of California. He attended three different colleges before graduating from San Francisco State. He and his wife have three sons, a daughter, and one grandson.

AVALON TRAVEL
publishing

How far will our travel guides take you? As far as you want.

Discover a rhumba-fueled nightspot in Old Havana, explore prehistoric tombs in Ireland, hike beneath California's centuries-old redwoods, or embark on a classic road trip along Route 66. Our guidebooks deliver solidly researched, trip-tested information—minus any generic froth—to help globetrotters or weekend warriors create an adventure uniquely their own.

And we're not just about the printed page. Public television viewers are tuning in to Rick Steves' new travel series, Rick Steves' Europe. On the Web, readers can cruise the virtual black top with Road Trip USA author Jamie Jensen and learn travel industry secrets from Edward Hasbrouck of The Practical Nomad. With Foghorn AnyWare eBooks, users of handheld devices can place themselves "inside" the content of the guidebooks.

In print. On TV. On the Internet. In the palm of your hand.
We supply the information. The rest is up to you.

Avalon Travel Publishing
Something for everyone

www.travelmatters.com

Avalon Travel Publishing guides are available at your favorite book or travel store.

MOON HANDBOOKS

provide comprehensive coverage of a region's arts, history, land, people, and social issues in addition to detailed practical listings for accommodations, food, outdoor recreation, and entertainment. Moon Handbooks allow complete immersion in a region's culture—ideal for travelers who want to combine sightseeing with insight for an extraordinary travel experience in destinations throughout North America, Hawaii, Latin America, the Caribbean, Asia, and the Pacific.

WWW.MOON.COM

Rick Steves shows you where to travel and how to travel—all while getting the most value for your dollar. His Back Door travel philosophy is about making friends, having fun, and avoiding tourist rip-offs.

Rick's been traveling to Europe for more than 25 years and is the author of 22 guidebooks, which have sold more than a million copies. He also hosts the award-winning public television series *Rick Steves' Europe*.

WWW.RICKSTEVES.COM

ROAD TRIP USA

Getting there is half the fun, and Road Trip USA guides are your ticket to driving adventure. Taking you off the interstates and onto less-traveled, two-lane highways, each guide is filled with fascinating trivia, historical information, photographs, facts about regional writers, and details on where to sleep and eat—all contributing to your exploration of the American road.

"[Books] so full of the pleasures of the American road, you can smell the upholstery."
~BBC radio

WWW.ROADTRIPUSA.COM

FOGHORN OUTDOORS guides are for campers, hikers, boaters, anglers, bikers, and golfers of all levels of daring and skill. Each guide focuses on a specific U.S. region and contains site descriptions and ratings, driving directions, facilities and fees information, and easy-to-read maps that leave only the task of deciding where to go.

"Foghorn Outdoors has established an ecological conservation standard unmatched by any other publisher."
~Sierra Club

WWW.FOGHORN.COM

TRAVEL SMART guidebooks are accessible, route-based driving guides focusing on regions throughout the United States and Canada. Special interest tours provide the most practical routes for family fun, outdoor activities, or regional history for a trip of anywhere from two to 22 days. Travel Smarts take the guesswork out of planning a trip by recommending only the most interesting places to eat, stay, and visit.

"One of the few travel series that rates sightseeing attractions. That's a handy feature. It helps to have some guidance so that every minute counts."
~San Diego Union-Tribune

CiTY·SMaRT™ guides are written by local authors with hometown perspectives who have personally selected the best places to eat, shop, sightsee, and simply hang out. The honest, lively, and opinionated advice is perfect for business travelers looking to relax with the locals or for longtime residents looking for something new to do Saturday night.